MW01641207

PREFACE

America's longest war ended in 1975, yet significant questions remain unanswered. Not the least of them is the character of the National Front for the Liberation of South Viet Nam (NLF) and its relationship with the Communists in Hanoi. From the birth of the NLF in 1960, Washington policy makers claimed that Hanoi alone directed the armed struggle in the South. Key members of the Kennedy and Johnson administrations argued that the insurgency was a war of aggression waged by Communist North Viet Nam against democratic South Viet Nam. Critics of American intervention, in contrast, insisted that the conflict in South Viet Nam was essentially a civil war and that the NLF had risen at southern initiative in response to southern demands. Neither of these views is entirely accurate and both ignore the complex set of circumstances that led to the formation of the NLF.

The NLF, derogatorily called the Viet Cong (abbreviated from Viet Cong-san or Vietnamese Communists) by its enemies, formed in 1960 after northern and southern Communists concluded that a new strategy was needed to overthrow the government of Ngo Dinh Diem and liberate Viet Nam south of the seventeenth parallel. For the next fifteen years, it combined political, diplomatic, and military struggle to win the anticolonial contest that had begun earlier in the century with the Thanh Nien resistance movement. Revolutionary continuity therefore links the NLF with its predecessors: the Viet Minh, the Lien Viet, and the Fatherland Front. The Lao Dong, Viet Nam's Communist Party, was, as Carlyle A. Thayer has correctly pointed out, a united nationwide organization that had used the front technique in the past to achieve its objectives.

The major purpose of this book is to examine the development and implementation of the NLF's international strategy and assess its impact on the war. Most previous accounts of the NLF's contribution to Viet Nam's modern revolution focus on the village war, virtually ignoring the important role of the Front's foreign relations campaigns. During the war, the Lao Dong skillfully used the NLF's diplomats to promote neutralism, soothe China's political wounds, engage the United States in secret peace contacts, foil Richard Nixon's plans to use superpower diplomacy to end the war, and drive a wedge between Washington and its allies in Saigon. The Front was quite successful in each of these endeavors, contributing significantly to the Lao Dong's political and military victories and frustrating the United States.

My second purpose is to examine the relationship between the Lao Dong's Political Bureau in Hanoi and the NLF's leadership. As the war dragged on in Viet Nam, several conflicts emerged within the Lao Dong over military tactics, strategy, and diplomacy. Some social scientists have emphasized psychocultural differences between northerners and southerners to explain divisions within the Lao Dong; I try to focus the discussion in a more concrete and historically grounded way. The vast differences of opinion between northerners and southerners in the Party were not the consequence of primordial loyalties or long-standing culturalist sentiments; rather they can be attributed to the significant differences in the ways northern and southern Communists responded to American intervention. The realpolitik of the southern revolution led many NLF leaders to pursue objectives that brought it into conflict with some Party leaders in Hanoi.

The division of Viet Nam in 1954 posed unique problems for the revolution, compelling it to adopt twin goals: to develop socialism in the North and to wage a war of liberation in the South. These two goals often competed for limited resources and at times were mutually exclusive. Whereas some Party members granted primacy to socialist development in the North and so sought to protect northern interests, southerners saw national liberation as the Party's priority and acted accordingly. The result was an often fierce debate within the Party that led to the South's estrangement at the war's end.

I hope this book will add to a fuller understanding of the Viet Nam War and the diplomatic environment associated with it. More important, I seek to revise our current understanding of the NLF and its role in the war. The Front was neither a puppet of Hanoi nor an autonomous organization. Its origins, development, and actions were a part of an evolving revolutionary process that shifted dramatically after the Communists' victory over the French in 1954. I argue essentially that the post–Dien Bien Phu division was an important geographic determinant of subsequent revolutionary national behavior. Since this book is an investigation of a Communist party's foreign relations, it naturally lends itself to a state-oriented approach. In many of my earlier writings, I have examined the impact of culture on foreign relations. In this book, however, I have relied on the shared strategic values of Vietnamese policy makers to tell the story.

The events of this period and the arguments contained in this book have been reconstructed from a wide variety of documents and oral histories. I traveled to Viet Nam several times each year between 1989 and 1997 for research in the various archives, libraries, and special collections in Hanoi and Ho Chi Minh City. Although many important collections remain closed to researchers, I was given access to sources only recently made available to scholars. Archivists and historians in Viet Nam showed me important internal documents and reports from NLF diplomats in the field. I also examined several Communist periodicals, including *Nhan Dan*, the Party's daily newspaper, and *Hoc Tap*, its theoretical journal. The daily broadcasts of Radio Hanoi and Liberation Radio were extremely informative, as were collections of Lao Dong resolutions and Political Bureau reports. The published materials on the war now located in Hanoi are rich and Western scholars have only begun to explore them.

In addition, I conducted well over one hundred interviews with former NLF officials and village cadres. Since many of the issues discussed in these pages remain controversial, some Vietnamese were willing to speak openly only on condition that they remain anonymous. I often delivered typed questions to my subjects before the actual interviews and was given typed answers. Sometimes I tape-recorded spontaneous responses to questions. In each case, however, I confirmed my informants' memories and comments with the written record. There are problems associated with oral histories and I have made every effort to minimize them. Former NLF officials who were overlooked by the central government after the war certainly have a particular viewpoint that is burdened with the political realities of their lives. Therefore, I have used most of the interviews to add a human touch to events described in the written record. Most cadres and former NLF officials appear in this manuscript in the form of quotations that highlight and expand upon an idea represented in the source material.

In the United States, I have relied heavily on the Douglas Pike Collection of NLF documents, located when I used them at the Indochina Archive of the University of California at Berkeley. Mr. Pike was kind enough to sit down for interviews with me three times in October 1992. The Jeffrey Race Collection of captured Communist documents and oral interviews at the Chicago Center for Research Libraries is invaluable for students of Viet Nam's modern revolution. I also consulted source material in Cornell University's Echols Collection, the Lyndon Baines Johnson Presidential Library, and the John F. Kennedy Presidential Library.

The bibliography on the Viet Nam War is immense, but four works are unique: Frances FitzGerald's *Fire in the Lake* (New York: Vintage, 1972); Carlyle A. Thayer's *War by Other Means: National Liberation and Revolution in Viet-Nam, 1954–1960* (Sydney/Boston: Allen & Unwin, 1989); George McT. Kahin's *Intervention: How the United States Became Involved in Vietnam* (New York: Doubleday/Anchor, 1986); and William Duiker's *Communist Road to Power in Vietnam* (Boulder: Westview, 1981). It is no exaggeration to confess that this book could not have been written without the work of these individuals.

In writing this book, I have incurred many debts both personal and intellectual. The National Endowment for the Humanities, the Society for Historians of American Foreign Relations, the Lyndon Baines Johnson Foundation, the Cold War History Project, the University of Kentucky, and Vassar College have all provided generous financial support. I thank David Anderson, Mark Bradley, Lloyd Gardner, Marc Gilbert, William Head, Gary Hess, Melvyn Leffler, Ngo Vinh Long, Robert McMahon, Martin Murray, Mari Olsen, Stein Tonnesson, and Marilyn Young for their comments on various parts of this book. William Duiker, Thomas Englebert, Andrew Rotter, Carlyle A. Thayer, and my colleague David Schalk read the entire manuscript and made valuable suggestions. John Prados shared his archive, comments, and friendship with me at every stage of this project. Several librarians paved the way for me to conduct efficient and useful research. John Wilson at the Lyndon Baines Johnson Presidential Library and Allen Riedy at the Echols Collection at Cornell were particularly helpful. Nguyen Trong Bien and Nguyen Minh Phuong at the State Archives Department of Viet Nam were very supportive.

I owe special thanks to Raymond Betts, Lady Borton, Darlene Calvert, Dan Duffy, David Hamilton, Carolyn Haynes, Mary Ann Heiss, Lynn Hyler, Dottie Leathers, Kyle Longley, John McAuliff, Theda Perdue, and Dana Sachs. My colleagues in the History Department at Vassar College have provided cheer and assistance. I am particularly grateful to Miriam Cohen, Rebecca Edwards, Maria Höhn, Ben Kohl, Jim Merrell, Leslie Offutt, Norma Torney, and Tony Wohl for their support. I also thank Jill Schneiderman, Pat Wallace, and Andy Watsky for their advice and friendship. My seminar students at Vassar have been a source of great inspiration and support. Their influence pervades these pages far more than these words of thanks indicate. My students Amanda Bennett, Megan Betts, and Keely Jones helped with the research. Le Phuong Anh, a young scholar from Hanoi, assisted me in translating Vietnamese documents. Peter Agree at Cornell University Press has been a kind and gentle editor. His equanimity and good humor have sustained me in many ways.

Since 1995, I have been involved in a critical oral history project on the Viet Nam War cosponsored by Brown University's Watson Institute for International Studies and Viet Nam's Institute for International Relations. This effort brought me into contact with several former officials in Hanoi and Washington, and many of their comments are present in these pages. I thank Jim Blight, Janet Lang, and Tom Biersteker of Brown, David Welch of the University of Toronto, and Malcolm Byrne and Tom Blanton of the National Security Archive for their support of this project. I also thank Jim Hershberg of the Woodrow Wilson Institute's Cold War History Project for showing me archival materials from China and the former Soviet Union.

In Viet Nam, my friends and colleagues at the History Institute and the Institute for International Relations were helpful in every way. I especially thank Nguyen Phuong Binh, Pham Sanh Chau, Nguyen Ngoc Dien, Do Van Dong, Ha Hong Hai, Vu The Hiep, Nguyen Dang Hung, Nguyen Khac Huynh, Le Lin Lan, Dao Huy Ngoc, Vu Huy Phuoc, Bui Thanh Son, Nguyen Vu Tung, Pham Ngoc Uyen, Nguyen Dinh Vinh, and Nguyen Si Xung. I profited as well from conversations with the historians Tranh Quynh Cu, Tran Huu Dinh, and Le Mau Han. I especially thank Luu Doan Huynh, who has become more than a colleague to me over the years. During each of my trips to Viet Nam, policy makers and scholars shared their time and ideas with me when I am sure they had more important matters at hand.

I am grateful for the patience and encouragement of Frank Costigliola and George C. Herring. Frank sparked my interest in diplomatic history when the war in Viet Nam was a recent memory. George Herring has been a friend to an entire generation of Viet Nam War scholars. It is difficult to categorize the many things he has done for the book and for me. I owe him more than I can ever repay.

An earlier version of Chapter 3 appeared as "Vietnamese-American Peace Negotiations: The Failed 1965 Initiatives" in *Journal of American–East Asian Relations* 4 (Winter 1995): 377–95. Parts of Chapter 4 appeared as "The NLF and the Tet Offensive," in *The Tet Offensive*, edited by Marc Jason Gilbert and William Head, published in 1996 by Praeger Publishers, an imprint of Greenwood Publishing Group, Inc., Westport, Conn.

From beginning to end of this project, my family has shared with me its frustrations and satisfactions. They have tolerated my long absences, and their support has sustained me over the years. This book is dedicated to my wife, Monica d. Church.

ROBERT K. BRIGHAM

Poughkeepsie, New York

DRAMATIS PERSONAE

Ball, George U.S. undersecretary of state, 1961–66.

Brezhnev, Leonid Secretary general of Central Committee and president of Presidium, Communist Party of the Soviet Union.

Bui Diem Ambassador of Republic of Viet Nam (RVN) to United States, 1966–72.

Bundy, McGeorge Assistant to U.S. president for national security affairs, 1961–66.

Burchett, Wilfred Australian journalist with close ties to National Liberation Front (NLF).

Byroade, Henry U.S. ambassador to Burma, 1963–68.

Chen Yi Foreign minister of People's Republic of China.

Chou En-lai Premier of People's Republic of China.

Clifford, Clark U.S. secretary of defense, 1968–69.

Cooper, Chester Special assistant to Ambassador-at-Large W. Averell Harriman.

Dang Quang Minh NLF diplomatic representative to Soviet Union.

Dinh Ba Thi NLF diplomat; led important tours in Belgium.

Duong Van Minh (Big Minh) RVN general and chief of state, 1963–65; presidential candidate, 1971; last RVN president, 1975.

Fanfani, Amintore Italian foreign minister.

Forrestal, Michael Member of White House national security staff, 1962–65.

Fulbright, J. William U.S. senator from Arkansas, 1945–74; chair of Senate Foreign Relations Committee, 1959–74.

Gromyko, Andrei Foreign minister of Soviet Union.

Gronouski, John U.S. ambassador to Poland, 1965–68.

Gullion, Edmund Unofficial U.S. envoy during 1965 peace contacts.

Harriman, W. Averell U.S. undersecretary of state for political affairs, 1963–65; ambassador at large ("peace ambassador").

Ho Chi Minh President and founder of Viet Nam's Communist Party, 1929–69.

Hoan Bich Son NLF diplomat.

Hoang Minh Thao General in People's Army of Viet Nam (PAVN).

Huynh Tan Phat NLF secretary general, 1964–75; chairman of Provisional Revolutionary Government (PRG), 1969–75.

Huynh Van Danh NLF revolutionary combat hero.

Janczewski, Zbigniew Official with Polish Foreign Ministry.

Kissinger, Henry U.S. national security adviser and secretary of state in Nixon administration.

Kosygin, Aleksei Chairman of Council of Ministers, Soviet Union.

Lam Ba Chau Vietnamese intellectual living in Paris.

Le Duan Secretary general of Lao Dong (Viet Nam's Communist Party), 1960–86.

Le Duc Tho Member of Lao Dong Political Bureau, 1951–86; chief negotiator for Democratic Republic of Viet Nam (DRV) at Paris peace talks.

Le Quang Dao PAVN general.

Le Thanh Nghi DRV vice premier and member of Political Bureau, 1960–86.

Lewandowski, Janucsz Polish representative to International Control Commission.

Lin Piao Minister of defense, People's Republic of China.

Lodge, Henry Cabot U.S. ambassador to RVN, 1963–64, 1965–67.

Ma Thi Chu NLF diplomat.

Mai Van Bo Chief of DRV's Commercial Delegation in Paris and secret peace contact.

McNamara, Robert S. U.S. secretary of defense, 1961–68.

Ngo Dinh Diem President of RVN, 1955–63.

Ngo Dinh Nhu Head of RVN Secret Forces, 1956–63; brother of Ngo Dinh Diem.

Nguyen Cao Ky Commander of RVN air force; RVN vice president, 1967–71.

Nguyen Chi Thanh PAVN general; director of Central Committee Directorate for South Viet Nam (COSVN), 1965–67; member of Political Bureau, 1951–67.

Nguyen Duy Trinh DRV foreign minister, 1965–75; member of Political Bureau, 1975–81.

Nguyen Huu Tho President of NLF, 1960–69.

Nguyen Khanh RVN general; prime minister, 1964; president, 1964–65.

Nguyen Luu Vien RVN representative at peace talks at La Celle St-Cloud, 1973–74.

Nguyen Minh Phuong NLF diplomat and acting representative to People's Republic of China, 1966–67.

Nguyen Thi Binh NLF diplomat, 1961–69; PRG foreign minister, 1969–75; vice president of Socialist Republic of Viet Nam from 1992.

Nguyen Tho Chan DRV ambassador to Soviet Union.

Nguyen Van Dong NLF diplomat; acting head of mission to Soviet Union.

Nguyen Van Hieu NLF diplomat, 1961–75; NLF secretary general, 1960–63.

Nguyen Van Thieu RVN chief of state, 1965–67; president, 1967–75.

Nguyen Van Tien NLF diplomat and representative to DRV.

Nguyen Van Vinh PAVN general.

Nguyen Xuan Long NLF diplomat; led delegation to People's Republic of China, 1966–67.

Orlandi, Giovanni d' Italian ambassador to RVN.

Pham Hung Member of Political Bureau, 1951–88; premier of Socialist Republic of Viet Nam, 1987–88.

Pham Van Dong Premier of DRV, 1955–87; member of Political Bureau, 1951–86.

Phan Chu Trinh Vietnamese patriot; grandfather of Nguyen Thi Binh.

Rapacki, Adam Foreign minister of Poland.

Rostow, Walt Whitman Assistant to U.S. president for national security affairs, 1966–69.

Rusk, Dean U.S. secretary of state, 1961–69.

Salisbury, Harrison American journalist.

Seaborn, J. Blair Canadian delegate to International Control Commission.

Souvanna Phouma Neutralist leader of Laos.

Taylor, Maxwell U.S. general; special assistant to President Kennedy, 1961–64; ambassador to RVN, 1964–65.

Thant, U Secretary general of United Nations, 1962–71.

Thich Quang Duc Buddhist monk who set himself on fire in Saigon, June 11, 1963.

Thich Tri Quang Leader of Buddhist Institute.

Tran Buu Kiem NLF diplomat; PRG representative to Paris peace talks.

Tran Dinh Thao Leader of National Alliance of Democratic and Peace Forces.

Tran Huu Thanh NLF diplomat; led delegation to People's Republic of China, 1966–67.

Tran Thiem Khiem Premier of Bao Dai regime.

Tran Van Thanh Catholic priest who organized anticorruption campaign against Nguyen Van Thieu, 1971.

Tran Van Tra PAVN general, B-2 theater.

Truong Chinh Secretary general of Lao Dong, 1954–56; president of National Assembly, 1958–76; member of Political Bureau, 1951–86.

Truong Nhu Tang NLF official; PRG minister of justice, 1969–75.

Van Tien Dung PAVN general; member of Political Bureau, 1972–86.

Vo Dong Giang NLF diplomat; member of NLF's Central Committee.

Vo Nguyen Giap PAVN general; minister of defense, 1941–81.

Vu Huu Binh DRV ambassador to Burma.

Xuan Thuy DRV minister for foreign affairs, 1963–65; DRV representative at Paris peace talks.

GUERRILLA DIPLOMACY

1

THE MAQUIS: ORIGINS OF THE NLF AND ITS DIPLOMATIC FRONT

On December 17, 1960, Nguyen Van Hieu, a journalist and schoolteacher, left Saigon secretly for the jungles of Tay Ninh province. He arrived at his rendezvous two days later and prepared for the business that had brought him to this remote corner of southern Viet Nam. That evening, Hieu and sixty other southern revolutionaries entered a makeshift meeting hall under a banner that read, "Welcome General Congress for the Foundation of the National Liberation Front for South Viet Nam." Before the evening was over, Hieu had supervised the creation of a new united front designed to overthrow the Saigon government and liberate Viet Nam south of the seventeenth parallel. The birth of the National Liberation Front, the NLF, ushered in a new phase in Viet Nam's modern revolution. After six years of trying to liberate the country through political means alone, the Lao Dong, Viet Nam's Communist Party, had approved the combination of political and military struggle movements to crush the American-backed Saigon regime. "The Maquis was organized with one simple purpose," an NLF cadre later commented, "and that was to liberate the South."[1]

From the birth of the NLF in 1960, officials in Washington claimed that Hanoi alone directed the armed struggle in the South. Key members of the Kennedy and Johnson administrations argued that the flow of men and supplies from north to south kept the revolution alive. Stop this externally supported insurgency, they insisted, and South Viet Nam could be stabilized. In December 1961, the Kennedy administration released a white paper titled "A Threat to Peace: North Viet Nam's Effort to Conquer South Viet Nam," which provided a rationale for the administration's policy toward the NLF. According to the document's authors, the NLF was nothing more than a "puppet on a string"; Communists in Hanoi had gone to great lengths to "conceal their direct participation in the program to conquer and absorb South Viet Nam."[2] The white paper was the underpinning of the Kennedy administration's explanation for the war and provided justification for its escalation. Since North Viet Nam had violated the letter and spirit of the 1954 Geneva Accords by invading South Viet Nam, Ngo Dinh Diem, the president of the newly formed Republic of Viet Nam (RVN), had the right to ask for outside assistance.

Critics of American intervention argued that the insurgency in South Viet Nam was essentially a civil war. Antiwar scholars suggested that the NLF was autonomous and independent of the Communists in Hanoi and that the Front had risen "at southern initiative in response to southern demands."[3] The French historian Philippe Devillers, a long-time student of Viet Nam, declared that southerners "were literally driven by Diem to take up arms in self-defence." He argued that the insurrection existed before the Communists decided to take part, and that "they were simply forced to join in" or risk losing control of the radical peasant movement in the South.[4]

As part of its overall strategy, the NLF publicly distanced itself from Hanoi. "We represent only the will of the people of South Viet Nam," one leading NLF official declared in 1962. "The Front stands for the creation of a coalition government that is independent of foreign interference and that has a neutral foreign policy."[5] Front strategists correctly predicted that they could exploit world opinion to frustrate the United States and its Saigon ally by making it impossible for them to build a cohort of supportive or at least sympathetic allies. By the mid-1960s, several world leaders and international organizations were convinced the Front was an independent actor in South Viet Nam. Postwar memoirs available in the West confirm this view. Truong Nhu Tang, a founding member of the Front, declared that he was never a Communist and that it was Diem who had in fact contributed to the formation of the NLF by "creating a swell of animosity throughout the country."[6] According to the NLF's own record, therefore, the Front had risen out of the tinder-dry fields of South Viet Nam in opposition to Diem with little outside influence or support.

In the postwar period, policy makers and scholars have not reached consensus on the makeup of the NLF. Instead, as Marvin Gettlemen has reported, Viet Nam War scholarship, "more than most areas of scholarly work, was and is an extension of the war by ideological means."[7] In this environment, it is difficult to track the complicated interplay of events and forces that led the Lao Dong to accept a united front strategy in South Viet Nam. It now seems clear, however, that the NLF was a classical Communist front organization that came to life in 1960 after the Party concluded that it could not unify the country through political means alone. The Lao Dong took advantage of its existing political structure in the South to mobilize Communists and noncommunists into a united front that opposed Ngo Dinh Diem and sought to liberate South Viet Nam from foreign influence. The Party's evolution toward a strategy of armed violence is one of the more interesting chapters in the war's history and tells us much about the nature of Viet Nam's modern revolution and the NLF.

A discussion of the origins of the NLF also tells us much about the development and implementation of its diplomatic strategy. The NLF's diplomatic corps had a decidedly southern worldview, and like most southern Communists, they gave primacy to the liberation war. The regional differences in tactics and strategy forced on the Party by the 1954 division of Viet Nam had a dramatic impact on the conduct and outcome of the war. Although the Party clearly controlled all policy decisions, southerners often pursued a foreign policy that brought them into conflict with some northerners. This conflict was born out of the events ending the First Indochina War and led to the creation of the NLF itself.

Of primary importance to the creation of the NLF were the provisions of the 1954 Geneva Accords and the failure of the Party to unify the country through the political protocols of this peace agreement. On July 20, 1954, after eight years of war and weeks of negotiations, representatives of the Democratic Republic of Viet Nam (DRV) met in Geneva with French officials to discuss the conditions and terms of France's withdrawal from Indochina. At the time, few observers could foresee the high human and ecological costs associated with the failure of the peace agreement. Nor could they have foretold the impact of the accord on the Lao Dong. The temporary division of Viet Nam at the seventeenth parallel and the delay of two years for unifying national elections set in motion a series of events that threatened the future of the Lao Dong and its modern revolution.[8]

The acceptance of the 1954 Geneva Accords marked a clear turning point in the Lao Dong's overall strategy. Since the beginning of the First Indochina War in 1946, the Party had supported the military struggle movement as the main method of achieving its goals. After years of bitter fighting, the People's Army of Viet Nam (PAVN) faced exhaustion and a decline in morale. One official source in Hanoi reported that PAVN regulars had to "overcome fatigue and weariness" to win at Dien Bien Phu and that "negative tendencies had appeared" within the armed forces.[9] President Ho Chi Minh told the plenary session of the Sixth Party Plenum in the summer of 1954 that "it was our aim to wipe out the puppet administration and army with a view to national reunification; now we practice a policy of leniency and seek reunification of the country through nationwide elections."[10] Although few Party leaders believed the elections would actually take place, most favored the respite from the burdens of war.

The changing international situation also had an impact on Lao Dong policy. In 1956, at the Soviet Union's Twentieth Party Congress, Premier Nikita Khrushchev denounced Joseph Stalin and outlined a policy of peaceful coexistence with the West. Khrushchev announced that the transition from capitalism to socialism could be peaceful if "parliamentary means" were applied adequately.[11] At Geneva, the Chinese Communists had made clear their reluctance to initiate a provocative action that might invite American intervention in Southeast Asia.[12] Having suffered heavy losses during the Korean War, Peking was not eager for another war. Pressured by the Soviets and the Chinese, the Viets agreed in July 1954 to accept the political compromise offered in Geneva. Accordingly, the Lao Dong also accepted the political struggle movement as its primary formula for unifying the country.

The political struggle movement required a massive restructuring of Party apparatus, particularly in the South, where the Communists had "surrendered" political control. The Party therefore disbanded the Lien Viet Front (1946–54), which had organized the population during the First Indochina War, and replaced it with the Fatherland Front. For the Lao Dong, the united front strategy had proved successful throughout the century in its domestic battles with the French. A united front was a tactical organization that mobilized all disaffected elements of society. According to General Vo Nguyen Giap, the front "must rally all the forces that are susceptible of being rallied" in opposition to the enemy.[13] In practice, the united front brought together trade union members, student associations, religious groups, political activists, and temporary allies of all social classes. Any individual or group that opposed "the enemy" could join, regardless of class.[14] These temporary alliances helped the Party achieve its objectives by putting enormous military and political pressure on the enemy, but they also neutralized potentially dangerous internal elements. In later years, noncommunists in the NLF did become a political liability and forced the Lao Dong to take drastic action.

Beginning in 1955, the Fatherland Front's objective was to organize cadres for political action and national elections in South Viet Nam. "We had less than two years before the national elections," one member of the Fatherland Front later explained, "and we had to prepare the population for political action."[15] According to Carlyle Thayer, an expert on the Lao Dong, the Party attempted to persuade legal and semilegal organizations to agitate for the implementation of the political provisions of the Geneva Accords.[16] Political agitation was to take place at the local level, where the bulk of mass association members felt most heavily the pressures of feudal land tenure policies. In 1955, Ngo Dinh Diem, soon to be elected president of the Republic of Viet Nam (RVN), passed a series of decrees that reversed many of the land reform measures outlined in the Geneva agreements. Under Diem's new laws, landlords could tax peasants and collect up to 25 percent of the main crop for land rents.[17] In addition, Diem applied new landownership criteria that made it impossible to hold title to land unless it had been approved in Saigon.[18] Sensing that most of the rural population opposed such measures, the Fatherland Front mobilized peasants to protest to the International Control Commission (ICC), an oversight body responsible for implementation of the Geneva Accords. Many peasants went far beyond protest of Diem's policies, however, to call for his ouster.

Ngo Dinh Diem had returned to Viet Nam in 1954, after a five-year absence, as Emperor Bao Dai's new prime minister. The third of nine children, he earned a law degree in 1924 and then accepted a position as provincial governor at the age of twenty-five.[19] In 1933, the newly crowned Bao Dai, last of the Nguyen emperors, appointed Diem as his minister of the interior.[20] A devout Catholic, Diem eventually abandoned political life for the seminary. In the early 1950s, he took up residence at the Maryknoll Seminary in Lakewood, New Jersey, supposedly with the intention of devoting the rest of his life to religious study. By 1953, however, Diem had made the acquaintance of several anticommunists in the United States Senate, including John F. Kennedy, Joseph P. McCarthy, and Mike Mansfield. He told of Communist atrocities in his homeland and of his lifelong refusal to cooperate with Ho Chi Minh. "I would rather die than make a pact with that devil," Diem reportedly told an eager Joe McCarthy.[21] Diem saw in the young Americans an opportunity, and by late 1953, he felt political stirrings once again.

Diem's opportunism met with the realities of the Cold War and events in Viet Nam in early 1954 when Bao Dai called him to Paris and offered him the position of prime minister if he pledged to "defend Viet Nam from the Communists and the French."[22] Sensing the emperor's political weakness, the astute Diem maneuvered the United States into supporting his own candidacy for the presidency of the Republic of Viet Nam. Buoyed by the fact that Washington wanted to "prevent a Communist victory through all Vietnamese elections," Diem in years ahead secured massive military and economic aid from his new partner.[23] Pointing to alleged DRV truce violations to justify their actions, American officials created a regional defense organization, the Southeast Asia Treaty Organization (SEATO), to repel any Communist aggression in the area. Claiming he was under attack from without, Diem with U.S. backing suspended the 1956 elections and presided over the birth of the Republic of Viet Nam, a counterrevolutionary alternative to the Lao Dong and the North.[24]

Once he consolidated power, Diem attacked the Fatherland Front. As early as August 1955 he launched a major drive against the various mass organizations that made up the Front. His newly created national police force arrested thousands of suspected Communists, who were jailed, perhaps at the former French prison on Poulo Condore Island, or executed. By early 1956, according to the journalist Stanley Karnow, Diem had reduced the former Communist cells south of the seventeenth parallel by 90 percent.[25] These political sweeps were some of the darkest days for the Party, and membership in the South dropped off significantly. Once it became clear that national elections would not take place so long as Diem was in power, several southerners urged the Party's Central Committee to reevaluate the political struggle movement.[26] "We had no recourse," complained one southern Communist. "Our families suffered at the hands of Diem and we could do nothing but sit back and watch. . . . It was disgusting."[27] Indeed, the Central Committee felt enormous pressure to launch retaliatory military strikes.

In late April 1956, however, at the Lao Dong's Ninth Plenum, the Party reaffirmed its commitment to unification "through political means."[28] This decision came after a heated debate between those Lao Dong officials who wanted to liberate Viet Nam by any means necessary and those who wanted to continue the political struggle while building socialism in the North. Le Duan, the Nam Bo [southern] regional secretary, argued vehemently for a renewed armed struggle against Diem. Truong Chinh, the Lao Dong's first secretary in 1956, believed that the political struggle promised new "reasons to be confident in the correctness of the policy . . . in the struggle for national reunification." Criticizing Le Duan, Chinh declared, "There are some people who do not yet believe in the correctness of this political program and in the policy of peaceful reunification of the country."[29] The Lao Dong's decision at the Ninth Party Plenum evoked protest in the South, but many Party strategists considered political struggle the only option.

In the mid-1950s, pursuing the political struggle was the pragmatic course for the Lao Dong. There was little international support for armed violence, and the United States was a formidable enemy. The Party had suffered tremendous losses at the hands of the French during its long struggle against colonialism, and most Vietnamese were not eager for another bloody encounter with the West. Developing socialism in the North remained the primary goal for many Party leaders because "all revolutionary efforts are meaningless without the reform of antisocialist economic elements. We must have a socialist base from which to expand and defeat the American puppets in the South."[30]

Still, many southerners, believing that the Party had lost the peace at Geneva by allowing the division of the country, called for an immediate reversal of policy and all-out attacks against the Saigon regime. Perhaps the most outspoken advocate of armed violence in the South was Le Duan.

Le Duan was born in 1908 in Quang Tri province, long a hotbed of anti-French activity.[31] He was a founding member of the Indochinese Communist Party in 1930, and like many others, he had spent time in French prisons. During his first incarceration, from 1931 to 1936, he learned revolutionary theory from his elders. When the French emptied their jails during the Popular Front period, 1936–39, Le Duan emerged as a committed revolutionary. From his earliest writings, we can see the clear identification with the region of his birth. Le Duan believed that the South had a unique colonial history and therefore suffered the heaviest burden.[32] During much of the Second World War, he was imprisoned by the Vichy French and their Japanese masters.[33] Once released, he returned to the South as a leader of the Lien Viet Front and quickly ascended to the position of regional secretary of Nam Bo, the southernmost region of the Party's political apparatus in Viet Nam.

At the Party's Tenth Plenum, in September 1956, a series of events propelled Le Duan into the national spotlight. Truong Chinh, the Party's secretary general, was forced to resign because of the failures of the Lao Dong's land reform policies. A Lao Dong spokesperson reported in September that "mistakes and shortcomings have been committed during the past period. In agrarian reform and the readjustment of organizations, grave mistakes have been committed."[34] Indeed, land reform had been an unmitigated disaster, with terror squads roaming the countryside and land distribution requirements suspect. Ho Chi Minh replaced Truong Chinh and immediately asked for the resignation of several other top Party officials, all of whom granted revolutionary primacy to building socialism in the North.[35] Finally, Vietnamese records indicate that the Party invited Le Duan to make a formal presentation on conditions in Nam Bo at its Eleventh Plenum, in December 1956.

Le Duan's report, "The Revolutionary Path in the South," was a forceful statement advocating the combination of political and military struggle movements in the South. This report grew out of a special conference of the Nam Bo Regional Committee held in April 1956, and its recommendations were widely supported. The lengthy chronicle concluded that there was "no other path for the people of the South but the path of revolution."[36] After careful consideration, the Lao Dong concurred with Le Duan's findings, concluding that "self-defense and armed propaganda forces are needed to support the political struggle, and eventually those armed forces must be used to carry out a revolution to overthrow U.S.-Diem. . . . The revolution in the South is to use a violent general uprising to win political power."[37] The Lao Dong's decision did not unleash armed violence unchecked. Instead, it encouraged southerners to shift the balance of forces in their favor through continued political agitation and to engage in limited political assassinations. "We were told to prepare for the armed uprising," one former NLF cadre later explained, "but we were not to attack prematurely."[38] Indeed, the Party would continue to rely on the political and diplomatic struggle movements to build up cadre levels in the South before it approved open hostilities against the Diem regime.

Le Duan's statement to the Lao Dong's plenum marked the beginning of his ascendancy to supreme power within the Party. In early 1957, senior Lao Dong officials invited him to join the Political Bureau, the Party's most important policy planning body.[39] From this vantage point, he continued to advocate armed violence in the South. The result was the expansion of the Party's revolutionary base in the South and an apparent shift in the balance of forces. By August 1958, the Party had carefully consolidated its apparatus and had successfully exploited Diem's political weaknesses. Cadre ranks had increased dramatically and new military bases appeared in all regions of the South. By the time the Nam Bo Regional Committee met in August 1958 at its third conference, Party leaders reported many positive developments to Le Duan. The newest Political Bureau member was cautious, however, and warned southern Communists to maintain control over the revolution. "We must not move into full armed rebellion too soon. The U.S.-Diem regime is capable of inflicting great terror on our people and we must retain the proper revolutionary balance."[40] For the increasingly pragmatic Le Duan, the proper balance required caution in the use of force.

Caution had a price, however, and in late October 1958 the Political Bureau ordered Le Duan to make an emergency inspection tour of the South.[41] Party leaders were concerned by recent reports that Diem had launched a new anticommunist campaign and that several radical peasant groups had retaliated. One brief suggested that cadres in the Central Highlands had openly rebelled, killing several Saigon troops.[42] Another report described attacks against key ARVN (Army of the Republic of Viet Nam) installations.[43] The results had been disastrous. Diem's secret police began, for the first time, to target urban areas in their anticommunist sweeps and had jailed, tortured, or executed thousands of southerners. More than one southern Communist has called these "the darkest days for the Party."[44]

Memoirs from this period only begin to tell of the cruelty and bloodshed. One young Communist, Nguyen Thi Dinh, described the situation in her province: "Sister, we must arm ourselves to survive, otherwise we'll die. If you let us kill the security police to get weapons, we'll do it right away. . . . We've heard that people in Hong Ngu and Dong Thap province have taken up arms. How about our province? Have we been allowed to strike back?"[45] Another Party cadre explained that "by 1959 the situation in the South had crossed to a stage which the Communists considered to be the darkest in their whole lives . . . there were instances of kidnappings and assassinations in order to resolve the problem of survival."[46] The regional nature of the debate over the use of armed violence is undeniable. As George Kahin points out, "the Central Committee faced disagreement with its southern branch; it was already losing influence over some southerners, and further delay would cause greater loss among those who were still active."[47] Le Duan was sympathetic to the southerners' plight, no doubt, and the Nam Bo Regional Committee still had considerable influence over the thinking of the Party's rising star.

Diem's reign of terror had a profound impact on Le Duan, and he returned to Hanoi more determined than ever to push the armed struggle. After his sorrowful trip south, Le Duan reported to the Party's Fifteenth Plenum, in January 1959, that conditions in the South had deteriorated and the political struggle movement seemed stalled. With American backing, Diem had initiated unprecedented purges in the South and thousands of cadres had suffered. To remedy the situation, Le Duan presented a list of recommendations. The Party must adopt a strategy of violence and must organize a broad-based united front directly under the control of the Central Committee. The armed struggle must be combined with the diplomatic struggle movement.[48] The Lao Dong accepted these "requirements" by passing what is now known as Resolution 15. In May 1959, the Political Bureau approved Resolution 15 and declared that "the time has come to push the armed struggle against the enemy."[49] Indeed, by midsummer, cadres in the Central Highlands had received word that "the green light for switching from political struggle alone to political struggle combined with armed struggle" had been approved.[50]

In September 1960, at its third national congress, the Lao Dong selected Le Duan as its new secretary general. Some former Communist Party officials have suggested that this promotion represented the dominance of the "southern view" in the Lao Dong, advocacy of armed violence. In any event, Le Duan used his new position to advocate the immediate creation of a broad-based front "to rally all patriotic classes and sections of the people . . . to oppose the U.S.-Diem regime."[51] Shortly after the congress, on December 19, 1960, at a secret meeting in the jungle of Tay Ninh province, near Viet Nam's border with Cambodia, sixty Vietnamese revolutionaries met to proclaim the formation of the National Front for the Liberation of South Viet Nam (NLF).

The founding of the NLF therefore resulted from a complex set of circumstances dating back to the signing of the Geneva Accords. Because the Lao Dong had agreed in 1954 to the temporary division of Viet Nam at the seventeenth parallel, it was forced to adopt twin revolutionary goals: to build socialism in the North and to liberate the South. Early pressure from the Soviets and Chinese compelled Party leaders to accept the political struggle as the primary means for national liberation. The Diem regime took advantage of the Lao Dong's unwillingness to engage in armed violence by launching massive anticommunist sweeps that depleted the Party's ranks in the South. After six years of trying to reunify the country through political means alone, Le Duan and the Nam Bo Regional Committee persuaded the Lao Dong's Political Bureau to combine the political and military struggle movements. At its Fifteenth Party Plenum, in January 1959, the Party recommended the formation of a broad-based united front to push the armed struggle forward and mobilize all anti-Diem forces. The Political Bureau affirmed the Party's recommendation at a meeting in May, and in September 1960 the Lao Dong approved the formation of the new united front.

The united front strategy in Viet Nam has deep historic roots. The Party had successfully used such a strategy to rally anticolonial forces under the Viet Minh and the Lien Viet fronts, and had used the Fatherland Front to harass Ngo Dinh Diem in the post-Geneva period. Essentially, the united front was a broad-based tactical organization that attempted to provide links between the Party and noncommunist elements. Any individual or group who opposed the Party's enemies might join the front, but its leadership was clearly dominated by Communists. The united front, according to the historian Huynh Kim Khanh, was supposed to be the Party's "architectural facade, composed of social and functional organizations whose dual function was to shield the Party from unfriendly forces and at the same time promote the Party's ideological values and policies as widely as possible."[52] In the case of the NLF, the Front was to unite all southerners opposed to Ngo Dinh Diem.

At the NLF's first meeting in December 1960, it established a provisional committee to oversee its operations. Dr. Phung Van Cung served as president and the schoolteacher Nguyen Van Hieu as secretary general.[53] During 1961 the provisional committee supervised the formation of local liberation associations that would eventually merge with the NLF during the Front's first national congress the following year. Of these local liberation associations, perhaps the most important was the Committee for the Saigon–Cholon–Gia Dinh Zone, headed by Vo Van Kiet. Kiet was active in the South during the French war and stayed behind in 1954 to help organize political opposition to Ngo Dinh Diem. As head of the newly formed Saigon committee of the NLF, he oversaw its recruitment operations. In 1961 the NLF was particularly interested in separating the Saigon regime from its urban support. Accordingly, the Saigon committee, under Kiet's direction, met frequently with noncommunists in the metropolitan region.[54] NLF officials worked cautiously and creatively to build a sophisticated network of professional allies. According to Truong Nhu Tang, a founding member of the NLF, recruiters made wide contacts in the government, business, and intellectual communities, "not merely to gain new members for the Front, but also to enlist the sympathy or strengthen those strands of opinion that bore an affinity with any of our positions."[55] By the end of 1961, most Party strategists concluded that the

NLF had won over nearly 40 percent of the urban middle class, Diem's only potential allies.[56] In later years, however, that group challenged Hanoi's authority over the southern revolution and forced the Lao Dong to distinguish forcefully and prematurely between southern Communists and noncommunists within the united front.

The NLF, of course, was also interested in winning over the rural areas. Throughout 1961 it relied on the combination of political and military struggle movements to enlist cadres. Its goals, as stated in a captured Party document, were to "lessen enemy pressure, oppose military operations and terrorism, oppose the strategic hamlet program, and halt the seizure of land and the corvée labor system."[57] To accomplish these objectives, the Front engaged in a "people's war" in villages throughout South Viet Nam. A concept borrowed in part from the Chinese Communists, people's war stressed the political nature of the military struggle.

In practice, people's war relied heavily on the NLF cadres' ability to communicate the ideas of the revolution to a war-ravaged rural population. According to one of the most important Lao Dong publications on the village war, "Needs of the Revolution," Party cadres should "choose the right moment to act . . . when the people's rights have been endangered." The Lao Dong defined these threats as "corruption, high taxation, forced money donations, land robbing, military draft." After these conditions have been identified, Party leaders explained, "struggle movements can then be launched in favor of freedom of travel, freedom to work, freedom of trade, freedom to move to a new part of the country, and for village council elections."[58] Cadres used this technique to convince villagers that they were the vanguard of a new social movement that would return control of their hamlets to them. They purposefully sought out for positions of leadership in the local liberation associations exactly those elements of rural society that the Saigon regime had excluded from power. NLF cadres drove repressive government officials out of many villages and harassed ARVN troops. In the countryside the NLF could provide security that the combined forces of the Saigon regime could not match. At the same time, cadres laid the foundation for the local liberation associations, controlled and directed by the Front. Traditional village councils were reinstituted and new local authorities replaced the RVN's district officials, many of whom lived in Saigon. Promotion in these liberation associations often depended on criteria that were the reverse of the Diem regime's and usually led to direct local control.

These measures, combined with selective acts of violence, forced the Saigon regime into a static position. As Jeffrey Race, an expert on the village war, has noted, "the Party's social strategy was preemptive . . . by developing policies more congenial to the interests of these classes than were the policies of the government, the Party ensured that when the conflict crossed into the military phase the majority of the population would choose to fight against the government."[59] Indeed, most village accounts portray the RVN as an intrusive force with little connection to the countryside.[60] Rural Viets saw in the Saigon regime a distant annoyance that instituted repressive policies, such as forced conscription, limitations on travel, and national identification cards.[61] Perhaps the most threatening Saigon policy was the so-called strategic hamlet program.

As part of its strategy to isolate the NLF from its base of support, the people of South Viet Nam, the Diem regime adopted a counterinsurgency plan based on the British experience in Malaya. The strategic hamlet program gathered peasants from scattered villages and brought them into safety zones controlled by Saigon. The hamlets were surrounded by moats, barbed wire, and military forces. Diem also planned to use the hamlets as a means of social and economic control, hoping to bind villagers to the government. Instead, most peasants resented being forced from their ancestral farmlands and distrusted the new village councils. In sharp contrast to Saigon's rural pacification program, the NLF offered a preemptive social revolution that promised local control, village security, and land and tax reform.

By the end of 1961, the NLF's provisional committee looked proudly upon its accomplishments. According to most estimates, the Front's ranks swelled by 300 percent a month in 1961, and it averaged more than three hundred political acts of violence each week.[62] The Front had made significant progress in the people's war, rallying rural Vietnamese to its cause. In the cities, Diem faced a similar crisis. Several of Saigon's leading noncommunists had publicly called for his ouster, and his own troops had attempted two unsuccessful coups.[63] Diem called the situation in South Viet Nam "perilous" and asked for increased American financial and political support.[64]

In Washington, the NLF's success caused the Kennedy administration to reevaluate American policy. In January 1961, ten days after taking office, the newly elected president underscored the Communists' victories in Viet Nam and elsewhere when he declared, "Our problems are critical . . . the tide is unfavorable . . . the news will be worse before it is better."[65] Kennedy's remarks foreshadowed significant Cold War confrontations. In midspring the United States launched the disastrous Bay of Pigs invasion. In Laos, Viet Nam's immediate neighbor, the Communist Pathet Lao was making headway against the American-sponsored government in Vientiane. In late April 1961, shortly after the catastrophic invasion of Cuba, the president concluded that a negotiated settlement in Laos was the best he could hope for, and the United States agreed to participate in a peace conference in Geneva.[66]

In June 1961, Kennedy met with Khrushchev in Vienna, where the Soviet leader again affirmed his support of wars for national liberation. Coming in the wake of the Bay of Pigs and Laos, the Vienna meeting haunted Kennedy. The president had refused to supply U.S. airpower to salvage the Cuban raid and had also expressed his unwillingness to intervene militarily in Laos. His browbeating by Khrushchev in Vienna convinced him that he had to take a stand somewhere. In mid-August the erection of the Berlin Wall stunned an already beleaguered White House. Berlin, however, was not going to be the administration's battleground, even though Secretary of Defense Robert McNamara later revealed that Washington was prepared for such a conflict.[67] Instead, Kennedy focused on Viet Nam.

In late October 1961, Kennedy sent General Maxwell Taylor, his personal military adviser, and Walt Whitman Rostow of the State Department to Viet Nam to assess the situation at first hand. They concluded that the NLF had made significant gains in the countryside and that the Saigon regime was plagued by a "deep crisis of confidence and a serious loss in national morale."[68] Taylor and Rostow recommended a significant increase in American economic and political aid to the RVN and the introduction of an 8,000-man "logistical task force," ostensibly to deal with flood control. In the past, Diem had rejected all of Washington's attempts to introduce American combat troops, but many in Saigon believed that the time had come for a greater U.S. military presence. If the NLF continued to grow unchecked, Taylor and Rostow warned, the future of South Viet Nam was in jeopardy.

As Taylor and Rostow's report circulated in Washington, key critics of American military intervention condemned the proposal. Undersecretary of State Chester Bowles and the diplomats John Kenneth Galbraith and W. Averell Harriman called for an expansion of the Laos negotiations to include Viet Nam. Harriman, who represented the United States in Geneva, claimed that Diem was "unpopular" and "dictatorial," and therefore unworthy of continued American support.[69] Galbraith agreed, calling Diem one of the most corrupt and ineffectual leaders in the world.[70] Bowles warned that in supporting Diem the United States was "headed full blast up a dead end street."[71] Other Washington insiders urged the president to force Diem to make some needed reforms before sending more aid or troops. Some low-ranking officials even recommended that Washington withdraw from Viet Nam immediately, "before the situation turned completely helpless."[72] The heated debate in Washington signified the changing conditions in South Viet Nam and offered the first post-1954 choice between military intervention and complete withdrawal.

Ultimately, Kennedy decided to take the middle road. He agreed to increase the number of American military advisers in Viet Nam, expanded military and economic aid to Saigon, and created a formal military command structure, the Military Assistance and Command–Vietnam (MACV), whose top official had the same status as the ambassador.[73] The White House then released the 1961 white paper, claiming that Hanoi had invaded South Viet Nam in clear violation of the 1954 Geneva Accords. The president stopped short of Taylor and Rostow's request for troops. Kennedy's new counterinsurgency measures, modeled on the British experience in Malaya, relied heavily on the strategic hamlet program. The objective was to isolate the NLF from the peasants by building new protected hamlets. American advisers and their ARVN counterparts relocated villagers to these newly constructed "safe havens" to separate them from the Communists and facilitate the predicted RVN social and economic revolution. The goal, according to the counterinsurgency expert Roger Hilsman, was to reduce NLF cadres to "hungry, marauding bands of outlaws devoting all their energies to remaining alive."[74] In the first year of Kennedy's new counterinsurgency program, the number of Americans in Viet Nam tripled.

The new American commitment had a dramatic impact on events in Viet Nam. Shortly after Washington's fateful decisions, the NLF met to assess what it called Kennedy's "special war." The Front's leaders concluded that the war had indeed entered a new phase and would require new tactics and strategic thinking. Accordingly, at its first congress, in February 1962, the Front asked the provisional committee to turn over its duties to the NLF's newly formed Central Committee. The Party correctly understood that Kennedy's counterinsurgency program laid the groundwork for future increases in American combat troops and aid to the RVN. The Front would face a changing enemy that brought to the field the latest technology and huge financial resources. The Front's people's war campaign, so successful in 1961, would face "new requirements in tactics, weaponry, and resources."[75] To meet these new requirements,

Party leaders determined that the Lao Dong's Political Bureau had to assume greater control over the Front's operations through a streamlined command structure.

The NLF's new command structure increased the Lao Dong's day-to-day control of operations and "regularized" strategic planning. In short, the Party assumed greater coordination and control of the decision-making process through the creation of the NLF's Central Committee and Presidium. Of the fifty-two members of the Central Committee, only twenty-seven were publicly identified.[76] The Central Committee's activities were closely coordinated by the NLF's Presidium, consisting of a president, a vice president, a general secretary, and five vice chairs. The NLF's Presidium reported directly to the Lao Dong's Central Committee Directorate for South Viet Nam, a Party structure that had been revitalized with the birth of the NLF. The Directorate, known in the West as COSVN, acted as liaison between the Lao Dong's Central Committee in Hanoi and the NLF's Presidium. Approved Party resolutions made their way to the Front via COSVN, and in return the NLF voiced its concerns through COSVN's director. From 1962 to 1964 that position was held by Nguyen Van Linh.[77] Nguyen Chi Thanh would assume the post in 1964. The COSVN's headquarters was located alongside the NLF's secret outpost in the jungle of Tay Ninh province, in South Viet Nam.[78] While the Front's Central Committee met infrequently, the Presidium operated on a daily basis.

In the first years of the NLF, three individuals dominated the Presidium: Nguyen Huu Tho, a Saigon lawyer, served as its president; the architect Huynh Tan Phat was vice president; and the teacher Nguyen Van Hieu was the secretary general. Tho was born in Cholon, a suburb of Saigon, in 1910. He studied law in France and returned to Viet Nam in the late 1930s as a successful barrister. In the late 1940s he headed several anti-French demonstrations in the Saigon area and in 1950 he was arrested by the French. The colonial administration later exiled him to the prison town of Lai Chau, and he remained there until 1952. Once freed, he returned to Saigon and helped organize the Saigon-Cholon Peace Committee, an anti-Diem organization that advocated national elections. Diem's secret police arrested Tho in 1954, and after several years in Saigon jails, he was transferred to Phu Yen under house arrest. When the NLF was founded, he was still in captivity.[79] NLF cadres freed him in early 1961 and rushed him to Tay Ninh.

Unlike Tho, Phat and Hieu had been long-time members of the Communist Party. Huynh Tan Phat was born in the delta town of My Tho in

1913. As a student in the 1930s he had led several anti-French demonstrations and founded the vanguard Youth Movement. During France's Vichy period he was arrested twice before participating in the August Revolution.[80] During the First Indochina War, Phat gained valuable experience as director of the Lao Dong's Information Service in Nam Bo.[81]

Nguyen Van Hieu was born in 1922 in the southernmost reaches of Viet Nam, on the Ca Mau peninsula. He studied history at university in Hanoi and Saigon before returning south to aid the Party's struggle against the French. In the fall of 1945 he participated in the Ca Mau Movement, one of the most successful anti-French uprisings during the war. After Dien Bien Phu, he worked for several Saigon newspapers, writing under the pseudonym Khai Minh (to declare clearly).[82] One expert on the Front has called him "the NLF's Lenin."[83]

Like many of their contemporaries, Phat and Hieu joined the Party in the late 1930s because of its position on national liberation. With its new command structure in place, the NLF moved to integrate the political, military, and diplomatic struggle movements into a unified whole. The Party had always emphasized that the modern revolution was fought on many fronts and had urged its cadres to think and act accordingly. As one former NLF leader explained, "every military clash, every demonstration, every propaganda appeal was seen as part of an integrated whole; each had consequences far beyond its immediately apparent results."[84] Communist Party leaders therefore placed considerable importance on public opinion, both domestic and international, as an "objective factor" that must be manipulated. According to an essay in *Nhan Dan* (The People), the Party's daily newspaper, international diplomacy was vital to the revolution's survival. "The more our just struggle wins the support of the people of the world, the better able we will be to demand the implementation of the Geneva Accords, including the most important clause, on reunification."[85] For many Lao Dong leaders, diplomacy was one of the most important weapons in war. Like the ancient Chinese military philosopher Sun Tzu, the Lao Dong believed that victory came to the side that could render the opponent's weapons useless in battle.[86] Throughout the American war, then, diplomacy occupied a special place in the minds and actions of Vietnamese revolutionaries.

In its first two years, the Front's diplomatic goals were simple: to introduce the NLF to the world, to create an aura of legitimacy, and to earn diplomatic recognition.[87] The Party tried to achieve these objectives with a massive outpouring of public pronouncements. Each condemned the Diem regime and claimed that the NLF represented the will of the people of South Viet Nam. By late 1961, most countries of the socialist bloc had recognized the NLF as the legitimate government of South Viet Nam through the press and at international conferences. At the NLF's first congress, in 1962, however, the Party realized that the time had come to increase the Front's diplomatic activities to "fully exploit the international situation."[88] Accordingly, the NLF created a Foreign Relations Commission, initially headed by Nguyen Van Hieu, that served as its foreign ministry from 1962 until the formation of the Provisional Revolutionary Government in 1969.

The formation of the Foreign Relations Commission brought the first stage of the southern revolution to its climax. After six years of trying to reunify the country through political means alone, the Lao Dong's Political Bureau accepted a combination of political and military struggle movements to overthrow the Diem regime and liberate Viet Nam south of the seventeenth parallel. The Party recommended the formation of a broad-based united front at its Fifteenth Plenum, in January 1959, to push the armed struggle forward and to mobilize all anti-Diem factions. The Political Bureau affirmed the Party's recommendation at a meeting in May 1959, and in September 1960, at the Lao Dong's third national congress, it approved the formation of the new united front. On December 20, 1960, the NLF was born in the mangrove swamps of Tay Ninh province in South Viet Nam. It quickly organized local liberation associations that launched preemptive political and military strikes against Ngo Dinh Diem's government. After many political and military successes, the NLF formed a foreign relations commission to exploit the international situation. By late spring 1962, therefore, it stood poised to launch a comprehensive political, military, and diplomatic attack against the Saigon regime.

2

OUR FRIENDS AROUND THE WORLD: THE NLF'S NEUTRALIST PLATFORM

"We believe in a neutral solution to the Viet Nam crisis," NLF Secretary General Nguyen Van Hieu stated in 1962. "Vietnam is capable of determining its own future without outside interference and the National Liberation Front is willing to engage in negotiations right now to produce a peace-loving and democratic government." It was a theme Hieu had sounded throughout the NLF's first year, and it set the tone for the NLF's diplomatic struggle movement. With careful coordination by the Lao Dong, the NLF launched a series of diplomatic initiatives in 1962 and 1963 to convince world leaders and international organizations that the Front was autonomous and independent of Hanoi. NLF diplomats claimed that the Front was the sole legitimate representative of the people of South Viet Nam, but that it was willing to negotiate with others in regard to a coalition government in Saigon. The NLF's neutralist platform, Hieu declared, had the support of "our friends around the world."[1]

The Party based its diplomatic strategy on the concept of "neutralism" and the growing nonalignment movement in Western Europe and the developing world. Since the 1940s, many developing nations and even France had seen neutralism as a middle ground in the Cold War. Caught between superpower rivals, many world leaders tried to chart a third course that offered their respective nations more freedom of action and less vulnerability. Lao Dong officials correctly predicted that they could exploit the sentiments expressed by many Asian and African nations at the 1955 Bandung Conference. President Achmed Sukarno of Indonesia was one of many leaders who claimed that the best political future for emerging nations rested with nonpartisanship in the struggle between communism and capitalism. Neutralism also had support in Western Europe, where several former colonial powers sought to gain influence with the newly independent nations by supporting nonalignment. Many important world organizations, such as the United Nations, had promoted neutralism as a way to stabilize the international situation after the superpower conflicts in Cuba and Laos. In the urban centers of South Viet Nam, thousands of noncommunists also supported what they called a "third alternative" because they feared the Saigon regime as much as the Communists.

Neutralism appealed to the Lao Dong for several pragmatic reasons as well. Understanding early on that the United States considered neutralist countries to be in the enemy camp, Party leaders sought to promote a coalition government in the South to undermine Washington's international position. "We believed from the outset of the Front's diplomatic program," a Party leader later commented, "that we could throw the Kennedy people off balance and make it difficult for Washington to find acts of support from its traditional allies by insisting on a neutralist solution."[2] Another senior Hanoi official added, "There was nothing for Washington to do," for the Party had "forced the Americans into a corner from which there was no easy exit." He concluded that "Kennedy either had to accept our compromise solution, which we knew he did not want to do," or "go against world opinion."[3] In the process, of course, the Party picked up domestic support for its policy of an "all-Vietnamese solution" to the political crisis in South Viet Nam. Unfortunately for the Lao Dong, the Party grossly underestimated the Kennedy administration's willingness to go it alone in Viet Nam. Rather than leading to a political settlement, the crisis caused in part by the NLF's diplomatic effort convinced Kennedy officials that military intervention was necessary. In any event, the NLF's neutralist platform remains an interesting chapter in the history of the war and tells us much about the way southern Communists used diplomacy as a weapon against their more powerful American adversaries. It also reveals hidden tensions between northern and southern Communists over the NLF's diplomatic strategy as neutralism failed to force the United States to withdraw.

In the early days of the NLF, northern and southern Communists saw great potential in promoting a coalition government in South Viet Nam. The decision to launch a neutralization campaign in the South was probably made at the Lao Dong's third national congress, in September 1960.[4] Although no documentary evidence exists to support this claim, a neutralist platform was included in the Ten-Point Manifesto that the NLF released shortly after its formation in December 1960.[5] On the surface, the Front's statement of neutrality seems to contradict the Party's overall goal of uniting Viet Nam under socialism.[6] Two prominent Vietnamese historians explained that at first reading, "the neutrality of the South means for Viet Nam a divergence of political character on the two sides of the seventeenth parallel, while our country has always constituted a single entity." They later concluded, however, that "neutralism is the solution acceptable to all patriots, and would constitute an important step forward compared with the present disguised colonial regime."[7] Northerners and southerners agreed that neutralism offered the Party an effective propaganda tool even though the Kennedy administration was unlikely to accept such a scheme in Viet Nam. "We can gain a tremendous diplomatic advantage and put the United States at a huge disadvantage," one Lao Dong official argued, "by promoting the neutralization of South Viet Nam."[8]

As we saw earlier, neutralism also had tremendous domestic appeal. The Communists hoped that in promoting an all-Vietnamese solution to the political and military crisis in South Viet Nam, they could gain converts from Diem's base of support. Urban professionals who understood the character of the worldwide neutralist movement were potential allies for the NLF if Diem failed to understand their political sympathies. "We opposed American intervention and foreign interference," one Saigon resident later reported, "and although none of my friends supported the Communists, we understood that they were the only ones who recognized the need for an all-Vietnamese answer to our pressing problems."[9] For a people free of French colonial rule less than a decade, neutralism was attractive.

When these domestic sensibilities were taken into account, neutralism emerged as the centerpiece of the Lao Dong's diplomatic strategy at the Front's First Congress, in February 1962. Promotion of this new policy was the responsibility of the NLF's nascent Foreign Relations Commission. According to approved strategic resolutions, the Foreign Relations Commission would launch an international offensive promoting the establishment of a coalition government in Saigon with a neutral foreign policy.[10] The Front's objective was to form a union of nonpartisan forces that would come to power in Saigon and then ask the Americans to leave. To accomplish this task, the NLF must promote itself as a separate entity, free of North Viet Nam's control.

The creation of the Front's domestic and international image was the responsibility of the NLF's diplomatic corps. These skillful propagandists were well-educated, urbane members of the bourgeoisie who felt comfortable in the international arena despite Viet Nam's relative isolation. Nguyen Van Hieu, the head of the Foreign Relations Commission, had little experience in foreign policy, but he had traveled extensively and had been a propaganda expert during the French war. According to one Party leader, Hieu was "theoretically sound without being an ideologue."[11] When the Kennedy administration began its counterinsurgency program in Viet Nam, Hieu was one of the first southern Communists to understand the importance of forcing an American withdrawal through the advancement of neutralism. In the early stages of the war, southerners alone suffered directly from U.S. intervention. Neutralism therefore was more than a diplomatic scheme; it provided an alternative to a costly military solution and the high price to be paid by southerners should the United States intervene. "All of our dreams, goals, aspirations are meaningless unless we can remove the foreigners from our land. We must adopt any means necessary to accomplish this task," Hieu explained, "including the promotion of a coalition government in South Viet Nam."[12] He realized that the United States would not drive a wedge between itself and the Saigon government by opening negotiations on Viet Nam, but Hieu also understood neutralism's broad appeal.

At the First Congress in February 1962, NLF leaders argued that a significant number of political elites inside and outside of Viet Nam would openly support neutralism because of the growing suspicion of Soviet and American hegemony. The urban petite bourgeoisie feared U.S. intervention even more than a Communist takeover, Hieu maintained, and would therefore back the NLF's neutralist proposal.[13] Since the urban areas supplied the Saigon government's only support, neutralism could divide the enemy from its potential allies and limit, if not nullify, the possibility of American intervention. Likewise, international support for South Vietnamese neutralism would undercut Washington's efforts to build a Western coalition, as it had done in Korea.

On June 26, 1962, the NLF's Foreign Relations Commission launched its diplomatic offensive. At its first stop, in Prague, Czechoslovakia, the delegation was met at the airport by representatives of the Socialist government, Viet nationals, and dozens of reporters. Hieu understood immediately that the life of an NLF diplomat was going to be far different "from the guerrilla life we were used to in the South." He would spend fourteen hours that day talking with reporters, despite a high fever and chronic dysentery. In his first speech on foreign soil, he outlined reasons for the creation of the NLF and explained that the Diem regime was ruling arbitrarily, without the support of the people of South Viet Nam. He claimed that the Front had risen at southern initiative in response to southern demands, and that it alone represented the aspirations of southern Viets.[14] The Party naturally presumed that such neutralist rhetoric helped swell the Front's ranks.

The next day, in an hour-long interview on Radio Prague, Hieu outlined the Front's Ten-Point Manifesto, highlighted American crimes in the South, and summarized the NLF's goals of peace and neutrality.[15] The NLF could achieve these goals, Hieu argued, once the Americans withdrew from Viet Nam. "Our struggle for the South is a long and hard battle," he warned, "but we solidly believe we will win and build the independence of the South based on democracy, peace, and neutrality." The NLF supported the creation of a neutral South Viet Nam and proposed the establishment of a federation of neutral states in all of Indochina. "We need a neutral zone in Indochina, one that is open to international inspection," Hieu stressed in conclusion.[16]

Perhaps the most effective element of Hieu's appeal was his promotion of the war in Viet Nam as "another holocaust." Hieu told his Czech audience that the Americans and the Saigon army had imprisoned and tortured innocent women and children and that "thousands had been killed in prison." "They are like Hitler," Hieu cried to members of the Czechoslovakian Antifascist League. Hieu visited several World War II sites, including former Nazi death camps. The image was powerful and the message clear: the United States was no better than the fascists. Several Western reporters accompanied Hieu on his tour of rural Czechoslovakia and these images made their way into the leading newspapers of Europe. Hieu's diary makes it clear that this visit was far more than a propaganda ploy; his emotions were real and his pain was genuine.[17]

After his emotional experience in Czechoslovakia, Hieu traveled to Moscow and repeated the Lao Dong's neutralist proposal in an interview with a *New York Times* reporter. The Western press had come to Moscow to cover the International Congress for Disarmament and Peace in July 1962. Hieu insisted that the NLF supported the creation of a coalition government in the South "that is independent of foreign interference and that has a neutral foreign policy."[18] He proposed open negotiations on Viet Nam, similar to the recent discussions on Laos. On July 20, 1962, the anniversary of the signing of the 1954 Geneva Accords, the NLF proclaimed its support for a new government in the South. "The National Liberation Front of South Viet Nam is ready to collaborate on an equal basis with all forces, parties, cliques, groups, associations, and individuals to oppose the aggressive war of U.S. imperialism in South Viet Nam."[19]

The NLF's Presidium carefully coordinated all of its declarations in 1962 with the important public stops of the Hieu mission. In August, while Hieu was in East Germany, the Presidium, acting on behalf of the Front's Central Committee, published a "Fourteen-Point Statement on Neutrality."[20] Hieu and the other diplomats included copies of the manifesto in all of their press releases in Eastern Europe. The document supported the nonalignment movement in South Viet Nam and insisted that all foreign military personnel must be withdrawn from the region. The neutralist government would accept economic aid from all countries without political conditions and would open the Vietnamese economy to foreign investment.

Two weeks after the release of this new statement on neutrality, the Hieu mission traveled to Indonesia and met with President Achmed Sukarno. Hieu told the president that the NLF comprised more than twenty organizations representing people from all strata of southern society. He linked the Saigon government to Viet Nam's colonial past and described Diem as a feudal lord. Sukarno praised the NLF, calling its struggle just and predicting that it "will surely win."[21] During a press conference on September 20, 1962, he supported the creation of a neutral zone in Southeast Asia and proposed open negotiations between the United States and the NLF to end hostilities.[22]

The Sukarno visit was perhaps the most important stop on the Hieu goodwill tour. The meetings in Djakarta were the NLF's first in the noncommunist world. During its initial strategy sessions in February 1962, the Front had purposefully marked Indonesia for support of its neutralist stance.[23] This Southeast Asian nation had been conspicuous by its absence from the Southeast Asian Treaty Organization in 1954 and had claimed that nonalignment represented the best future for Asian nations. Sukarno himself had pursued a vigorously neutral line and had championed nonpartisanship at the 1955 Bandung Conference.[24] Sukarno's tilt toward neutralism had troubled American policy makers for some time. In late 1959, the Eisenhower administration launched an unsuccessful coup attempt against the popular Indonesian president. Allen Dulles, the head of the

Central Intelligence Agency (CIA) and brother of the secretary of state, gave $10 million to anti-Sukarno rebels, but even that enormous sum produced no results. Frustrated, Dulles approved secret air attacks against Sukarno. They ended in bitter failure and the loss of at least one CIA plane.[25] By 1960, relations between the United States and Southeast Asia's largest country had reached an all-time low. Indonesia's neutralist position clearly frustrated SEATO and American efforts to enlarge the war.

The NLF also targeted Prince Norodom Sihanouk of Cambodia and Prince Souvanna Phouma of Laos, two supporters of the growing nonalignment movement. Sihanouk had proposed a similar neutral zone as early as 1961. He believed that the presence of Americans in Indochina represented a return to colonial-style politics and economics and thought the military buildup dangerous to the future of all Indochina. Ever mindful of Cambodia's precarious position between capitalists in Thailand and Communists to the north and east, the young prince continually asserted Khmer neutrality. Sihanouk favored the creation of a neutralized Federation of Indochina comprising Cambodia and South Viet Nam.[26] All political matters would be handled jointly, and all foreign influences would be removed from the region. Such a federation, the prince argued, would bring Cambodia and South Viet Nam unprecedented economic opportunities.[27]

Representatives of the NLF had met with Sihanouk in February 1962, shortly after the First Congress. They apprised him of their neutralist stance and showed him a copy of their program, which referred to the "experiences of peaceful and neutral Cambodia" as proof that neutralism could work in Viet Nam.[28] Two weeks after Hieu began his world tour, Sihanouk told a reporter, "South Viet Nam is an international issue, and should be treated as Laos was treated. South Viet Nam should become a neutral zone."[29] Contact between Sihanouk and the NLF diplomats was regular, usually carried out through Phnom Penh, where the NLF had an extensive political and propaganda network.[30]

Prince Souvanna had come to power in Laos as a result of the three-year negotiations that had brought the United States, the Soviet Union, and China to the bargaining table in Geneva. On July 23, 1962, the participating countries agreed to the withdrawal of all foreign troops and the permanent neutralization of Laos under a coalition representing the country's three main political factions—royalists, neutralists, and Communists.[31] An International Control Commission (ICC) comprising representatives of Canada, Poland, and India would oversee implementation of the agreement. Souvanna, the neutralist leader, believed that such a scheme could work in Laos and in all of Indochina if the Soviet Union, China, and the United States respected its terms.[32] The Kennedy administration left Geneva believing it had made enormous sacrifices for neutralism. Years later, Secretary of State Dean Rusk reported that the prospects for peace in Laos were decent because Souvanna was the "Soviet candidate and not our own." When the PAVN continued to use Laos as a staging area and route of infiltration, Rusk explained, the agreement broke down.[33]

The Kennedy administration declared the neutralist solution in Laos a bitter disappointment as early as October 1962.[34] Robert S. McNamara, Kennedy's secretary of defense, has reported that the failure in Laos had a profound impact on the president, forcing him to reject negotiations in Viet Nam in favor of military action. "He was convinced neutralization had not worked in Laos," McNamara wrote in 1995, "and doubted that it would work next door."[35] According to Dean Rusk, Kennedy made up his mind that if he had to fight international communism, "we'll fight in South Vietnam."[36] Although several scholars have highlighted the "Laos first" aspect of Kennedy's Asian policy, the Lao Dong never doubted the president's intentions to bring American firepower to Viet Nam.[37] Accordingly, the Party placed great importance on the NLF's first diplomatic visit to the People's Republic of China in the fall of 1962.

The Lao Dong realized that Peking was likely to embrace neutralism and a coalition government in the South because it had supported the 1962 Geneva Accords on Laos. Contrary to Washington's later claims, China thought its interests were "sufficiently served" by the Laos settlement because it removed the United States from its southern border.[38] Although Peking saw the Soviet move toward détente as "dangerous revisionism," in 1962 it did support neutralism and a negotiated settlement in Viet Nam.[39] Perhaps China believed that neutralism would lead to an early American withdrawal and diminish Soviet influence in Viet Nam. The growing Sino-Soviet dispute was certainly foremost in the minds of China's leading strategists as they considered the merits of the NLF's neutralist platform.

In September 1962, the NLF representatives were the guests of honor at a state banquet in Peking attended by Chairman Mao Tse-tung, Premier Chou En-lai, Vice Premier Ch'en Yi, and Chu Teh, the chairman of the People's Congress. At this reception and at stops in Shanghai, Foochow, Fukien, and Canton, the Chinese pledged support for the creation of a coalition government composed of nationalists. The Chinese Peace Committee and the Chinese Afro-Asian People's Solidarity Committee, the

NLF's hosts, released a statement on September 25, 1962, that pledged Chinese support for South Vietnamese neutralism.[40]

Three weeks later, the "largest crowd ever assembled at the railway station" greeted the NLF delegates in Hanoi.[41] Leaders of the Lao Dong were careful to treat the Front's representatives as foreign emissaries, but the Fatherland Front embraced the NLF as fraternal Communists. On October 19, 1962, the Fatherland Front held a reception for the Hieu mission attended by diplomats from the Soviet Union and all Eastern bloc countries and from China, North Korea, Mongolia, Cuba, Indonesia, and Laos. The delegates toasted the Front and pledged support for the liberation movement in the South. No one mentioned the neutralist platform. The next day, October 20, President Ho Chi Minh warmly welcomed Hieu and the other "sons of the suffering, but undaunted South."[42] Hieu was given a book of poetry written by a southern patriot who had died in an RVN prison. In return, Hieu gave Ho a leather-bound copy of the NLF's original 1960 manifesto and a vase made from an American artillery shell. Ho was shown photographs of the NLF's activities against the RVN and Americans in the South. He tearfully placed his hand over his heart and said, "I carry here a picture of South Vietnam."[43]

While in Hanoi, Hieu learned of the Military Commission's plans to launch a strategic offensive in early 1963. The Party's Political Bureau always coordinated the diplomatic and military struggles, and in the wake of the Front's world tour it decided to initiate a strike deep into government territory. The target was Ap Bac, a hamlet in the town of Tay Phu, just twenty kilometers from My Tho, one of the most strategically important and well defended cities in the Mekong Delta. According to Lao Dong military records, the battle of Ap Bac on January 2, 1963, was a clear-cut victory for the Communists. "After suffering heavy losses . . . 450 wounded or dead . . . the enemy had to accept defeat," an official history from Hanoi reads, "and called off the operation." The Communists had met three ARVN battalions with American air support at Ap Bac. The battle carried strategic significance for the Lao Dong because its guerrillas had finally learned to shoot down American helicopters. "After Ap Bac," one official reported, "the enemy realized it would be difficult to defeat us."[44]

In a pattern it was to use repeatedly, the Lao Dong instructed the NLF to introduce another diplomatic offensive shortly after the battle of Ap Bac. "We always launched a diplomatic initiative after a battlefield victory," Nguyen Co Thach, the former foreign minister, later confided.[45]

Agreeably, the Front sent several of its diplomats to Eastern Europe, northern Africa, Cuba, and Asia armed with photographs of suspected Communists being tortured by the RVN Secret Police in Saigon and of Americans using chemical defoliants in the countryside. The photographs were supplied by the *giao lien*, a "battlefield diplomat" who constantly provided the Front with physical proof of RVN/American atrocities.[46] The *giao lien* was a propaganda expert who went into the theater of operations to secure physical evidence for the NLF's diplomatic initiatives. The NLF correctly believed that it could exploit the evidence she collected to increase international support for neutralism in Viet Nam. By the spring of 1963, the impact of the NLF's neutralist platform was already manifesting itself in street demonstrations throughout South Viet Nam and through pledges of support from world leaders. The Communist Party had successfully predicted the debilitating impact of its neutralist scheme on the Saigon regime, but it was unprepared for the quick changes taking place in the South. International pressure for political and social reform coupled with growing support for the creation of a coalition government caused a crisis in Saigon. Had the Party been more alert to the success of its international campaign, it might have further exploited the turmoil in the South.

On May 8, RVN troops fired into a crowd of Buddhists who had gathered in Hue to protest Diem's decision not to allow the display of flags on Buddha's birthday. Buddhist leaders accused the RVN of religious persecution and organized a series of street protests and hunger strikes. Diem denied the charges and blamed the disturbances on the NLF, which he said had infiltrated the Buddhists. On June 11, 1963, the crisis intensified as an elderly bonze named Thich Quang Duc set himself afire in the middle of Saigon. The Buddhist protest raged throughout the summer. More bonzes immolated themselves. Finally, on August 21, Ngo Dinh Nhu, Diem's brother, who directed Saigon's special forces, ordered raids on the major pagodas in Saigon, Hue, Da Nang, and other key cities. RVN special forces arrested over 1,500 people and destroyed many temples.

The fallout from the Buddhist crisis was swift and heavy. Buddhists all over Asia criticized the raids, and Nhu's own father-in-law resigned as RVN ambassador to the United States.[47] On September 11, 1963, as the crisis entered its fourth month, the NLF issued its "Three-Point Peace Plan," which Hieu sent to the United Nations' secretary general, U Thant. The plan called for an end to American military assistance to the RVN, withdrawal of U.S. forces, and the formation of a coalition government of political and religious organizations.[48] The NLF timed its petition to coincide with the opening of the United Nations' eighteenth session, which was already committed to a discussion of Malaysian neutralism and to investigating human rights violations in South Viet Nam. At a press conference on September 13, 1963, Thant publicly chastised the Diem regime and criticized American intervention in Viet Nam. He labeled the RVN one of the most corrupt governments in the world and claimed that Diem remained in power only through force. He declared his support for an international conference to end the war, perhaps the reconvening of the 1954 Geneva group, and the creation of a coalition government.[49]

Thant's press conference came only weeks after President Charles de Gaulle of France announced his support of neutralization and the reunification of North and South Viet Nam. On August 29, 1963, de Gaulle declared that the United States should withdraw from Viet Nam and that the contesting groups should negotiate a settlement.[50] He determined at an early stage that the United States would not succeed where France had failed and that the conflict required a political settlement. He believed that nationalism would prevail in the developing world, even over forces as powerful as the United States. Neutralization in Viet Nam, he argued, would not be tantamount to the surrender of democracy in Southeast Asia; rather it would bring peace to the region, and democracy would prosper in neighboring countries.[51] The Lao Dong had long suspected that de Gaulle would support neutralism in Viet Nam and had directed the NLF to try to influence the general. Through its Cambodian contacts, the Front urged Prince Sihanouk to use his considerable prestige to sway de Gaulle to support the neutralization of South Viet Nam.[52]

De Gaulle needed little convincing. He was determined to rescue France from the shadow of Washington and establish what he often referred to as a "new global role" for his country. He believed that France should be an "umpire" in the Cold War and a valued defender of national independence in Asia, Africa, and Latin America. Supposedly he once commented that France "struck an out-and-out neutralist attitude in relation to the two foreign hegemonies of the United States and the Soviet Union."[53] The Americans and Soviets having signed a test-ban treaty in August 1963, France found itself out of the center of Cold War politics in Europe. As a result, in September 1963 de Gaulle moved toward normalization of relations with the People's Republic of China. Perhaps he believed that a Franco-Chinese rapprochement would heighten French prestige among developing nations. This independent course, however, was consistent with de Gaulle's post–Dien Bien Phu policy.

Curiously, despite pressure from de Gaulle and others to adopt a more comprehensive political program in South Viet Nam, U.S. policy makers appeared handcuffed and reactive. The Buddhist crisis made Kennedy insiders most uncomfortable, and after Nhu's August 20 raid on the pagodas, some supported a group of RVN generals who had begun to plan a coup against Diem and Nhu. The "generals' coup," as Kennedy officials called it, had the support of many American officials who felt the United States could not defeat the NLF with Diem and Nhu in charge.[54] The generals had produced significant victories in the countryside, according to American accounts, but now they had lost confidence in the Saigon government.

As Washington went forward with coup plans, officials in the Kennedy administration assessed de Gaulle's position. Secretary of State Dean Rusk believed that the French president understood that the NLF's proposal "for the neutralization of South Vietnam was a phony" and that de Gaulle really meant that the North and South must neutralize—a position, Rusk said, "that is very close to our own."[55] Rusk's position on the NLF and neutralization was unequivocal. During much of the war, he completely ignored the NLF as a political force. For him, it was nothing more than "a puppet on a string," a classic Communist front organization created by Hanoi to assist in the violent overthrow of the RVN.[56] Rusk refused to separate the NLF from Hanoi, and the idea of neutralization or open negotiations on Viet Nam therefore seemed absurd. The secretary believed that neutralization or a shared power scheme in Viet Nam would be tantamount to a Communist takeover.[57] The Communists, according to Rusk, wanted to gain a political foothold in South Viet Nam without surrendering any control in the North. The NLF's appeals for power sharing and neutralism therefore amounted to little more than "a one-sided bargain."[58]

On the surface, Rusk's assessment of the Lao Dong's strategy in promoting neutralism was correct. Hanoi saw neutralism as a way of arresting political control in South Viet Nam while avoiding a full-scale American military intervention. A significant number of southern supporters of the Front's neutralist policies, however, believed that they could control a coalition government. "One always assumes that the Communists would dominate any southern political arrangement," one noncommunist later commented, "but I believe we had just as much influence on our Communist brothers and sisters in the Front as they had on us."[59] Nguyen Van Hieu's own regional sensibilities suggest that the transition period from coalition government to reunification under the socialist banner might have taken longer than Rusk assumed.

In any event, by mid-1963, the Front's effective diplomatic offensive had forced the United States into a static position by linking South Vietnamese neutralism with recognition of the NLF as a separate entity, free of North Viet Nam's control. One Communist leader later explained, "We understood that the United States was not willing to accept our neutralist program, so we used it for its propaganda value."[60] "The only thing the United States could do," reported another Party leader, "was to criticize its Western allies for joining the growing international movement toward a neutralist solution in Viet Nam."[61] Indeed, by mid-1963 the United States was spending most of its diplomatic energies trying to persuade its friends in Europe and elsewhere "to get on board."[62] Rusk warned foreign leaders not to be duped by Communist propaganda ploys, but offered few alternatives.

Many U.S. officials shared Rusk's attitude. American foreign policy experts chided world leaders for aiding the Communist cause in Viet Nam. "The NLF is not serious about negotiations," one State Department official warned, "it only wants to use smoke and mirrors to cover Communist activities in Viet Nam."[63] Another claimed that "the NLF's frequently used terms such as neutrality, negotiations, or coalition government have considerable propaganda impact in the democratically oriented West," but they are merely for public consumption and "possess quite different meanings from those commonly accepted in the United States."[64] One State Department spokesperson argued that Vietnamese unity under a neutralist regime was "no solution at all."[65] Many supporters of U.S. policy in Viet Nam feared that de Gaulle and U Thant had taken too much interest in the Communists' propaganda appeals. Several State Department strategists urged the president to reject such proposals publicly.[66]

Kennedy, of course, could not easily dismiss de Gaulle's statement. According to American intelligence assessments, there was a growing "world-wide trend toward consideration of de Gaulle's proposals" on neutralization and reunification in Viet Nam.[67] A member of the National Security Council staff warned the president in September 1963 that a "number of Governments, including some friendly ones, would begin pressuring for a Laotian-type solution in Vietnam" soon.[68] Shortly after U Thant's critical United Nations speech, the two leading newspapers in India and several African leaders pledged support for South Vietnamese neutralism.[69] After the August raid on the pagodas, students and intellectuals in South Viet Nam embraced the NLF and neutralization in unprecedented numbers because they preferred "the devil we do not know to the one we do."[70]

Compounding Kennedy's dilemma were rumors that Nhu had begun talks with Hanoi and that even the RVN might support the neutralization of the South. The administration was aware of de Gaulle's efforts to open secret contacts between the RVN and the Communists. On September 15, 1963, de Gaulle had instructed the French ambassador in Saigon to promote the neutralization concept to both sides. The ambassador, Roger Lalouette, contacted the Polish representative to the International Control Commission, Mieczylsaw Maneli, who approached Hanoi and Nhu on the possibilities of a real bargain. Maneli felt encouraged by his first contacts and pursued the matter throughout the fall. Washington now had to respond to neutralization to ensure that Nhu did not "give it all away."[71]

In a television interview with Walter Cronkite, Kennedy finally responded to de Gaulle by suggesting that the general was entitled to his opinion, but "he doesn't have any forces there or any program of economic assistance, so that while these expressions are welcome, the burden is carried, as it usually is, by the United States."[72] Kennedy had been critical of de Gaulle's Asian policy for years, and the administration made no secret of its displeasure at the timing of his remarks. In a meeting with the French ambassador to the United States, Herve Alphand, Michael Forrestal of the National Security Council staff complained that de Gaulle had supported the NLF's neutralist platform without consulting the United States. The ambassador responded that the Americans never consulted France on Southeast Asia, so Kennedy should not be surprised when the French acted without consulting the United States.[73]

Two weeks after the Alphand-Forrestal meeting, Diem was overthrown and killed, and just three weeks later Kennedy was assassinated. De Gaulle flew to the United States for the president's funeral and met with President Lyndon Johnson at the White House. Johnson was prepared for harsh criticism of American policy in Viet Nam, but, according to Rusk, the meeting was "very amiable."[74] Johnson opposed neutralism vigorously, however. So did Walt Rostow of the State Department's Policy Planning Staff. He argued that the growing interest in neutralism in South Viet Nam could potentially result in "the greatest setback to American interests on the world scene in many years." Rostow called for a direct military confrontation with Hanoi and argued that international pressure for South Vietnamese neutralism would subside once the Saigon government was stabilized.[75]

In the late fall of 1963, a second wave of support for South Vietnamese neutralism swelled. On November 30, after a visit to Peking, Prince Sihanouk released to the press his most ambitious neutralization program.[76] His call for the immediate establishment of a Federation of Indochina States was broader than his 1962 appeal; now he was calling for the neutralization of the entire region. In an interview with a Cambodian newspaper, Nguyen Huu Tho hailed Sihanouk's proposal as "one of lasting vision" and pledged the Front's full support.[77] Sihanouk, naturally, had frustrated American policy makers since the 1955 agreement with France that brought him to real political power in Phnom Penh. Cambodia's relative economic prosperity gave Sihanouk a certain amount of political flexibility and reduced his dependence on foreign aid, especially from the United States. By 1963, Cambodia had refused all U.S. military aid and Sihanouk had condemned America's Southeast Asia program. Cambodia's refusal to support U.S. objectives in Viet Nam encouraged many critics of American policy to step forward and embrace neutralization.

In Washington, the president's closest Senate friends, Mike Mansfield (D-Montana) and Richard Russell (D-Georgia), endorsed South Vietnamese neutralism.[78] Johnson admired and respected both senators, and no doubt their support of a negotiated peace through neutralism caused considerable problems at the White House. Mansfield, by training an Asian historian, advised Johnson privately that he doubted whether military intervention in Viet Nam was in the United States' interest and urged him to go on the "diplomatic offensive based on de Gaulle's appeals for a neutral Vietnam."[79] The United States, he suggested, should listen "most intently" to "whatever the French had to say" regarding peace in Viet Nam.[80] Likewise, the *New York Times* editorialized that neutralism should not "be ruled out" in Viet Nam.[81]

Johnson's closest advisers did rule it out. Ambassador Henry Cabot Lodge Jr. and Defense Secretary Robert McNamara joined Rostow's sharp criticism of the various neutralization schemes being promoted in late 1963. Lodge told the president that he should not listen to Sihanouk's repeated proposals for an international conference on Indochina and called the neutralization plans "disastrous."[82] McNamara agreed that any plan to neutralize Viet Nam would mean that the Saigon government "would in short order become Communist-dominated."[83] The secretary of defense argued that de Gaulle, Sihanouk, Mansfield, and Russell were naive and shortsighted.

"Neutralist fever," as one State Department official called it, swept through Saigon as well.[84] In mid-January 1964, rumors surfaced that the generals who had overthrown Diem were planning to negotiate a neutralist settlement with the NLF. Lodge warned the president of these developments and suggested that the generals "did favor the French neutrality solution at that time."[85] On January 28, General Nguyen Khanh, a self-promoter and opportunist, warned American officials in Saigon that the coup leaders were "pro-French and pro-neutralist."[86] Khanh indicated that another coup would take place within a matter of days to replace the neutralist generals.[87] On January 30, he led a palace coup, placed the neutralist generals under arrest, and consolidated his political and military control in Saigon by declaring war against communism and neutralism.

After the Khanh coup, Lodge urged the president to disclose to de Gaulle American concerns over his policy toward Viet Nam.[88] Before Johnson could act, de Gaulle at a lengthy press conference again proclaimed his support for South Vietnamese neutralism. The general's statement came only days after his country officially recognized the People's Republic of China. The timing of de Gaulle's actions provoked severe criticism from State Department officials, who were convinced that he was trying to embarrass the United States and "ensure that America not succeed where France had failed so miserably."[89]

Editorials in the *New York Times* and *Le Monde* on January 30 and 31, 1964, suggested that the neutralist movement in Saigon experienced significant growth only after de Gaulle's August comments. Indeed, as Johnson administrators assessed the collapse of yet another Saigon regime, most blamed de Gaulle for the groundswell of neutralist support. The United States therefore made several attempts to change French policy. In March 1964, Ambassador Charles Bohlen warned the French president that his policy toward Viet Nam had produced a tremendous strain on successive Saigon regimes. Bohlen asked if the United States and France shared a commitment to a noncommunist Viet Nam. De Gaulle replied that French and American goals were similar, but that a military solution was not possible. He concluded that the United States must withdraw from Viet Nam if meaningful political changes were to be made to save the country from the Communists.[90] Undersecretary of State George Ball met with de Gaulle three months later, with the same results. The United States could not solve the problem of Viet Nam with its superior military force, de Gaulle argued, because the problem was political. He believed that the more force the United States committed, the more the population of Viet Nam would turn against it.[91]

Washington's attempts to solve the crisis in Saigon by promoting a change in French policy symbolized its Western bias and lack of understanding of the political situation in Viet Nam. The neutralist sentiment embraced by the RVN generals and by Khanh himself one year later did not originate in France. Modern Vietnamese neutralism was born in the Ba Dinh quarter of Hanoi with the full support of the Communist Party. That so many world leaders supported neutralism and proved less than enthusiastic supporters of American policy illuminates the Party's early international success.[92]

The Lao Dong had correctly predicted the debilitating effect of neutralism on the United States and continued to find supporters in unusual places, including the United Nations. On July 8, U Thant, the United Nations' secretary general, called for the reconvening of the Geneva Conference on Viet Nam, declaring that the "diplomatic method of negotiations" was the only "sensible alternative" to an escalating military conflict.[93] De Gaulle likewise supported an international meeting "of the same order . . . as the Geneva Conference."[94] Later in the month, the NLF joined Peking, Moscow, Phnom Penh, Vientiane, and Hanoi in appealing for such a conference.[95] The NLF's president, Nguyen Huu Tho, declared: "The people's front is prepared to begin negotiations with all parties, groups, religious sects, and patriotic persons, without regard to differences of political views or past actions."[96]

Johnson rejected the conference outright: "We do not believe in conferences to ratify terror."[97] The president correctly believed that an international conference might end with a request for an immediate American withdrawal. Since the Honolulu conference in early June, the Johnson administration had debated the prospects of "taking the war north" to stop the flow of men and supplies and to "teach the Communists that they could not wage war in the South without reprisal."[98] The new American ambassador in Saigon, General Maxwell Taylor, warned that Washington needed to get more directly involved in the war to stabilize the Khanh regime.[99] By late July, the president had accepted the recommendations of his advisers. Any doubt about the American rejection of neutralism disappeared in August 1964 with the bombing raids against DRV navy bases near Vinh and the Tonkin Gulf Resolution, which endorsed them.[100]

The hope for a more stable and unified Saigon government that had accompanied the Tonkin Gulf Resolution disappeared quickly. By mid-August, Khanh was under attack in most cities for curtailing civil liberties under his wartime state of emergency and for supporting American military intervention.[101] The Self-Determination Movement coordinated many of the protests with the aid of the Buddhist Institute, a politically active group of monks led by Thich Tri Quang.[102] The NLF's influence on both groups was undeniable. Khanh was particularly sensitive to the Buddhists, however. The general had an inordinate preoccupation with self-preservation, and when he felt he was losing power in Saigon's ruling Military Council, he embraced the Buddhists in what George Kahin has called "strictly a marriage of convenience."[103]

Khanh's courting of the Buddhists cost him considerable political support in Washington. Secretary Rusk believed that the Buddhists' position on neutralism could easily be exploited by the Communists and that Khanh should distance himself from Tri Quang immediately. General William Westmoreland, the commander of American forces in Viet Nam, had convinced McNamara that the Buddhists had not denounced the Communists and that they seemed willing to enter into an alliance with the NLF.[104] Ambassador Taylor likewise warned that Khanh's relationship with the Buddhists threatened American objectives in Viet Nam.[105] Washington's assessment of the Buddhists was accurate: they did favor a negotiated peace with the NLF and the formation of a broad coalition government.[106]

U.S. support for Khanh declined considerably as the fall progressed. Taylor was especially eager to replace Khanh with a government that would be more receptive to American military plans. Khanh knew of Taylor's efforts to unseat him and understood that the coups against his government in the fall of 1964 failed only because of Taylor's earlier support. With the ambassador's approval shaken, Khanh saw no choice but to rely on the Buddhists. Thus he had to support their objectives, including a negotiated settlement with the NLF and a neutralized South Viet Nam.

Khanh's flirtation with the Buddhists and the NLF suggests that the Party's neutralist policy had produced the desired results. The leader of the Saigon regime was willing to recognize the political legitimacy of the Front and enter into a political agreement to cut the Americans out and preserve Vietnamese sovereignty. Khanh's secret contacts with the NLF began in December 1964.[107] He wrote several letters to Huynh Tan Phat, the NLF's new secretary general, and even released Phat's wife from jail.[108] Phat told Khanh that the Front supported his public stand against American intervention and that "whatever our differences of political opinion, we can join together and coordinate our efforts to accomplish our supreme mission, which is to save our homeland." The NLF leader congratulated Khanh for his "ardent patriotism" and determination to "oppose any kind of intervention by outsiders."[109] At the same time, Phat persuaded the Self-Determination Movement to increase its public demands for a negotiated settlement. On February 1, 1965, the movement's leaders held a press conference to announce the gathering of thousands of names on a petition that called for an immediate end to the war based on an all-Vietnamese settlement. Several noncommunists delivered the petition to the Presidential Palace and the headquarters of the International Control Commission.[110] After many important figures in the Self-Determination Movement were arrested, Saigon's streets once again erupted with protests. In mid-February, Khanh moved even closer to an accord with the Buddhists and the NLF, knowing that his American support was rapidly fading.[111]

Sensing that Khanh was desperate and that the NLF had "gotten inside the presidential palace," U.S. intelligence experts in Saigon uncovered Khanh's indiscretions in early January 1965. When word reached Washington, even his most ardent supporters backed off. Khanh's secret talks with the Front threatened not only the political future of the Saigon regime but also the prospects for the new American bombing campaign then being discussed in Washington. Khanh had grown increasingly unmanageable over the bombing issue. With Khanh in charge, it was unlikely that the Americans would have the RVN's complete support. His secret negotiations with the NLF therefore provided the United States with a pretext for bringing to power a more cooperative and hawkish ally. On February 24, under enormous pressure from Taylor, Khanh capitulated and left Viet Nam for exile in France.

In a matter of fourteen months, then, three separate Saigon governments had collapsed. NLF leaders boasted that their neutralist platform was partly responsible.[112] The Front's diplomatic strategy had isolated the United States from several of its Southeast Asian and Western European allies, and the Saigon regime had lost control of the urban elite, its only base of support. Government leaders around the world had accepted the Front's claims that it had risen at southern initiative in response to southern demands, and domestic and international support for the southern revolution increased accordingly. Cadre ranks swelled as the revolution gained legitimacy in the urban areas, and the Front scored significant political victories in South Viet Nam through its promotion of neutralism.

The success of the neutralist platform in South Viet Nam, however, caused the NLF serious problems with the Lao Dong's Political Bureau in Hanoi. Some northern Party leaders complained that neutralism had not stopped the Johnson administration from escalating the war, so the NLF's diplomatic strategy seemed hardly as effective as the Front claimed. By 1963, a significant number of Party strategists who had once supported neutralism condemned the policy as counterrevolutionary. Apparently several northern representatives of the Central Committee were angered that Diem's own officers and not the NLF had removed him from power. In addition, some northerners had grown increasingly concerned that the NLF had become too independent in its diplomatic activities and that it "had relied too much on Western-style diplomacy and personalities" to achieve its goals.[113] "We needed more action aligned with the correct political and military thinking," one Communist official later complained, "and fewer cocktail parties."[114]

At the Lao Dong's Ninth Plenum, in December 1963, critics of the NLF's neutralist platform secretly launched a vicious attack on the policy and the diplomats who had promoted it.[115] They privately called for censure of the Front's most outspoken advocates of South Vietnamese neutralism and demanded that the Central Committee in Hanoi assume control of the NLF's foreign affairs. Since NLF diplomats traveled with Hanoi passports and usually reported to the DRV's foreign missions, some Party officials argued that northern oversight would be easy to accomplish. Because the Party had approved the NLF's neutralist platform, Lao Dong leaders faced a difficult problem. To calm northern fears and ensure Party unity, Nguyen Van Hieu was made the scapegoat. Shortly after the plenum, the Lao Dong formally replaced Hieu as the NLF's secretary general and head of its Foreign Relations Commission.[116] The neutralist platform, however, remained a crucial element of the diplomatic struggle movement in the South largely because of the support of Le Duan, the Party's secretary general.

Neutralism was attractive to Le Duan because it had enabled revolutionary forces in neighboring Laos to win a significant victory at the conference table. In February 1965 Duan reported: "Neutralism can serve a tremendous purpose. . . . If several divisions of the puppet's army could be crushed and others lured away from the cities, urban uprisings would then have a good chance of success. Then politics would become a key factor. A coalition of neutralist forces could form a government in Saigon," which "would ask the Americans to leave."[117] Le Duan has often been portrayed in the West as an uncompromising hard-liner who was determined to seize power by violence.[118] His stance toward the southern revolution in the late 1950s helped to create this perception. It now seems clear, however, that his thinking on these matters was never static and that he advocated battlefield victory and political struggle simultaneously. His support of South Vietnamese neutralism illustrates his flexibility regarding the southern revolution. He accepted neutralism as a transitional phase in the battle, according to William Duiker, "in order to give the United States a face-saving way out of its predicament."[119] He was also prepared, however, to increase the military pressure if the Johnson administration rejected the NLF's neutralist proposals.

Le Duan's support of the Party's neutralist platform tells us much about the character of the relationship between the NLF and the Lao Dong by 1965. It is difficult to imagine what might have happened had he not used his considerable political capital to save neutralism, and therefore the NLF, but it is conceivable that the Front could have taken on a more subordinate role in foreign affairs. "It is quite possible that the NLF would have been cut out of the diplomatic loop altogether," a Lao Dong official later speculated, "because some in the Central Committee and the Political Bureau believed it to be a loose cannon."[120] The Lao Dong, in the early years of the war against the Americans, had not figured out how to use the NLF's diplomatic corps effectively, and as a result, relations between northern and southern Communists grew strained.

By the time of General Khanh's ouster in February 1965, some Lao Dong officials claimed that the NLF had pursued a faulty strategic line. The political crisis in Saigon, caused in part by the NLF's efforts, had precipitated Khanh's collapse, yet in a strange way this Communist political "victory" had persuaded the United States to pursue a new policy line that included the introduction of ground troops to South Viet Nam and an intensification of the air war against the North. Southern revolutionaries had failed to meet their primary objective, an American withdrawal. Instead the war intensified, causing new problems for a people already overburdened with hardship.

Despite the severe criticism, the NLF's diplomatic initiatives had served the revolution well. The broad international support that the United States had counted on proved increasingly elusive as the war progressed and more and more governments accepted the NLF's platform. Understandably, American escalation rendered a political solution to the Viet Nam crisis impossible and convinced a significant number of Communists that they must win on the battlefield. As time progressed, the Political Bureau would grow more skillful and sophisticated in its use of the Front's diplomatic corps, but bitter memories from this period stayed with many southern Communists indefinitely.

3

HAUNTED BY GENEVA: THE BOMBING PAUSES OF 1965

"We still believe in neutralism," Nguyen Van Hieu declared in August 1965, "but the conditions have changed. The formation of a coalition government can take place only after all American troops have been withdrawn. The Vietnamese people can solve their own problems through open negotiations, but these talks will not begin until the last American has left our soil." Negotiations were useless, Hieu went on to say, "until the Americans have accepted our Five Points, including acknowledgment that the National Liberation Front is the sole representative of the people of South Viet Nam." Vietnamese revolutionaries had been deceived in 1954 at Geneva, Hieu stressed, and they would not make that mistake again. "We will not surrender at the negotiating table what we have rightly won on the battlefield."[1]

Hieu was addressing the Czechoslovakian Democratic Student League in Prague shortly after the Johnson administration had announced its latest troop increase in Viet Nam. His hard-line position represented his rehabilitation in the Party and a dramatic shift in thinking among important southern Communists who had once supported neutralism as an expeditious way to achieve victory in the South. After the introduction of American combat troops to Viet Nam in March 1965, many southerners, including Hieu, abandoned neutralism in favor of a decisive battlefield victory. Southern hard-liners in the Party feared that northern doves wanted to avoid a direct confrontation with the United States and would seek a political settlement to limit the war to the South. "We feared that northerners, especially members of the National Assembly who had friends in the Political Bureau, were so blinded by socialism," a southern Communist reported, "that they would sacrifice the South to save the North."[2] Interestingly, many southerners believed that Hanoi put the long-term interests of the North before southern liberation. "We were always the ones to suffer," an NLF cadre complained. "We had to live with the impostor government, we had to live with Americans in our backyard. . . . We needed a commitment from Hanoi that the liberation of South Viet Nam was primary."[3]

Indeed, the introduction of American ground troops to Viet Nam in March 1965 had a profound impact on strategic thinking in Hanoi. For the first time since the late 1950s, there were serious ideological divisions within the Lao Dong's Political Bureau over the future of the southern revolution and the allocation of limited resources. As Washington unleashed its deadly air war against the North, a small but vocal minority called for a reexamination of the Party's priorities. Worried that American bombing threatened socialist construction in the North, some members wondered aloud if the southern insurgency was worth the high price all Vietnamese had to pay to ensure success. Some Party leaders asked if there was not some way to limit the war to the South and save northern industries from American bombs. A people's war, they argued, must be self-sufficient. If Hanoi could distance itself publicly from the southern insurgency and provide Washington with certain guarantees, perhaps the Johnson administration would call off its deadly attacks. In 1965, therefore, the Party approved secret and controversial contacts with the United States.

Hanoi's brief Party debate over the secret contacts tells us much about the character and nature of the Lao Dong. At times the Party's two objectives—to develop socialism in the DRV and to liberate Viet Nam south of the seventeenth parallel—were mutually exclusive, and they temporarily divided the membership along ideological and sometimes regional lines. It is important to note that the Lao Dong was a united, nationwide organization and that Party members in all regions of Viet Nam took part in policy debates.[4] Apparently some northern members feared that provocative actions in the South threatened what they perceived as the revolution's primary goal, the construction of socialism in the North.

The antagonism between doves and hawks in the Lao Dong began with the American escalation in early 1965. After months of debate, Lyndon Johnson agreed in February to the strategic bombing of the North to save the RVN. Communist attacks against U.S. Army installations at Play Ku and Quy Nhon convinced the president that something had to be done to stop the infiltration of men and supplies. It was impossible, Johnson concluded, to build a stable and democratic government in Saigon while Hanoi and its Communist supporters waged a war of aggression. Accordingly, he ordered retaliatory attacks on DRV targets that paved the way for Operation ROLLING THUNDER, the sustained bombing policy many of his advisers had long advocated.[5]

The expanded air war also changed the scope of U.S. military requirements on the ground. In late February, General William C. Westmoreland, the commanding officer of the U.S. Military Assistance Command–Vietnam, requested two Marine battalions to protect the air base at Da Nang from Communist reprisal attacks. Over Ambassador Maxwell Taylor's muted objections, Johnson approved Westmoreland's request, and on March 8, 1965, the first American combat troops arrived in Viet Nam. As Taylor predicted, however, once the United States had "gone that final step" with the introduction of ground combat forces, it was "difficult to hold the line."[6] In a matter of weeks, the president deployed an additional 40,000 American troops. In July, Johnson granted Westmoreland approval to "commit U.S. troops to combat independent of or in conjunction with RVN forces in any situation," thus changing their mission.[7] On July 17 he asked Congress for $700 million for expanded military operations. At the end of the month, an additional 50,000 troops were sent to Viet Nam. The president also authorized the use of B-52s for the saturation bombing of Communist sanctuaries in the South and the intensification of the bombing of the North. The historian George C. Herring has called these July decisions among "the most important in the history of American involvement in Vietnam."[8]

American intervention caused consternation in Hanoi, and signs of conflict in the Party emerged in late May 1965 during an initial U.S. bombing pause. Before undertaking a major escalation, the Johnson administration decided to suspend the bombing for a brief period to explore the meaning of Hanoi's recent "Four-Point Plan for Peace" and see if the Communists had any interest in negotiations.[9] The NLF, too, had announced a peace plan, shortly after the introduction of U.S. combat troops in March. Since the "Five-Point Plan for Peace in Viet Nam" provided the basis for the Front's negotiating stance until August 1967, the full text should be noted:

> Facing the present situation of utmost gravity, the South Viet Nam National Front for Liberation deems it necessary to reaffirm once again its ironlike and unswerving stand to carry through the war of resistance against the American imperialists.
>
> (1) The U.S. imperialists are the saboteurs of the Geneva Accords, the most brazen warmonger and aggressor and the sworn enemy of the Vietnamese people.
>
> (2) The heroic South Vietnamese people are resolved to drive out the U.S. imperialists in order to liberate South Viet Nam and achieve an independent, democratic, peaceful, and neutral South Viet Nam, with a view to national reunification.
>
> (3) The valiant South Vietnamese people and the South Viet Nam Liberation Army are resolved to carry out fully their sacred duty to drive out the U.S. imperialists so as to liberate South Viet Nam and defend North Viet Nam.
>
> (4) The South Vietnamese people express their profound gratitude for the wholehearted support of the people of the world who cherish peace and justice and declare their readiness to receive all assistance, including weapons and all other war matériel, from their friends on five continents.
>
> (5) To unite the whole people, to arm the whole people, to continue to march forward heroically, and to resolve to fight and defeat the U.S. aggressors and the Vietnamese traitors.[10]

Behind the polemics lay the NLF's refusal to enter negotiations until all U.S. troops were withdrawn. Although the Front had supported discussions to create a coalition government from 1962 through January 1965, the increased presence of American combat troops in the spring of 1965 made negotiations impossible. The aggressive language of the Front's five-point peace plan concerned the Lao Dong's Political Bureau, and before Nguyen Huu Tho read the declaration over Liberation Radio, political strategists in Hanoi had modified the statement.[11] These changes brought the NLF's five-point plan more in line with Hanoi's four-point plan. No reference was made to the necessity of an American withdrawal before negotiations could begin.

Clearly, the Lao Dong's Political Bureau had fashioned the Party's negotiating position and the NLF had no independent course of action. "The four-point plan of Hanoi and the NLF's five-point plan," according to Hanoi's former foreign minister, Nguyen Co Thach, "were two sides of the same coin."[12] The Front's political leaders, however, continued to insist that no negotiations were possible while Americans were still in the South—a view that on the surface looked like an independent stand to many northern Communists. "We had to watch the NLF carefully in those days," a former Lao Dong official noted. "We were not sure what they would say on one day that we had to undo the next."[13] Another Party official claimed that Hanoi "had long feared that the noncommunist elements of the Front had too much influence on their southern partners."[14] The NLF was not an independent actor, however, and it had to work within the Lao Dong's command structure to have any effect on strategic decisions. The NLF did have powerful friends in the Political Bureau, most notably Le Duan and Nguyen Chi Thanh, director of COSVN (the Party's southern office), but they alone could not influence Party policy. Interestingly, the NLF used its public pronouncements to sway events in Hanoi and the Political Bureau's thinking. "We had to push our point on negotiations in the public forum," a former NLF diplomat later confided, "in the hope that the Party would see how serious we were about an American withdrawal."[15] Not everyone in Hanoi appreciated such a public airing of southern sentiments, especially when they clashed with northern attitudes.

The U.S. embassy in Saigon noticed the distinctions between Hanoi's four-point plan and the NLF's original five-point plan but concluded that the contrasts did not reflect "differences in basic position," and U.S. intelligence experts believed that they were more "apt to reflect different tactics, local situations, and at times lack of immediate coordination. These were differences of tone rather than substance," the embassy concluded, "the Front's tone being somewhat sharper."[16] These intelligence assessments were perhaps shortsighted. Clearly, by the spring of 1965 regional distinctions had surfaced within the Party. Exploration of these differences could have provided the Johnson administration with a more nuanced view of events in Hanoi, and therefore perhaps a more sophisticated approach to negotiations. Instead, Johnson and his advisers rejected all attempts to learn more about the enemy, and as a result they stumbled through negotiations. This lack of sophisticated analysis of political divisions within the Lao Dong was especially acute in the State Department, where Secretary Rusk saw no difference between Hanoi and the NLF and suggested that the president proceed with his dubious spring 1965 peace feeler.[17]

On May 10, therefore, Johnson informed Taylor that there would be a "brief halt to the air attacks." Secretary of Defense McNamara followed Johnson's message with the specifics that called for a five-to seven-day pause starting May 12. American officials gave the operation the code name MAYFLOWER. Rusk had the responsibility of informing Hanoi that a pause would soon be in place and of its political purpose. On May 11 he instructed Foy Kohler, the U.S. Ambassador to Moscow, to tell Nguyen Tho Chan, DRV ambassador to the Soviet Union, that the United States had initiated the pause because it had been told that "there can be no progress toward peace while there are air attacks on North Viet Nam." Rusk's message concluded with assurances that if Hanoi scaled down its military activities in the South, the pause would remain in place. If the Communists took military advantage of the bombing halt, however, the United States would resume the attacks.[18]

Delivering Rusk's message was not as easy as declaring the bombing pause. On the morning of May 12, Kohler's assistant telephoned the Vietnamese embassy to request an immediate and urgent appointment with the DRV ambassador. The Vietnamese emissary refused to grant an appointment and suggested that Kohler instead send his message to the Soviet Union in its capacity as co-chair of the Geneva Conference. Rusk had already tried the Soviets as an intermediary, but Ambassador Anatoly Dobrynin had refused the role. Kohler made several other attempts to contact Chan, usually through letters, but Chan returned them all unopened.[19]

In a radio address on May 15, Ho Chi Minh criticized the bombing pause as a "worn-out trick of deceit and threat."[20] *Nhan Dan* [The People], the Lao Dong's daily newspaper, followed on May 17 with an editorial condemning the pause as "a deceitful maneuver to pave the way for American escalation."

Ironically, several Western observers agreed. On May 19 the *New York Times* editorialized that there were strong indications that the Johnson administration had hastily called a bombing pause "to convince critics at home and abroad that North Vietnam and China were preventing negotiations, not the United States." On April 7, in a major speech at Johns Hopkins University, the president had stressed his administration's desire to engage in "unconditional discussions" to end the war.[21] "I am ready to go anywhere at any time, and meet with anyone whenever there is promise of progress towards an honorable peace," Johnson told an audience two weeks earlier.[22] The administration was feeling pressure from Congress and the American public when it announced the bombing pause. According to some critics, it managed the entire MAYFLOWER affair for its public relations value and, as several scholars have noted, as a pretext for further escalating the war.[23]

When Hanoi refused to respond to the MAYFLOWER initiative, Johnson went public, claiming that the Communists had no interest in negotiations.[24] Therefore, he declared, he must resume bombing the North until it stopped its aggression toward the RVN.[25] On the morning of May 18, the air attacks began.

In a pattern it was to use repeatedly, the Lao Dong communicated with the United States hours after the bombing had resumed. On the morning of May 18, Mai Van Bo, chief of the DRV's commercial delegation in Paris, approached the French Foreign Ministry with some minor complaints concerning troops along the seventeenth parallel.[26] Soon, however, Bo revealed the true nature of his visit. He told the French that the withdrawal of American troops was not a precondition for negotiations, but rather an expected result of talks.[27] On May 20, the French relayed Bo's message to the State Department. The State Department, however, concluded that Bo's message should be disregarded, since a subsequent conversation between Blair Seaborn, the Canadian representative to the ICC, and the DRV's foreign minister, Nguyen Duy Trinh, stressed Hanoi's four points as prerequisites to any talks.[28] The French concurred, stating that "Bo did not give the impression of urgency" when he presented Hanoi's clarification.[29]

On June 14, Bo met again with French officials to discuss his May 18 message. He asked if the Americans had responded to his initiative and was quite despondent when told they had not. The Lao Dong realized that failure to acknowledge Bo's inquiry indicated that the United States was considering a major escalation.[30] In fact, Westmoreland had requested an additional forty-four battalions "to establish a favorable balance of forces" and "seize the initiative from the Viet Cong."[31] After a month-long debate, Johnson approved Westmoreland's request, but not without taking political consequences into consideration. As Wallace Thies has noted, he "apparently shared the view that the summer of 1965 would be an opportune time to probe the DRV's willingness to continue the struggle, especially if the probe could be completed before American troops began fighting and dying in large numbers."[32] This maneuver seemed typical of Johnson: escalating while pursuing peace, holding the middle ground while fending off hawks and doves at home. With troop increases planned for late July, Johnson had but a few weeks to launch his initiative.

As the Johnson administration made plans to contact the DRV, an unplanned event brought the two together again in Paris. On July 16, an American businessman, Urah Arkas-Duntov, arranged a meeting with Mai Van Bo through two French journalists.[33] After a short and somewhat unproductive interview, Bo informed Duntov that he would talk with an American official if the United States recognized the four points. Duntov relayed this message to State Department officials, who immediately contacted Edmund Gullion, a retired Foreign Service officer and the dean of the Fletcher School of International Diplomacy at Tufts University. George Ball, the White House dove and undersecretary of state, asked Gullion to take over the Paris contact with Bo and briefed him on the administration's negotiating position. Gullion was to tell Bo that the United States desired peace in Viet Nam and that the Johnson administration wanted to end the conflict along lines compatible with the DRV's four points, but he was also to say that the prolongation of the war was bound to lead to a greater American military presence.

Bo and Gullion met four times in August and September 1965. They seemed to make substantial progress during their August 15 meeting, when both sides agreed to the reconvening of the Geneva Conference. They also made considerable headway concerning the issue of troop withdrawals. Bo and Gullion agreed that all foreign troops must be withdrawn from the South before a final settlement, but that negotiations could start once "both sides agreed in principle to troop withdrawals."[34] Although Hanoi had issued a statement in early August declaring that the United States must show "tangible proof" of its acceptance of the four points, on August 15 Bo assured Gullion that the DRV stood behind his statements on troop withdrawals.[35]

By the time they met again on September 3, Bo and Gullion seemed to have made substantial progress toward serious negotiations to end the war. They had reached a tentative accord on a conference and apparently had settled the question of the four points as a precondition for negotiations. Bo's reversal during the fourth meeting therefore stunned Gullion. "Until the last meeting between X [Gullion] and R [Bo]," wrote the *Pentagon Papers* analyst, "all was proceeding at a better than expected pace. At this September 3rd conversation, R turned cold. He insisted on immediate cessation of U.S. bombings, and he pulled back on his agreement for the staged withdrawal of forces from South Vietnam." Bo now demanded that all American troops be withdrawn from Viet Nam before national elections took place in the South. He insisted that the United States stop the bombing "unilaterally, immediately, totally, and definitively." When Gullion suggested that Bo's conditions had changed dramatically and were inconsistent with his earlier statements, Bo became quite agitated. He demanded that Gullion acknowledge that he had been consistent and firm in their previous meetings and that the DRV's four points had always been a condition for any settlement. When Gullion refused, the talks broke down.[36]

Western experts have long speculated on the reasons for Bo's sudden change. The analyst of *The Pentagon Papers* has suggested that Johnson's July 28 announcement of troop increases and his pledge to send additional troops triggered a negative response in Hanoi. The impact of the additional U.S. forces may have taken a month to reach the Lao Dong's Military Commission, so Bo's September 3 reversal could have been timely. Another possibility is that the bombing raids against the North in August had struck civilian targets, angering Hanoi enough to cause a change in negotiating policy. Perhaps the DRV broke off contact with Gullion because it had achieved its goal: Hanoi may have been using the meetings as a measuring stick to judge how the United States viewed the war in the South.[37]

While all of these explanations are plausible, it now seems clear that in ending the talks Bo and the Lao Dong were responding to pressure from the hard-liners, especially the COSVN director, Nguyen Chi Thanh, and his NLF allies.[38] Several southern Communists compared Bo's negotiating stance to the Viets' position during the 1954 Geneva talks. According to one revolutionary, "when the Geneva agreements were signed, there was already much ill will against the Lao Dong Central Committee and Ho Chi Minh, because people felt that the South was always to be treated as a sacrificial animal when it came to reunification. Now southerners were called upon to sit by and tolerate more sacrifices. They felt that the Party and Ho Chi Minh had turned out to be more stupid than the French, the Americans, and even Diem himself."[39] Although it seems unlikely now that Hanoi was willing to engage in serious discussions to end the war in 1965, many southerners thought that possibility existed. "We were haunted by Geneva," one NLF member later commented.[40]

The hard-liners had a growing number of allies in the Lao Dong's Political Bureau, and the issue of negotiations and withdrawal of American troops sparked a heated and often acrimonious debate.[41] Three powerful Lao Dong officials—Le Duan, the Party's secretary general; Deputy Premier Pham Hung; and Nguyen Chi Thanh, director of COSVN—led the call for an immediate end to the Paris talks in favor of a decisive military victory in the South.[42] Opposing them were a small but powerful cadre of doves who wanted to avoid a direct confrontation with the United States and seek a negotiated settlement. Understandably, these Party moderates feared the awesome firepower of the United States and questioned the wisdom of inviting war upon the North when a diplomatic solution promised to confine hostilities to the South.[43] The moderates had a powerful ally in the president of the National Assembly, Truong Chinh, who had long supported a self-sufficient people's war in the South to save limited Party resources. Ho and Pham Van Dong, Party premier, were sensitive to this position, although they hoped to appease both groups.[44]

The debate intensified in late July with Johnson's new troop commitments. General Van Tien Dung, second in command to General Vo Nguyen Giap, launched the new controversy with a scathing attack on negotiations in *Nhan Dan*.[45] The essay appeared on the day of Bo's first meeting with Gullion and added significantly to the conflict. The Political Bureau member Le Duc Tho complained bitterly about calls for negotiations to end the war issued by "a small number of comrades who had developed erroneous thoughts and views."[46] Tho summarized the debate six months later when he wrote that those favoring discussions with the United States "fail to realize clearly the deceptiveness of the enemy's peace negotiation plot."[47] Nguyen Chi Thanh criticized "ideological wavering" in the face of the American buildup and argued that a renewed military commitment to the southern revolution was needed because victory was at hand.[48] Thanh had long supported Carl von Clausewitz's theory of decisive battles and believed that victory came only on the battlefield. "If we feared the United States," Thanh declared earlier in the war, "we would have called on the people of southern Viet Nam to wait and coexist peacefully with the U.S.-Diem clique. We are not afraid of the United States."[49]

Still, those favoring negotiations had an audience in the Political Bureau in August 1965 because some Lao Dong leaders feared that the bombings would damage the DRV's industrial base. A significant number of Central Committee members, led by Truong Chinh, argued that an aggressive offensive war in the South would deplete the North's resources and increase the likelihood of further American bombing raids.[50] The character and nature of the Party debate were not unusual. Since the founding of the modern revolutionary movement in the 1920s, the Party had often experienced periods of intense conflict and turmoil. During the 1950s, the Lao Dong constantly worried about the proper balance between building socialism and carrying out the war of national liberation, and in fact had granted primacy to the political struggle for several years.[51] The NLF had been born of this conflict, as southerners insisted on revolutionary violence to overthrow Diem. By 1965, the southerners once again were demanding a more militant and aggressive line, promoting battlefield victory and condemning negotiations with the United States.

In one of the most important decisions of the war, the Party's leadership temporarily resolved the crisis by deciding to pursue both policies at once.

Hanoi would increase its military commitment to the southern battlefield and at the same time pursue negotiations to limit the war. Specifically, this plan called for a "decisive victory" in the South through a protracted war. The Lao Dong resolved to "endeavor to limit the enemy's war and defeat the enemy in that limited war, inflict heavy casualties on them, and force them to become bogged down and heavily defeated."[52] Negotiations played a significant role in the strategy of protracted war because they allowed the North to limit the ground war to the South. At the same time, Party leaders hoped to use negotiations to get the bombing stopped at limited cost to revolutionary objectives.

Although Nguyen Chi Thanh never accepted the new protracted war strategy, Le Duan soon became one of its most outspoken advocates. He admitted that his earlier predictions of a quick military victory in the South were overly optimistic and that the combination of political, military, and diplomatic techniques represented the best strategy to defeat the Americans.[53] Duan's evolution marked the significant changes that were taking place in Hanoi among those who had once predicted a swift and total military victory. Le Duan, Pham Hung, and General Nguyen Van Vinh now conceded that negotiations might be necessary at some point to force the Americans to withdraw.[54]

To assuage southern fears, however, the Political Bureau agreed that Bo's contacts with Gullion in Paris must end. This decision was actually made before the September Political Bureau meeting because Le Duan had convinced Party leaders that they had to settle this issue immediately.[55] As the debate between hawks and doves raged on in Hanoi, Le Duc Tho led a DRV delegation to Paris. He met with Bo on August 26 and presumably told him of the Party's problems concerning his contacts with the American. Tho apparently suggested that Bo "harden" his position and stress that the DRV's four points must be met as a condition for a political settlement.[56] Six days later, Pham Van Dong, the DRV's prime minister, stated in a radio broadcast that the "Four Points stand must be solemnly accepted by the U.S. government before a political settlement of the Viet Nam problem can be contemplated."[57] Dong could not make the four points a condition for talks when Bo and Gullion had already met, but he did say that talks and negotiations were not necessarily the same thing, and that Bo's meetings with Gullion represented only "a willingness to express our commitment to the NFLSV's Five Points and our Four Points as the basis for any political settlement."[58] Within the week, the Lao Dong's Political Bureau and its Military Commission also endorsed the creation of several main force infantry divisions in the People's Liberation

Armed Forces, the NLF's army, to show the Party's support for the southern revolution.[59] In addition, Hanoi began a major military operation in the Central Highlands that culminated in the battles of the Ia Drang Valley.[60] Hanoi also agreed to increase the number of PAVN regulars in the South.

Although the Lao Dong had agreed to terminate Bo's contacts with the Americans and had renewed its military commitment to the South, some southerners still feared that Hanoi might enter into serious negotiations to stop the bombings. When they conveyed these fears to Le Duan, he assured them that the Lao Dong would "never abandon the southern battlefield."[61] In a letter to Nguyen Chi Thanh in November, Duan explained the Party's new protracted war strategy. He told Thanh that the revolutionary forces lacked the capacity to achieve a complete military victory in the South, as both had hoped. The United States still remained vulnerable, however, because it lacked the patience to fight and win a protracted war. This new revolutionary tactic required "heavy emphasis . . . on the political struggle, which includes the diplomatic struggle"; but, Duan added, the basic problem "is to defeat the imperialists on the battlefield."[62]

At the core of Le Duan's new thinking lay the political reality of American escalation. The first secretary had concluded that "the Americans' bringing hundreds of thousands of troops into the South is an important step in the development of the war. This proves that the United States is more determined to cling to the South," he warned, "and with the current balance of forces . . . we have to prepare to fight them . . . over the long term." The increasingly pragmatic Le Duan was convinced that "the United States cannot struggle with us for long or win over us; in the long resistance war we shall definitely win the final victory."[63] Nguyen Chi Thanh was outraged, and is said to have felt betrayed by his former ally.[64]

Nguyen Chi Thanh's frustration did have an impact on the Lao Dong's Political Bureau, which feared that the southern armed forces would feel betrayed if they believed the Party was negotiating with the United States. Accordingly, the Lao Dong decided to send the NLF's diplomatic corps on a world tour to promote the hard line. As one Party official later commented, "We did not want to dampen the spirits of the fighting forces in the South by creating the illusion that we were serious about negotiations."[65] Of course, the Front was more than willing to promote the hard-liners' position, since it had opposed any talks with the United States until all Americans were withdrawn from the South. While doves and hawks in the Party represented various regions and ideological interests, almost everyone in the NLF supported Nguyen Chi Thanh's hard-line stance in 1965 and rejected the secret contacts. The Lao Dong understood that its southern comrades would hold such feelings, and therefore knew that the Front's diplomats would be excellent spokesmen abroad for the antinegotiations position.

With the Lao Dong coordinating the effort, the NLF launched the initiative in October 1965 with a visit to Helsinki, Finland. The Front had carefully selected Nguyen Van Dong, the acting head of its permanent mission to the Soviet Union, to lead the delegation. Apparently Front strategists believed that Dong's ties to the more moderate Soviets were important. In Finland, Dong met with representatives of the Finnish Social Democratic Party, the Finnish Peace Committee, and students from Helsinki's two universities. During each of these meetings he stressed the hard-liners' position. There could be no negotiations while American troops remained in the South, and nothing the Johnson administration did short of full withdrawal would lead to talks.[66]

In late October, Dong traveled to Stockholm, where he repeated the hard-line position in interviews with the Western press. "There can be no negotiations to end the war while American troops and the army of the Saigon puppets continue to devastate our homeland," he declared. During a television interview, Dong categorically rejected "Johnson's deceitful talks about peace and unconditional discussions."[67] On October 28 at a reception for the NLF delegation, the mayor of Stockholm toasted the struggle for self-liberation in South Viet Nam and pledged his support for neutralism "after all American troops had been withdrawn."[68] At each stop, Dong supplied the Western press with copies of the NLF's Five-Point Plan for Peace and the Front's July 1965 announcement demanding an American troop withdrawal. On October 30, the delegation returned to Moscow and filed its report.

Dong concluded that the mission had been a success. He believed that most Western leaders had readily accepted the NLF's position, that the withdrawal of American troops was a precondition for talks. He had eliminated the issue of bombings from the discussions; to his way of thinking, silence on that subject would be of tremendous benefit among revolutionary armed forces. Party leaders hoped that Dong's diplomatic offensive would produce the desired results in the South, but to make sure, the Lao Dong sent the rehabilitated and seasoned NLF diplomat Nguyen Van Hieu to the Afro-Asian People's Solidarity Conference in Syria to reiterate the hard-line position.

Hieu landed in Damascus on November 14, and in a speech at the airport proclaimed that "the only way to settle the South Viet Nam problem is to recognize and respect the South Vietnamese people's rights, put an end to U.S. aggression, drive out U.S. troops from this area, and recognize the NLF as the only genuine representative of the South Vietnamese people."[69] Hieu had once been considered a moderate in the West; now he declared, "Neither napalm bombs nor poison gases can quench the Vietnamese people's will to fight. . . . The only solution to the Viet Nam problem is the total expulsion of the U.S. imperialist aggressors from Viet Nam."[70] The Americans used napalm and Agent Orange only in the South; Hieu did not mention the bombing of the North.

It now seems clear that the NLF used Hanoi's approval of the latest diplomatic tour to stress southerners' antinegotiations stance and that perhaps the Front was more vigorous in its promotion of the hard line than many in Hanoi had wished. With Hanoi's tacit approval, NLF diplomats carefully coordinated a massive international propaganda campaign that drew on southern passions and southern interests. On November 6 the NLF's president, Nguyen Huu Tho, gave an interview to the Japanese newspaper *Asahi Shimbun*, and he was again interviewed by a Japanese newspaper on November 19.[71] On the same day, the Chinese News Agency released a full-page story headed "Viet Cong Commander," in which a southern military leader stressed battlefield victory. Wilfred Burchett, an Australian journalist, published a lengthy interview with several Front leaders in early December.[72]

The most important public relations campaign was a planned speech by Nguyen Huu Tho on the fifth anniversary of the founding of the NLF. An advance copy of the speech was circulated by Front diplomats throughout the world. The usually reserved Tho called for offensive action against the Americans and victory on the battlefield. "Point your rifles and shoot at the heads of the U.S. aggressors," Tho implored. "Strike night and day. Strike when it rains as well as when it is sunny. Strike at the enemy in the forest, on the mountains, in the delta, and in the cities. Strike at the enemy in large as well as small battles. All of you rush ahead and strike deadly blows at the heads of the U.S. aggressors in order to exterminate them."[73] Tho left no doubt where southerners stood on negotiations in 1965.

By mid-December 1965, Party hard-liners believed they had "tipped the balance against the pro-negotiations forces," thanks in part to the NLF's diplomatic efforts.[74] When the Lao Dong met at its twelfth Party plenum in December, debate was intense over the protracted war strategy. Three distinct positions emerged. The first was advocated by those who supported negotiations within the limited war strategy. Under this scenario, Hanoi appeared eager for negotiations, but at the same time used the pause to rush men and supplies south. Le Duan argued this position most forcefully. He believed that the Party should dangle tantalizing diplomatic leads in front of the United States to keep the Johnson administration off balance. By taking advantage of the bombing pauses, he argued, revolutionary forces could destroy the bulk of ARVN troops while inflicting sufficient damage on American forces to compel the United States to withdraw.[75] The second position, probably supported by Truong Chinh, called for negotiations with the United States to create a coalition government in the South in exchange for a bombing halt. To this end, Wallace Thies has suggested, those favoring this negotiating track promised a limited role for the Front in a coalition government if the United States agreed.[76] Truong Chinh and other influential northerners were most interested in socialist construction in the North and wanted the southern liberation war to be self-sufficient. The third group, represented by Nguyen Chi Thanh and most southerners, argued that it was not possible to negotiate with the United States while American troops were still in the South.[77]

The Lao Dong ultimately sided with Le Duan and adopted a resolution (Resolution 12) approving the two-track protracted war strategy. Under this new policy, the DRV increased its military commitment to the southern battlefield by sending additional regiments from the People's Army, and the Party prepared to open negotiations with the United States.[78] According to captured Communist documents, the Party would engage the Johnson administration in talks "to project an image of concern for peace," but it would "negotiate nothing away."[79] Le Duan and other Lao Dong leaders predicted that the Johnson administration would undertake another peace initiative soon because they suspected Washington wanted to increase its troop levels and expand the air war over the DRV.[80] Indeed, rumors had circulated throughout Viet Nam that a truce would take place shortly after the Twelfth Plenum, during the Christian holiday season.[81]

On December 24, the White House announced the anticipated ceasefire in the North. Johnson decided to launch a bombing pause on the strong recommendation of Secretary of Defense McNamara. McNamara had long advocated a bombing pause accompanied by another peace initiative before an anticipated American escalation. A pause, he argued, would test Hanoi's interest in negotiations and silence the administration's critics. Over the strong objections of the Joint Chiefs of Staff, Johnson reluctantly agreed to a brief holiday truce. "I pressed my case hard," McNamara would later report, "laying out my deepest concerns and fragile hopes."[82]

In typical Johnson style, the president used the pause to launch his own peace offensive, designed at least in part to quiet his critics. He dispatched Ambassador-at-Large W. Averell Harriman, Vice President Hubert H. Humphrey, and Assistant Secretary of State G. Mennen Williams to thirty countries to talk to representatives of over one hundred nations. Johnson's message was clear: he was willing to negotiate without conditions, but he was looking for signs that the Communists desired peace. At the same time, Secretary of State Rusk released the administration's "Fourteen Points" for peace, which amounted to little more than a recapitulation of Washington's position on the need to stop the Communist insurgency.[83] In this environment, as Harriman's aide Chester Cooper has noted, the administration expected little. "The efforts in December of '65 and January '66 were not the kind that would be likely to elicit a response. They were just much too flamboyant, noisy, more form than substance."[84]

To coincide with the truce and Harriman's effort, the State Department instructed Henry Byroade, the U.S. ambassador to Burma, to convey to the DRV representative, Vu Huu Binh, that Washington might extend the bombing pause if Hanoi "will now reciprocate" by taking meaningful steps toward peace, presumably a moratorium on the shipment of arms and personnel across the Demilitarized Zone.[85] The two diplomats met face to face on December 29 and Binh promised to deliver Byroade's message to Hanoi. Weeks passed before Byroade met with Binh again. The DRV delegate informed Byroade that he had not received any message from Hanoi, but that the Lao Dong's recent public announcements stated its position clearly. Binh was probably referring to the January 4, 1966, statement released by Foreign Minister Nguyen Duy Trinh denouncing the bombing pause as a trick.[86] Three weeks later, with the pause still in effect, Ho Chi Minh sent a dispatch to various heads of state accusing the United States of deceit and hypocrisy, demanding an immediate American troop withdrawal, and claiming that the NLF was the only true representative of the people of South Viet Nam.[87]

The Byroade-Binh contact, code-named PINTA by U.S. officials, resembled the Bo-Gullion meetings in Paris in that serious discussions did not get under way until the bombing had resumed. On January 31, Binh invited Byroade to the DRV embassy and informed him that Hanoi's official response to his December inquiry was now ready. Byroade read the statement, which offered nothing new, and promised Binh an immediate response. On February 19 the two met again, but by that time Hanoi seemed to have lost interest in negotiations. Binh declared that "since the United States has resumed the bombing, I hold that it is inappropriate to continue our contacts."[88] This time pressure from the hard-liners had little to do with the breakdown of talks. It seems likely that those Political Bureau members who preferred a compromise settlement to the continuation of the war grew disenchanted when the Johnson administration and the Saigon government ruled out such a possibility at their meeting in Honolulu in February 1966.[89] These doves also realized that each bombing pause and secret contact had been accompanied by a corresponding escalation of U.S. efforts. Similarly, advocates of the limited war strategy had achieved their goal, as Hanoi had increased its shipments to the South twofold during the bombing pause.[90] Le Duan and others probably concluded that the Party had taken full advantage of the pause, and that since the bombings had resumed, there was no reason to continue negotiations.

The White House blamed the Communists for PINTA's failure. The Johnson administration pointed to the increase in men and matériel shipped south and Ho's January 28 letter to various heads of state condemning the pause as proof that the Communists had no interest in talks. Rusk concluded that the peace offensive produced "no runs, no hits, no errors," and held that the Communists, not the Americans, had canceled the talks in Burma.[91] With virtually no debate, the bombing resumed on January 31.

Resumption of the bombing ended the first chapter in the long history of diplomatic contacts between Washington and the Lao Dong. The failure of the 1965 initiatives can be attributed to the unwillingness of either side to negotiate while the balance of forces south of the seventeenth parallel remained unclear. Since neither side had a decisive military edge, both used the bombing pauses and secret discussions as pretexts for further escalation and for scoring propaganda and public relations points. Any chance of moving the Lao Dong to the negotiating table by cultivating the doves in Hanoi was undermined, ironically, by Washington's provocative actions and the Party's own hard-liners. Communists in Hanoi who favored negotiations in an effort to limit the war in the South and concentrate on building socialism in the North failed to convince Party hard-liners that the southern revolution was a drain on limited resources. Support for negotiations dwindled in Hanoi as the Johnson administration continued to increase its bombing campaigns and escalate its military efforts in the South. Southerners, who had long opposed negotiations while American troops occupied their territory, played a crucial role in promoting the hard-liners' position throughout the world. The Lao Dong used the Front's experienced diplomats to calm the fears of revolutionary forces concerning the likelihood of negotiations.

By December 1965 the Party had rejected negotiations with the United States and adopted the two-track strategy of a protracted war. According to Lao Dong strategists, the Party would dangle tantalizing diplomatic leads in front of the Johnson administration to keep it off balance, and at the same time would increase its military commitment to the South. Of course, this plan resembled Washington's own. In the end, the war dragged on as both sides adopted a strategy of "fighting and talking" while waiting for the balance of forces to shift. Southerners seemed satisfied with Hanoi's strategic decisions, but regional differences would surface once again as the Party continued to struggle with its twin revolutionary objectives.

4

GLORY DAYS: THE NLF'S DIPLOMATIC VICTORIES OF 1966–1967

In the two years that followed the Lao Dong's decision to adopt a protracted war strategy, the military conflict in Viet Nam reached a stalemate. The introduction of American combat troops to Viet Nam had not produced the quick and easy victory that many in Washington had predicted. As a counter, Hanoi had increased its commitment to the southern battlefield, tripling the number of combat troops it sent south from 1965 to 1967.[1] In 1966 and 1967, PAVN regulars and PLAF guerrillas engaged U.S. combat forces in major military actions in the Western Highlands and near the Demilitarized Zone (DMZ), hoping to draw the Americans away from the protection of South Viet Nam's major cities. Despite his 430,000 American troops in the field, General William C. Westmoreland could not destroy PAVN main force units or seize the military initiative.

The American air war against the North also produced limited results. Although the United States had destroyed many major targets by 1967, Hanoi showed no signs of weakening.[2] The gradualist approach to air strikes gave the DRV time to prepare its major cities and military targets against American bombing raids and seek alternative ways of sending supplies south. It is unlikely, however, that the massive, unrestricted air war advocated by the Joint Chiefs of Staff would have produced different results. The DRV's anti-aircraft defense system was superb, and it seems doubtful that Americans would have accepted the huge losses such raids would have required.

As the Americans became bogged down in Viet Nam, they joined their Vietnamese counterparts in using diplomacy as a weapon of war. According to George C. Herring, American officials counted as many as 2,000 attempts to initiate peace talks between 1965 and 1967. "Neither side could afford to appear indifferent," Herring wrote in 1979, "but neither was willing to make the concessions necessary to make negotiations a reality."[3] Public pressure on Lyndon Johnson from the left and the right required him to "do something" in Viet Nam. From 1965 to 1967 he pursued his own two-track strategy of increasing the U.S. military commitment to the South and engaging the Communists in meaningless talks. That was the limit of American diplomatic efforts, however, and as a result, the Lao Dong was able to use the NLF's diplomats for more constructive measures.

In 1966 and 1967, the Political Bureau mobilized the Front's diplomatic corps to help secure Chinese military assistance. In addition, the NLF created political and military divisions between Saigon and Washington that set the stage for the series of military offensives known in the West as the Tet Offensive. These diplomatic victories increased the NLF's influence and prestige in Hanoi and signaled that relations between northern and southern Communists were close and warm. Although this closeness was short-lived, the NLF's diplomats were instrumental in ushering in a new phase of the war, "fighting while talking." The Political Bureau's handling of the Front during 1966 and 1967 was sophisticated and nuanced, and as a result, the Party scored significant victories. Perhaps its most important achievement was steering clear of the conflict between China and the Soviet Union.

The Sino-Soviet dispute had threatened to disrupt Viet Nam's struggle, and Hanoi understood that it needed China to be successful. For years Hanoi had managed to stay clear of the quarrel and had often been a buffer between the two powers.[4] Peking had always assumed that the Lao Dong was on China's side in the struggle against "Soviet revisionism." Visits to Peking in April 1965 by Le Duan and Vo Nguyen Giap seemed to confirm this view, and China's support for the Vietnamese revolution increased dramatically. From 1965 to 1968 Peking provided the Lao Dong with engineers, anti-aircraft artillery troops, and substantial military supplies. Mindful of its precarious position in the growing Sino-Soviet dispute, Hanoi carefully steered a middle course.

Relations between Moscow and Peking had soured as early as 1956, when Nikita Khrushchev had denounced Stalin and invited the United States to a summit meeting in Moscow "to come to terms on major East-West issues."[5] In 1960, at a meeting of Warsaw Pact countries in Moscow, the Soviets pushed through a declaration that "the world has now entered on a period of negotiations about the settlement of the main international issues in dispute with the aim of establishing a lasting peace, while the advocates of cold war are sustaining a defeat."[6] The declaration was clearly aimed at China and its policy of "continued revolution."

According to Peking, China served as the vanguard for all revolutionary movements in the developing world, and its strategy of people's war remained the model for all liberation wars. The Soviet Union, its Chinese critics claimed, had betrayed revolutions by promoting peaceful coexistence with the West and advocating negotiations over battlefield victory. China insisted that the world was divided into two camps—socialist and capitalist—and that there could be no collaboration and ultimately no compromise. Once the war in Viet Nam heated up, China charged that the Soviet Union, with its policy of détente, had abandoned wars for national liberation.[7]

Indeed, by early 1965 the Soviet Union had modified its position on Viet Nam. According to Anatoly Dobrynin, the Soviet ambassador to Washington, Moscow's leaders "unanimously recognized that our relations with the United States were a priority, while Viet Nam was not that vital to our national interest." Accordingly, Moscow sought to reduce international tension and end the conflict in Viet Nam through negotiations. Of course, the United States would have to agree to a meaningful compromise in Viet Nam. To underscore its commitment to détente, in January 1967 the Soviet Foreign Ministry circulated a top-secret document outlining Moscow's Viet Nam policy. The document condemned "Chinese adventurous schemes" and insisted that the "development of the [domestic] economy calls for the maintenance of peace."[8] By 1966, therefore, working with Washington toward a negotiated settlement in Viet Nam became Moscow's top foreign policy priority.

As Moscow promoted détente, Hanoi felt compelled to accept its benefactor's new ideological stance. Hanoi's move toward Moscow in 1966 was subtle and the Lao Dong was sensitive to its precarious position between the two Communist powers. In the past, the Lao Dong had boasted that "we use Moscow's technology and Peking's strategy."[9] By the summer of 1966, however, the Political Bureau in Hanoi became convinced that it needed the Soviets' more sophisticated anti-aircraft weapons to defend the North. Several leaders of the Lao Dong, including Vo Nguyen Giap and Truong Chinh, also argued that the offensive strategy in the South was going badly.[10] These factors, combined with Peking's less than cooperative attitude toward the passage of Soviet arms shipments through China, persuaded many Lao Dong leaders to accept Moscow's policy line. China did help deliver limited Soviet war matériel to Viet Nam, but only on condition that the operation remain under its control and be seen in Hanoi as a tremendous favor.[11]

Hanoi hoped to distance itself from China in Soviet eyes but simultaneously to use the NLF's diplomatic corps to court China. In January 1966, therefore, the Party adopted an informal policy line that directed the NLF to embrace the People's Republic of China publicly while the Lao Dong carefully negotiated the best course for Viet Nam's future. This new line would downplay divisions in the Communist camp in favor of international solidarity. "I told the crowd in Peking," an NLF diplomat would later report, "that China and Viet Nam are as close as lips and teeth."[12] "There was a little something for everybody," a Lao Dong official explained. "We would bend toward Moscow and then send the NLF to China to sing its praises."[13]

By the fall of 1966, however, Hanoi had downplayed the significance of Mao's doctrine of people's war in its attempt to win favor in Moscow. In an essay written for *Hoc Tap*, the Party's theoretical journal, Brigadier General Hoang Minh Thao explained that "the people's war outlook of our party is a new, creative development of the Marxist-Leninist ideas of revolutionary violence and revolutionary war."[14] In September, *Hoc Tap* editorialized that the Vietnamese struggle was unique in the history of liberation movements and was based on the country's past experiences with foreign invaders.[15] Both of these essays were thinly veiled criticisms of Peking's policy of "continuous revolution," a worldwide movement centered in China. In December 1965, Le Duan argued that the Vietnamese revolution could never be led by the peasant class, a position quite different from that advocated in the People's Republic of China.[16] The Lao Dong also attacked China's cultural revolution and decried the deification of Mao "to the detriment of close Party relations with the masses."[17]

At the same time, however, the NLF purposefully reinvented its ideological roots and manipulated its public image to make it acceptable to Peking. The Front sent several delegates to China, all to reject Soviet-style revisionism in favor of a military victory through people's war. According to Mao's theory, people's war depended on the power of the individual over modern weapons. Through superior morale and organization, relatively untrained and poorly armed soldiers defeated a militarily more sophisticated and modern enemy. The "people" acted locally and in defense of broadly defined national interests. The guerrilla movement in South Viet Nam was a carbon copy of people's war, according to the NLF's touring diplomats.

Tran Van Thanh and Nguyen Xuan Long headed the first of these NLF legations. Thanh had been born in 1921 in Vinh Long, in the heart of the Mekong Delta. The French imprisoned him during World War II for trade union activities. He was freed after the August Revolution in 1945, and he worked for several industrial unions in Saigon. He had had diplomatic experience in Cuba before his visit to the People's Republic of China in 1964 as the NLF's official representative.[18] Much less is known about Long. A Saigon intellectual, he had apparently been active in the NLF since its founding. He had traveled with other Front delegations to Cuba and Eastern Europe and had been active in the NLF-sponsored self-determination movement.[19]

On December 19, 1966, Thanh prepared the Chinese people for the arrival of the NLF delegation with an hour-long broadcast on Radio Peking.[20] This was an unusual occurrence, as foreign diplomats were rarely given access to Peking's propaganda network. Thanh boasted that the efforts of the NLF in Viet Nam were a major contribution to national liberation movements throughout the world. He challenged other nations to "pick up the banner of national liberation" and flatly reject "the revisionist policies of those who help the imperialists through their naive talk of peaceful coexistence." Thanh concluded that "if the United States can be defeated in South Viet Nam, it will be possible to defeat it anywhere in the world."[21] His speech pleased the Chinese Communists, who had predicted the same outcome.

More than two thousand people greeted the NLF delegation in the South China city of Kwangchow. The ostensible purpose of the visit was to celebrate the sixth anniversary of the founding of the NLF, but Long and his Chinese hosts used the occasion to promote the Front's new policy line. Wang Shou-tao of the Kwangtung Provincial Revolutionary Committee spoke first. He praised the NLF's battlefield victories "against the U.S. imperialists," which he described as upseting the counterrevolutionary goals of the United States and contributing to national liberation movements all over the world.[22]

Nguyen Xuan Long also condemned Soviet revisionists for "working in the service of U.S. imperialism." The revisionists were "like brokers peddling U.S. imperialism's peace fraud," and Long vowed that the South Vietnamese people would not be swayed by such transparent peace overtures and would continue to fight the Americans on the battlefield. He then paid tribute to the "700 million Chinese people for following Chairman Mao's teachings to make the vast territory of China the reliable rear area for the Vietnamese people." He concluded by praising the fraternal solidarity between Viet Nam and China.[23]

In Peking, on December 20, the sixth anniversary of the founding of the NLF, Chen Yi, the Chinese foreign minister, addressed a crowd of over 100,000. He declared that the Chinese people were fully prepared to march to the front any time the Vietnamese people required their aid. He also chastised the revisionists for supporting peace talks.[24] *People's Daily*, the Chinese Communist Party's newspaper, welcomed the NLF delegation to China and warned the United States and the Soviet Union that their "conspiracy of forcing peace talks by coercion, inducement, or persuasion would be futile."[25] Chou En-lai sent a message to Nguyen Huu Tho urging the Front "to fight the war to the end."[26]

Coinciding with the Front's diplomatic offensive in China were public assurances from leading NLF officials in Hanoi that the southern revolution spoke for itself. In mid-December the NLF had opened a permanent mission in Hanoi headed by Nguyen Van Tien. Tien used the visibility of his new appointment to highlight policy differences between Hanoi and the NLF, as if they were actually two separate entities. A former Saigon professor, Tien told the American journalist Harrison Salisbury that the "Front is an independent entity." "The North cannot speak for the South," Tien claimed, "anyone who has to discuss South Viet Nam must speak with the Front."[27] He reiterated these sentiments two weeks later when he reported, "Reunification is a matter that will require substantial time and a careful working out of details"—perhaps "ten, fifteen, maybe twenty years. . . . We have to make sure that southerners are comfortable with any arrangement agreed upon."[28] Nguyen Van Hieu, now serving as a roving NLF ambassador, echoed Tien, stating that "an unconditional cessation of the bombing of the North will not in itself lead to a settlement in the South. Of course to talk to Hanoi you [the United States] have to stop the bombing of the North, but that is to talk to Hanoi."[29] Douglas Pike, the government's expert on the NLF during the war's early years, has suggested that Tien's and Hieu's comments were just diplomatic ploys to demonstrate the Front's independence.[30] "Won't they drop the mask and eliminate all their supposed differences if they win the war?" one journalist asked.[31] Although Tien and Hieu were loyal Party members, neither could hide his regionalist sentiments and both enjoyed the NLF's renewed prestige.

Apparently the Front's diplomatic offensive produced the desired results. In late June, Chen Yi officially recognized the NLF, stating that "the Chinese government has considered the NLF delegates in China the only foreign representatives of South Viet Nam. The Government now recognizes the NLF group here as the staffers of the embassy of South Viet Nam."[32] The Chinese timed the announcement to coincide with the explosion of their first hydrogen bomb.[33] Their actions allowed the NLF to continue to promote its antinegotiations message without fear of reprisal from Hanoi. Even though relations between Hanoi and Peking had cooled, the Lao Dong could not afford to alienate its northern neighbor completely. For the Chinese, the NLF represented the success of their people's war strategy. Support for the Front gave Peking an elevated standing in the developing world. The Chinese used their special relationship with the NLF against the Soviet Union, claiming that Moscow did not support the anti-imperialist struggle in Asia and Africa. In Viet Nam, Mao's Communists supported the Front to influence one of the major revolutionary groups. It now seems clear that Peking preferred a pro-China southern regime to a Moscow-leaning unified Viet Nam.

In mid-August 1967, the NLF held its third national congress at the Central Committee headquarters in Tay Ninh province. The congress was called ostensibly to endorse the Party's resolutions approved at the Thirteenth Plenum in January, which included stepping up the diplomatic struggle.[34] The Party apparently decided that the time had come to create a broad-based front in the South to unite the Vietnamese people against the Saigon government and the United States.[35] Over the course of the war, NLF officials argued, the Front had abandoned its more subtle attempts to win popular support. Now, with U.S.-sponsored elections scheduled in South Viet Nam for early September, the time had come for the NLF to "create conditions in which the South Vietnamese people will unite to persuade the United States to withdraw."[36] The goal was to launch a campaign in South Viet Nam with broad nationalist appeal to encourage Vietnamese, "irrespective of political tendencies," to work together against the Saigon regime. The NLF pledged to welcome "all patriotic forces and individuals into the Front," even if they disliked the Communists, "to take joint action against the common enemy—the U.S. aggressors and their lackeys."[37] This had been the NLF's goal at its founding, leaders explained, but the war had produced conditions that detracted from their original intentions. For instance, the NLF had once won people to its side by adopting tactics that forced the Saigon government into repressive action. Peasants overburdened by taxes and resentful of the draft volunteered for service with the NLF to strike back at the government.[38] As the war widened, however, the Front itself had been forced to increase its levies and draft recruits. The Congress now planned to correct that flawed strategy by "following more closely the path of revolution laid down by our brothers in China."[39]

Several NLF leaders promoted the new united front policy as a faithful copy of the formula for people's war put forth in Lin Piao's *Long Live the Victory of the People's War*, distributed in Viet Nam shortly before the Front's third congress. Piao wrote, "Holding aloft the banner of national revolution, our party issued the call for national unity and united resistance to Japanese imperialism, a call which won fervent support from the people of the whole country."[40] In people's war, a disciplined party of revolutionaries acted as the vanguard of the movement. They directed a united front with mass support and controlled an organized army loyal to the Party. These revolutionaries, through their united front strategy, secured rural areas as strategic havens or reserves to support the fighting and develop showcase alternatives of the political system to come.[41] During the final phase of people's war, revolutionaries combined political, diplomatic, and military action for victory. According to Mao, the final stage of people's war had three phases. The first was the enemy's strategic offensive and the people's strategic defensive. The second was a period of the enemy's strategic consolidation and the people's preparation for the counteroffensive. The third and final phase was a period of strategic counteroffensive against enemy forces. Conventional forces won the decisive victory on the battlefield.[42]

Peking interpreted the NLF's new fourteen-point manifesto, approved at its third congress, as a commitment to the Chinese revolutionary path. The Front resolved to create an honest government by dissolving Saigon's National Assembly and holding free elections to create a new one. The NLF platform also supported a variety of economic and land reforms and endorsed efforts to encourage private industry and trade. The document affirmed the Front's respect for religious freedom, rights for women, and democracy. Like the original 1960 manifesto, the August 1967 resolutions endorsed a foreign policy of neutrality.[43] All of these measures were designed to create favorable conditions for the establishment of the new united front. One interesting provision was a promise to abolish the regulation requiring resident Chinese to become Vietnamese citizens.[44]

In early September 1967, the NLF launched a major propaganda and diplomatic offensive to highlight the results of the Third Congress and promote the close relationship with China. Nguyen Minh Phuong, the acting ambassador of the NLF's mission in Peking, headed the first of these legations. Touring the major cities of China, Phuong released statements concerning the Front's new political program and its dependence on Mao's revolutionary theory. On September 4, Premier Chou En-lai received Phuong, who later reported that the two spoke at length about "the U.S. imperialists' new war escalation and peace talk frauds."[45] In an uncharacteristically long radio broadcast from Peking, Phuong outlined the new political platform confirming the Front's determination "to strengthen the unity of the entire people, to resolutely defeat the U.S. imperialist war of aggression, to overthrow the puppet regime of U.S. imperialism, to establish a broad national, democratic coalition regime, to build an independent, democratic, peaceful, neutral and prosperous South Vietnam, and to reunify the fatherland."[46] He then announced that the Front's combat hero, Huynh Van Danh, would embark on a two-month tour.

Danh was sent to China, according to the NLF's president, Nguyen Huu Tho, to publicize the Front's commitment to "continue the sacred war against U.S. aggression and for national salvation with redoubled efforts till not a single U.S. aggressor remains in our beloved South Viet Nam."[47] Tho assured the Chinese that the NLF's new political program followed Mao's revolutionary path and flatly rejected the "Soviets' leftist revisionism."[48] The Front chose Danh because of his extraordinary combat record—he was reported to have killed "over one hundred U.S. aggressors."[49] On September 29, he gave a saber-rattling speech at a banquet sponsored by Chou En-lai, boasting that the NLF boldly followed the revolutionary example of the Chinese people and that "the people of South Vietnam and Chinese people will always fight shoulder to shoulder and win victory together."[50] Despite the presence of three DRV representatives, Danh claimed that, "while continuing to perpetrate monstrous crimes in South Viet Nam, the U.S. is clamoring for peace negotiations in a vain attempt to achieve its criminal designs. The South Vietnamese people are determined to advance on the crest of victory with their guns firmly in hand."[51]

On October 7, the Chinese Ministry of National Defense sponsored a meeting in the Great Hall of the People where Danh was the featured speaker. Before over ten thousand members of the three services of the People's Liberation Army, Danh declared that "reality on the battlefields has clearly shown that the armymen and people of South Vietnam have grown stronger and stronger and won more and more victories in their fighting. The graves of U.S. soldiers were to be found everywhere on the South Vietnam battlefield."[52] Danh then introduced Ngo Thi Tuyet, an eighteen-year-old from Long An province, who had already been fighting the Saigon forces for six years. She recounted several battlefield stories and assured the gathering that the people of the South were willing to fight as long as it took to drive the Americans from Viet Nam. "We will not stop our struggle for national salvation until the U.S. aggressors have been soundly defeated on the battlefield." Nieh Jung-chen, the vice premier and vice chair of the Chinese National Defense Council, ended the ceremony by declaring, "China and Vietnam are neighbors as intimately dependent on one another as lips and teeth."[53] Danh made several other stops in China. In Shanghai, he spoke before a crowd of 100,000 backed by a banner that read, "Down with Modern Revisionism with the Soviet Revisionist Leading Clique at Its Center!!"[54] He visited revolutionary fighters in Changsha, a bicycle assembly plant, an East China Sea fleet of the PLA navy, and a medical supplies center.[55] At each stop he praised the Chinese for following the path of people's war to victory and thanked them for their support of the NLF's new political platform.

By late October, therefore, the NLF had launched two separate diplomatic initiatives to highlight its acceptance of Mao's strategy of people's war and publicly reject Soviet revisionism. This Janus-faced Lao Dong policy had delayed the inevitable, but it did not stop relations between Hanoi and Peking from deteriorating. China began to drift from its "brotherly comrades" in early 1966, and the Front's diplomatic effort merely bought two additional years of support. Without this aid, however, the war might have taken a different course. Even Hanoi's most severe critics of China understand the valuable contribution that Peking made to Viet Nam's modern revolution and underscore the "effort of the NLF in keeping Chinese support for the revolution."[56]

As relations with the Chinese cooled, the Political Bureau mobilized the NLF's diplomatic corps for another major maneuver. By the summer of 1967, Hanoi had grown increasingly anxious about the tensions between the fraternal socialist allies and therefore moved forward with its plans to force the Johnson administration to the bargaining table and end the long and costly war. Party leaders feared that a continued military stalemate might result in Chinese or Soviet intervention, with possibly disastrous results. In October, therefore, the Lao Dong moved forward with a bold plan that had been in existence in theory at least since 1960. The plan was not based on a strategy endorsed by Moscow or Peking, but instead relied on the Vietnamese concept of *tong cong kich/tong khoi nghia*, "general offensive/general uprising."

On October 25, 1967, the Central Committee approved Resolution 14, or the Quang Trung Resolution, named for the emperor who had defeated the Chinese invaders during Tet of 1789. The Party's new strategy combined a protracted war of attrition with morale-shattering attacks on southern urban centers. Its centerpiece was a projected three-phase offensive in South Viet Nam. The Political Bureau reasoned that widespread attacks against southern urban centers would compel the United States to pull back its firepower to defend southern cities and thereby deescalate the war against the North.[57] The offensive would show the Americans that they had to choose one of two alternatives: to step up the war substantially —difficult to do in an election year—or go to the negotiating table. In either case, the Lao Dong was committed to continue the war until the United States withdrew from Viet Nam under terms favorable to it.

In late spring, plans for the general offensive/general uprising circulated at the highest levels. In most reports, the Political Bureau predicted that "the upcoming general offensive/general uprising will be a period, a process, of intense and complicated strategic offensives by military, political, and diplomatic means. . . . It is a process in which we will attack and advance on the enemy continuously both militarily and politically as well as a process in which the enemy will counterattack ferociously in order to wrest back and to reoccupy important positions that will have been lost."[58] When word of the planned general offensive/general uprising reached the South, there was considerable debate among Party members as to its efficacy. Some southern Communists in the Tri-Thien region criticized the plan because the Party would not be able to carry out continuous attacks. Military leaders also feared that they did not have the personnel to launch such an offensive.[59]

In addition, many southern military leaders balked at the notion of a general offensive/general uprising at this stage of the war. While most southerners had favored a battlefield victory and refused to support negotiations with Washington until after an American troop withdrawal, few supported the idea of a decisive offensive to end the war. The COSVN director, Nguyen Chi Thanh, remained steadfast in his belief in the potential of a decisive military encounter, but in midsummer 1967 Thanh was killed. After his death, few in the South supported the Clausewitzian battle he had hoped for. Throughout the war, southerners had used the tactic of *tien cong va noi day, noi day va tan cong* (attack and uprise, uprise and attack). This tactic required the support of the local population, and once this support was guaranteed and sustained, future attacks could take place. As the war progressed, the NLF modified the tactic to include *noi day dong loat* (simultaneous uprising), a series of military attacks with logistical support by the local population over a large area to avoid concentrated counterattacks by the Americans and the ARVN. According to many southern revolutionaries, the Tet Offensive relied too heavily on the notion of *dut diem* (to take over a target completely).[60] This concept, as carried out in the three phases of the offensive, opened the door for reprisal attacks and exposed the PLAF to the full power of the American armed forces. Postwar criticisms of the Political Bureau's decision making during Tet by Senior General Tran Van Tra and other high-ranking officials confirm this view.[61]

In any event, by the summer of 1967, plans for the general offensive/general uprising were taking shape and the Party called on the NLF's diplomats once again to set the stage. Focusing its efforts now on domestic conditions, the Front's diplomatic team worked closely with the Political Bureau to drive a wedge between Saigon's political and military leaders. The plan was based on the Party's concept of *dau tranh—dich van*, or "struggle action—against the enemy." The goal was to neutralize or win over government troops, the secret police, and civilian officials. The Front promised "an unblemished biography" to anyone who would join the fight against the Americans. Those who collaborated with the NLF, the propaganda teams announced, would be rewarded and promoted to "adequate positions" and have their past indiscretions erased. Those who sympathized with the Front or refused to "carry out the orders of the aggressor American imperialists" would have "their merits recorded."[62]

Le Ngoc Lan, brother-in-law of Dr. Phung Van Cung, the vice chairman of the NLF's Central Committee, directed the Front's effort in Saigon. Known in the South as Ba Tra, or Brother Three Tea, Lan had been a key figure in the NLF since its founding in 1960. In 1967 he was to mobilize Saigon business leaders and intellectuals, who would announce their support for a coalition government at the proper time. He promised them cabinet-level appointments in such a government and encouraged them to work closely with NLF leaders in Saigon. His early effort was timed to create a groundswell of opposition to the national elections scheduled in South Viet Nam for early September.

In late March, Lyndon Johnson had met with Air Marshal Nguyen Cao Ky, the prime minister of South Viet Nam, and begged him to hold national elections. "My birthday is in late August," Johnson reportedly said, and the "greatest birthday present you could give me is a national election."[63] Ky agreed, and Saigon officials moved forward toward what would become the first national election since the referendums that brought Ngo Dinh Diem to power in 1955 and 1956. In the short term, Lan hoped that this coalition of opposition forces would boycott the election, thus proving that it was a farce and creating further problems between Saigon and Washington. By late April, however, it became apparent to those most closely connected with events in the South that the United States was prepared to back the elections no matter what form they took. Ky and his only real opponent, General Nguyen Van Thieu, South Viet Nam's chief of state in 1967, eliminated most candidates early on through a series of questionable actions. The United States raised few objections, so the NLF strategists decided to change their tactics.

Instead of boycotting the election, the Front secretly promoted a candidate of its own. Truong Dinh Dzu, a Saigon lawyer and friend of Lan's, agreed to run for the presidency. As instructed, Dzu promoted a neutralist solution in South Viet Nam. The Front held no illusions that he would win, but encouraged him to "take away as much support from the American lackeys" as possible.[64] Dzu's candidacy did have a dramatic impact on the outcome of the election, as Thieu and Ky decided to pool their resources and run on a joint ticket, Thieu as president and Ky as vice president. In the end, Dzu won 17 percent of the vote and the Saigon regime garnered only 35 percent.[65] The September elections, originally designed to show democracy at work in South Viet Nam, instead highlighted the political weaknesses of America's ally. Air Marshal Ky, analyzing Thieu's poor showing in the presidential race, boasted, "I would have won sixty to seventy percent of the vote if I had wanted to cheat." He then explained, "I was the very person who organized and controlled the election. There was no reason for me to cheat in favor of Thieu and get the blame, when I had given up my own chance for the presidency."[66]

Thieu's narrow victory convinced NLF leaders that they should encourage their urban allies to move quickly. Beginning in late September, hundreds of Saigon's leading business people and intellectuals ridiculed the election results and called for a coalition government and a new constitution. Many of the city's daily newspapers criticized the new Thieu-Ky regime openly and blamed them for the rampant corruption. Buddhist leaders condemned police brutality under the Saigon regime, claiming that South Viet Nam's prisons were filled with innocent people. Street protests in early October pointed to the government's growing political problems, and news of PLAF military advances in nearby Long An province intensified the problem. By mid-October, a Washington skeptic charged, "We praise the Saigon regime and democracy in South Viet Nam, but all around us the walls are tumbling down."[67]

Despite these political victories, the NLF did suffer a serious setback. In May, Saigon authorities, on a tip from a double agent, arrested Lan and forced him to name names. He quickly admitted that he had already converted to the NLF's cause three top-level government officials, the chief of the Saigon River Port Authority, the city's leading engineer, a prominent bank director, and several lawyers and university professors. The nucleus of this group would surface after the general uprising as the Alliance of National, Democratic, and Peace Forces. In addition, Lan named most of his secret contacts in the NLF. According to Truong Nhu Tang, Lan had "denounced all the secret cadres with whom his job as liaison agent put him in contact."[68]

Shortly after Lan's arrest, Tran Bach Dang, the NLF's secretary of the Saigon–Cholon–Gia Dinh region, and his assistant, Sau Ha, made contact with the American embassy in an attempt to establish a prisoner exchange. The NLF, naturally, was interested in getting these prisoners back and believed that the United States would be interested in getting its own high-ranking captives in return. According to one of the NLF's prisoners, "Both sides strove mightily to keep these negotiations secret from other parties."[69] After two weeks of talks, however, the Saigon regime learned of the secret contact and had Sau Ha arrested. During his painful interrogation, Ha produced the names of over a dozen NLF leaders being held in Saigon jails whose release was being negotiated with the United States.[70] Saigon officials were outraged, but reported their findings to the American embassy. Embassy staff now felt compelled to disclose their dealings with the NLF to the State Department.

In Washington, the prisoner exchange negotiations assumed greater significance than they deserved. According to the journalist Don Oberdorfer, "there was speculation that the North Vietnamese might finally be ready to settle," and that Hanoi had "chosen the Viet Cong to make the bid."[71] The State Department gave the contact the code name BUTTERCUP and encouraged the embassy in Saigon to pursue every possible avenue with the Communists. Pressuring the Saigon regime to cooperate, embassy officials approached the NLF through channels Ha had previously opened. They sent a letter directly to Dang stating that the United States was interested in listening to what he had to say. In addition, they forced the newly elected Thieu-Ky regime to release some prisoners on the BUTTERCUP list as a good-faith gesture.[72]

The NLF's reply in mid-October contained familiar and frustrating language: there was no possibility of a political settlement to the crisis in South Viet Nam unless the United States accepted the four-and five-point peace plans. The Johnson administration had to understand, the Front said, that it could not force its will on the people of South Viet Nam; they themselves would determine the nation's future.[73] As puzzled State Department officials met to get a better grip on BUTTERCUP, the entire affair created a political nightmare in Saigon.

Rumors circulated throughout the city that the Americans were negotiating with the NLF. General Nguyen Ngoc Loan, the head of the national police, was reported to have resigned in protest against orders to free prisoners.[74] The National Assembly voted almost unanimously to condemn Washington's actions, claiming that "the United States is seeking to sell out the nationalist cause."[75] Simultaneously, at instructions from the NLF, many of Saigon's elite renewed their calls for a coalition government. "It was a hornets' nest," reported a Saigon official. "The level of secrecy and distrust was at an all-time high."[76] Another complained, "The Americans' secret contacts with the NLF came at the worst time for us—just as we were trying to establish a liberal democracy through national elections."[77]

In Washington, some American officials correctly concluded that BUTTERCUP had served the NLF's purposes well. The entire diplomatic episode, according to an American journalist, had sown "doubt and suspicion in South Viet Nam" and had given "credence to the coalition government rumor."[78] BUTTERCUP was perfectly timed to disrupt political events in South Viet Nam, but it happened also to coincide with Johnson's effort to put a positive face on the war. Since early fall, the State Department and other government agencies had been gearing up their propaganda machines to match the Communists'. Movies, posters, and public speakers all spoke of American gains in Viet Nam. In the last months of 1967, Johnson formed a task force headed by the CIA director to demonstrate that U.S. figures and optimism about the war were well founded. MACV got involved in the act too, issuing report after report that showed progress in the war.[79] In mid-November, General Westmoreland returned to Washington for a series of reports to the nation. The general told a national radio audience that the war was winding down. "We have reached an important point where the end begins to come in view," Westmoreland optimistically predicted.[80]

In one of the greatest ironies of a war rich in irony, the Johnson administration's newfound optimism ran headfirst into the NLF's last diplomatic ploy before the major offensive. In late fall, the NLF carefully coordinated rehearsals of the offensive. On December 20, 1967, the seventh anniversary of the Front's founding, students launched a general strike, flying NLF flags from schools and universities and handing out pro-NLF literature on Saigon's streets. PLAF units simultaneously attacked several strategic targets in the center of the city. The Lao Dong also went on the diplomatic offensive, trying to throw the Johnson administration off guard. On December 21 the NLF proposed three-day cease-fires at Christmas and the Western New Year. These short truces would be followed by a seven-day respite at the Vietnamese New Year. In the North, the major diplomatic announcement was reserved for the DRV's foreign minister, Nguyen Duy Trinh.

On December 30, at Hanoi's City Hall, during a routine government reception for a diplomatic delegation from the Mongolian People's Republic, Trinh announced for the first time that talks with the United States "will begin" when the bombing was stopped unconditionally.[81] The use of the future tense represented a dramatic departure from all previous DRV statements. In January, Trinh himself had announced, "It is only after the unconditional cessation of U.S. bombing and all other acts of war against the DRV that there *could be* talks between the DRV and the U.S."[82] For years policy makers and scholars have wondered whether Trinh's December 30 comment was simply an oversight or an error in translation. It now seems clear that the Party had purposefully introduced the change to coincide with the NLF's peace overtures in preparation for the general offensive. The Political Bureau correctly interpreted Johnson's September message in San Antonio, Texas, as an effort to end the military stalemate. Johnson had expressed his willingness to stop the bombing if Hanoi assured the United States that this action would lead promptly to substantive discussions. The president also expected North Viet Nam to refrain from sending troops and supplies south.[83]

After hearing Trinh's remarks, a determined and curious Johnson pursued another secret contact through Romania. The president dispatched his chief negotiator, Averell Harriman, to Bucharest to test Hanoi's interest. Harriman reported that the Lao Dong was indeed interested in a "no advantage" formula as originally outlined in San Antonio, and that Trinh's comments seemed to reflect the current thinking in Hanoi. The Romanian contact, Deputy Foreign Minister Gheorghe Macovescu, traveled to Hanoi in early January and reported startling news: the DRV was apparently willing to drop its four points as the basis for negotiations, suggesting instead that "each side would come with its own view." In addition, Macovescu received confirmation that the DRV was willing "to receive any person, or even a representative of the United States," to discuss peace once the bombing stopped.[84] Macovescu was still in Hanoi when PLAF forces fired the first shots of the Tet Offensive, changing the course of the war forever.

The NLF's diplomatic efforts had clearly created the proper atmosphere for the attacks. Saigon was in political chaos, with its only base of support, the educated elite, calling for a coalition government daily. The Thieu and Ky regime had won a narrow victory over the NLF's candidate, but in victory the weakness of the American-backed government was exposed. The Front had used a secret contact over a prisoner exchange to sow doubt and confusion among its enemies, and as a result, the Johnson administration ignored early warning signals of the impending military offensive and went on a propaganda offensive of its own. The result of the NLF's diplomatic and political barrage was that neither Saigon nor Washington was fully prepared for the military attacks that came in January 1968.

On the eve of the Tet Offensive, with several important diplomatic objectives achieved, relations between the NLF and the Political Bureau were at their closest. At no other time during the war did the Front have so much influence or prestige in Hanoi. The Party had successfully used the NLF's diplomatic corps to placate China and disrupt the political and military situation in Saigon, and as a result, the Front gained stature. "A southern wind came over Hanoi," one former Lao Dong official commented, "and we could feel a closeness with our southern brothers and sisters that was indeed unique in our experience."[85] Southern Communists held out hope that Hanoi would be more sensitive to the South's needs and that the liberation war would move to the top of the Political Bureau's agenda. The fallout from the New Year's attacks shattered those illusions, however, and relations between northern and southern Communists were never again the same.

5

OLD WINE IN NEW BOTTLES: JOHNSON, NIXON, AND THE PRG, 1968–1969

On January 30, 1968, in the early-morning hours, combined PLAF and PAVN forces launched a series of raids on key district and provincial towns. The Communists also attacked five of South Viet Nam's six major cities; the attack on Saigon targeted the American embassy. Over the next ten months, the Communists initiated two more massive attacks on southern urban areas, leading to some of the bloodiest fighting of the war. In Hue, the Nguyen dynasty's imperial capital, ARVN and PLAF forces fought hand to hand and from house to house. Early press reports exaggerated Communist military advances, and even the venerable newscaster Walter Cronkite, an early supporter of American intervention in Viet Nam, exclaimed, "What the hell is going on here! . . . I thought we were winning the war."[1] Almost overnight, Johnson's approval rating for his handling of the war plummeted to 26 percent, an all-time low.[2]

Fearful that the war was getting out of control and that domestic public opinion threatened his presidency, Johnson reevaluated his Viet Nam policy in mid-March. Particularly important to the president was General Westmoreland's proposal to add 206,000 American combat troops to the U.S. arsenal, most of them destined for Viet Nam. Westmoreland had made the request in late 1967, before Tet, but it now seems clear that the

Communists' offensive provided Johnson with an opportunity for a full policy review. Although the president decided not to alter U.S. goals or objectives in Viet Nam, he did reject Westmoreland's request. Clark Clifford, who had replaced McNamara as Johnson's secretary of defense during Tet, concluded that the United States was in a "hopeless bog" in Viet Nam and that a negotiated settlement was necessary.[3] Secretary of State Rusk urged Johnson to launch a peace initiative to quiet domestic critics and stabilize the Saigon regime. In addition, domestic political events worked against the president. On March 12, Senator Eugene McCarthy, a peace candidate who opposed Johnson in the Democratic Party's presidential race, won 42 percent of the vote in the New Hampshire primary.[4] Although Johnson had not been on the ballot, most political experts quickly labeled McCarthy's showing a resounding defeat for the president and those who wanted to continue the war.[5] With the debate raging in the administration over the future of U.S. policy in Viet Nam and his own political future in doubt, the president shocked the nation with a surprise announcement.

On March 31, 1968, before a nationwide television audience, Lyndon Johnson announced that he would commit all his energy to ending the war, and therefore would not accept his party's nomination for another term as president. Johnson announced that he was limiting the bombing to the area just north of the Demilitarized Zone and that he had instructed his diplomatic team to "search for peace." The president understood that the Tet Offensive undermined his administration's plans to "fight this war in cold blood," and the Communists' military raids had come at the most inopportune time for the United States.[6] Washington was overextended militarily and financially in Viet Nam, and Johnson could not grant Westmoreland's troop request without dire economic and political consequences at home. The administration assumed that Hanoi would reject the offer to negotiate, since it was not connected to an unconditional bombing halt, and that the refusal might buy the president some time.[7] Johnson was thus unprepared for Hanoi's private assurances that it was ready to open negotiations.

For some time, Party leaders in Hanoi had expected Johnson to launch a peace initiative.[8] The Political Bureau had carefully prepared for a new round of negotiations, since the Tet Offensive had been planned to precipitate such a move. Some Party leaders warned, however, that any meaningful concessions by the United States were not to be expected. The Johnson administration was unlikely to give in on key issues and intended to use the negotiations only to calm domestic public opinion. Although some

Lao Dong officials had hoped Tet would end the war, they also realized that they could take advantage of Johnson's need merely to engage in talks. They were equally committed to a "no concessions" policy, and therefore predicted that they could exploit the growing contradictions between the United States and its southern ally.[9] As one Lao Dong leader later explained, "Of course, we hoped to persuade the Johnson people to end their involvement in Viet Nam, but we also saw a tremendous opportunity in talks."[10] Even the NLF saw the advantage in beginning negotiations. "While there was some disagreement over tactics before Tet," one former NLF official explained, "there was complete agreement on the idea that Tet had changed everything. We were now prepared to negotiate from a position of strength, and Johnson was in a position of weakness."[11] Indeed, most southerners understood that Tet was a tremendous psychological defeat for Washington.

After several false starts, the talks finally began on May 13, 1968, in Paris. Party leaders moved quickly to exploit the talks for their full propaganda value, but understood all along that the chances for peace were slim. "When the peace talks opened in Paris," a Lao Dong official remembered in 1995, "we knew not to expect major concessions from the United States right away. They would continue to wage a war of aggression and their talk of peace would amount to little more than old wine in new bottles."[12] Still, the Lao Dong's Tet Offensive had forced the United States to the bargaining table in the spring of 1968, and the Communists did see a tremendous political and military advantage to the negotiations.

Once the talks began, the Political Bureau in Hanoi skillfully used the NLF's seasoned diplomats to drive a wedge between the United States and its South Vietnamese ally. As a result, relations between the Johnson administration and the Saigon government reached an all-time low, and the Front scored significant diplomatic victories. In 1969, the Political Bureau called upon the NLF's diplomats once again, this time to frustrate Richard Nixon's effort to use superpower diplomacy to end the war. What is significant and interesting about this period is the way the Political Bureau used the NLF as its front line in international diplomacy, skillfully moving the Front's diplomats from one situation to the next.

Problems were growing, however, between northerners and southerners. NLF losses during the Tet Offensive were oppressively high, and critics argued that Hanoi was gaining too much control over the southern revolution. This had always been a problem, as southern Communists balanced the Party's interests against the region's needs. As one NLF member recounted, "North Viet Nam had committed more and more of its resources to the war, until it had become . . . a giant rear area supporting the front lines. As a result, the NLF had found itself ever more obviously dominated by the northern government." Another southerner complained that "the blue half of the NLF flag had become too red."[13] The losses of the Tet Offensive had a dramatic impact on the internal dynamics of the Party, threatening to destroy what had taken years to construct. Few policy analysts in Washington understood the nature of the conflict, and as a result, the Lao Dong continued to score significant diplomatic victories.

In late March, the Lao Dong's Political Bureau had adopted a two-pronged negotiating strategy. In the best-case scenario, the Party would press the United States into meaningful concessions, including a total bombing halt, a planned withdrawal, and the creation of a coalition government in the South. Most Political Bureau members conceded that this scenario was highly unlikely, so they concentrated on using the talks to drive a wedge between Washington and Saigon. Party leaders correctly predicted that they could use the NLF's participation in the upcoming negotiations to alienate the United States from Saigon. In a secret meeting in Hanoi in early April, the Political Bureau instructed the southern diplomats to promote the NLF as a political entity with a significant role in the settlement.[14] In creating this perception, the Front could isolate the United States from its South Vietnamese ally because Washington was eager to point to negotiations as proof that it was doing everything it could to end the war. The Communists therefore linked the negotiations to the Front's right to participate, a position the Saigon government had opposed from the beginning.

On May 13, 1968, when the talks finally began, the NLF was not officially present, but for the next six months it actively promoted four-sided negotiations through its overseas representatives. The Communists believed that support for the Front as an equal partner in negotiations was growing and that the Western press was also sympathetic. As one Party leader later commented, "We believed that the Western press would do for us what Johnson did not—recognize the NLF as the legitimate representative of the South Vietnamese people."[15]

The Front began its international propaganda campaign in early June. In Paris, Nguyen Thi Binh and Tran Buu Kiem, its chief negotiators, told the Western press that southerners would never agree to a settlement unless the NLF signed the accord independently. "We represent the aspirations of the southern people and will never surrender our sacred bond with our brothers and sisters in South Viet Nam. We must be an equal and willing participant in any negotiations."[16]

Born in Saigon in 1927, Binh was the granddaughter of Phan Chu Trinh, one of Viet Nam's most celebrated patriots.[17] She had been a student leader during the First Indochina War and was arrested by the French in 1950. Having served four years in a French prison, she was set free after the signing of the Geneva Accords. During the next six years, she was one of the most important members of the resistance to Diem and organized Saigon's intellectuals and students against the American-backed regime. Kiem, for his part, was born in the delta town of Can Tho in 1921. He graduated from law school at Hanoi University and joined the Party in 1944. For years he assumed important functions in the resistance movement. At length he became a member of the NLF's Central Committee and chair of its Foreign Relations Commission.[18]

Working closely with Binh and Kiem in Paris, the NLF diplomat Le Anh Kiet toured the Middle East and southern Europe in early June, insisting that the Front deserved its own seat at the Paris negotiations.[19] In the same month, Xuan Thuy, the DRV's official representative at the Paris talks, reiterated Hanoi's commitment to NLF participation in the current discussions. "The only way peace can be achieved in South Viet Nam," Thuy declared, "is with the NLF's full participation in negotiations to end the war."[20]

Although press coverage of the Communists' public statements was adequate, the Party believed it could be improved. In October, therefore, the NLF opened fully operational propaganda offices in Paris and Stockholm.[21] In the Paris office, Pham Van Ba was the information director and Ha Thanh Lam his deputy. Both had extensive experience with the NLF's Foreign Relations Commission and had previously been assigned to various missions in Europe. More important, Ba and Lam had been long-time supporters of the Front's neutralist platform.[22] Before coming to Paris, Ba had spent a month in Hanoi discussing propaganda strategy.[23] During a press conference on October 11, he outlined the bureau's aim to publish an information bulletin concerning the negotiations and provide Western leaders with material concerning NLF activities.[24] At an opening reception, more than a thousand Vietnamese nationals gathered at the Information Bureau to hear Lam Ba Chu, an intellectual living in Paris, announce the establishment of the mission. The Information Bureau, he declared, "brings joy to all Vietnamese residents and is consonant with their earnest desires to keep in close contact with the NLF."[25]

The Saigon government, fearing that the Front would use its propaganda missions to establish a full-fledged negotiating delegation, immediately voiced its displeasure over the opening of the NLF agency. In a letter to the French Foreign Ministry, the RVN declared that "the opening of this bureau will considerably strengthen the propaganda means of the Hanoi regime." In addition, Saigon officials warned that "the French government's decision to authorize the operation of this agency is in contradiction with the neutrality and impartiality implied in the role the host government has agreed to assume."[26] The letter failed to mention, of course, that the Saigon regime had previously established its own press office in Paris.[27]

For weeks the RVN president, Nguyen Van Thieu, had urged the Americans to press the French government to withdraw the NLF's visas. In the process, an embarrassed Thieu discovered that the French Republic had invited the NLF to establish a news bureau in Paris long before negotiations had started.[28] W. Averell Harriman, the chief U.S. negotiator, was clearly worried about the impropriety of Thieu's comments.[29] Restricting a news bureau in the capital city of a Western democracy reeked of the censorship that had plagued the Saigon government since its establishment in 1955. Thieu's public demands made it difficult for the United States not to respond negatively to its ally.

While the Saigon regime centered its tirade on the Paris office, the NLF opened another information bureau in Stockholm, where it used its considerable propaganda expertise to coordinate its first major diplomatic foray to Western democracies. The new mission opened on October 28 and was headed by Le Phuong, who had spent the previous six months in Hanoi preparing for his new post.[30] Dag Maln, head of the Political Department and counselor of Sweden's foreign ministry, welcomed Phuong to Stockholm at a public reception and pledged his government's support for the bureau's operation.[31] Foreign Minister Torsten Nilsson assured the NLF that no government would interfere with the work of its diplomats and hoped that it would find the liberties of Sweden satisfactory.[32] Many Western experts had long predicted a break between Sweden and Saigon, and the opening of the NLF mission seemed to confirm this opinion.[33] For the Front, however, the bureau served as a staging area for diplomats preparing for trips to Western Europe.

In late October, the Front launched the second phase of its Western European diplomatic initiative. The first stop on the tour was on October 24, in Belgium. The delegation, led by Dinh Ba Thi, visited several cities and held a peace rally in Brussels.[34] At each stop, Thi read a statement prepared by Xuan Thuy, Hanoi's representative in Paris: "After the U.S. unconditionally stops the bombing and all other acts of war against the Democratic Republic of Vietnam, the DRV side will accept a conference with the participation of four delegations, namely, the delegation of the South Vietnam National Liberation Front, the delegation of the United States, and the delegation of the Saigon administration, to discuss a political solution to the Vietnam problem."[35] The Communists promoted the four-sided negotiations at diplomatic stops in Rome, Milan, London, and Montreal.[36] Each visit was the first of its kind for the NLF, and its diplomats took full advantage of Western press coverage.

That same week, the NLF diplomat Hoang Bich Son traveled to Italy, where he praised Western nations for inviting the Front's representatives to speak about peace. He declared that the NLF stood ready to negotiate with the United States and the Saigon government with no preconditions. When a reporter asked if negotiations had any chance of ending the war, Son replied, "We are firmly committed to negotiations and are prepared to meet with President Johnson and President Thieu immediately."[37] Several Western newspapers reported the NLF's readiness to negotiate, and in the process elevated it to full diplomatic standing. The *New York Times* wrote that "an NLF representative has expressed the view that negotiations with the United States and the Saigon government are more promising than ever." The *Washington Post* likewise suggested that "peace talks between the four sides appear likely in the near future." In the last week of October, the *Wall Street Journal*, the *Christian Science Monitor*, and the *Far Eastern Economic Review* all indicated that negotiations between the four belligerents would take place soon, in the process conferring a kind of political legitimacy on the NLF.[38]

The reaction in Western Europe was the same. The French journalist Jacques Amalric, writing in *Le Monde*, claimed that the Tet Offensive had changed the scope of the war and that negotiations with the NLF seemed like the only logical course.[39] In London, the left-leaning *Tribune* editorialized that "the world is tired of hearing excuses from warring powers for not negotiating."[40] Throughout the spring and summer of 1968, protest rippled through Europe. In Norway, Prime Minister Per Borten's conservative government had "difficulty in fending off protests against its support of the American war effort."[41] In France, Charles de Gaulle's political reorganization efforts were defeated in national elections as students protested a variety of French policies, including its tacit support of the United States in the Cold War. In Sweden, Tage Erlander faced a serious political challenge from Olof Palme, who attacked him for his failure to back the

NLF. Erlander had openly criticized the radical groups that were calling for negotiations with the Front. "It is patently impossible to carry on a rational discussion with any group that uses such faulty methods and that advocates violence and anarchy," he concluded.[42] One year later, de Gaulle and Erlander suffered political defeat at the hands of those who wanted to negotiate with the NLF.

In Saigon, the RVN leadership responded quickly to the Front's propaganda campaign. Vice President Nguyen Cao Ky declared that the "Western press has fallen under the spell of the Communists. They have reported that negotiations with the Communists will soon be under way. This could not be further from the truth. We will never be told to sit down with the group that Hanoi calls the National Front for the Liberation of South Viet Nam."[43] Indeed, in late October the Saigon government again vetoed the start of talks, claiming that its participation would be a "clear admission of defeat."[44] President Thieu insisted that his administration would never participate in negotiations with the NLF, and demanded that the DRV publicly pledge that the Front would not have a seat at the conference table.[45] When Deputy Ambassador Anthony Berger later made clear that the United States could not support such a demand, Thieu replied angrily, "You sound more like a representative of Hanoi rather than the United States."[46]

The Johnson administration suspected that Thieu and Nguyen Cao Ky were stalling to gain more favorable concessions from the Republicans. With the U.S. presidential election just weeks away, many Washington insiders suspected that Bui Diem, South Viet Nam's ambassador to the United States, had made a deal with Richard Nixon to delay talks until after the November election, thus depriving the Democrats of the political advantage of a major diplomatic breakthrough.[47]

On October 31, therefore, Johnson ordered a full bombing halt without South Vietnamese approval. The president feared that Thieu's conditions threatened the entire peace process, and would hurt Hubert Humphrey's election bid. He also realized he needed the negotiations to quiet domestic critics. Whether he was convinced of a sellout remains unclear. Johnson decided, however, to announce the pause and pressure the Saigon regime to participate in negotiations, assuring Thieu that Washington would not recognize the NLF or agree to a coalition government. On November 11, Secretary of Defense Clifford threatened to go ahead with the negotiations even if Saigon refused to attend.[48] Two weeks later, after Nixon had narrowly defeated Humphrey, Thieu agreed to send a delegation to Paris.[49]

Once in Paris, the Saigon representatives protested the logistical arrangements for the delegates. Vice President Nguyen Cao Ky led the RVN negotiating team and rejected a variety of seating arrangements proposed by the U.S. envoy, Cyrus Vance. Vance had first suggested two long tables, to support the contention that it was a two-sided conference. The NLF representatives, Nguyen Thi Binh and Tran Buu Kiem, objected strenuously. Xuan Thuy, the DRV delegate, insisted on a square table, one side for each delegation, thus giving the Front equal status with the Saigon government. Ky naturally protested. In a mood of desperation, Vance and Harriman suggested a round table and the Communists quickly agreed. Once again, however, Ky balked, claiming that that arrangement, too, would give the NLF undue political legitimacy. With the help of the Soviet Union, Harriman finally persuaded Hanoi to accept two rectangular tables separated by a large round table.[50]

The resolution of the table issue was seen as a victory for the Communists, since the RVN could not claim any special political status over the NLF. The administration's position all along had been that to grant the Front equal status at the negotiating table was to prejudice the final outcome of the talks; that in giving in on the point Washington was responding to its critics at home and abroad seems abundantly clear. The president needed the negotiations to quiet his opponents, and he was willing to sacrifice the RVN's needs to ensure that talks got under way. The Western press also made it difficult for Johnson to deny the NLF a seat at the talks. When Washington finally caved in, relations between the Johnson administration and the Saigon regime sank to an all-time low. The NLF had effectively alienated the RVN from its Western ally by manipulating international public opinion and Washington's need for negotiations. The growing power of leftists in France, Britain, Norway, and Sweden persuaded many political leaders there to give open support to the four-party peace talks.

For the remainder of the war, the Front had a significant role in the peace talks, and the Saigon regime never completely trusted the United States. More important, the Political Bureau had learned how to use the NLF's skilled and experienced diplomats as the front line of its propaganda efforts. By the end of 1968, northern and southern Communists had united behind an international strategy that had won significant victories.

In some southern circles, however, discontent was growing concerning the prosecution of the war. Critics of the Tet Offensive charged that Hanoi had deliberately used southern cadres as cannon fodder. General Tran Van Tra, who oversaw most military operations near Saigon, claimed that

Hanoi "did not correctly evaluate the specific balance of forces . . . did not fully realize that our capabilities were limited . . . and set requirements that were beyond our actual strength." Tra believed that Hanoi based Tet calculations not on "science" but on "subjective desires." The general concluded that the South had suffered "great sacrifices and losses with regard to manpower and matériel . . . which clearly weakened us. Afterward we not only were unable to retain the gains we had made but had to overcome myriad difficulties in 1969 and 1970 so that the revolution could stand firm in the storm."[51]

Southern discontent mounted throughout 1969, but during Richard Nixon's first year in office, the Political Bureau once again enlisted the NLF to foil Washington's war plans. During the presidential campaign, Nixon claimed he had a secret plan to end the war, and insisted privately that he was the only man on earth who could do so.[52] Like Johnson, Nixon was committed to the independence of the Saigon government, and he pledged never to surrender Thieu's monopoly of power. The new president likewise refused to recognize the NLF, and he steadfastly opposed an American withdrawal and the creation of a coalition government.

Interestingly, Nixon's secret plan to end the war involved the Soviet Union. He hoped to use Moscow's interest in détente to pressure Hanoi to withdraw DRV troops from the South and accede in the continued dominance of the Saigon regime. In 1968, Nixon had declared, "If the Soviets were disposed to see the war ended and a compromise settlement negotiated, they have the means to move Ho Chi Minh to the conference table."[53] The key, Nixon argued, was to convince Moscow that he would escalate the war to a more menacing level. He would go to the Soviets and explain, "Look, if you go on supporting North Vietnam, we will have to act dramatically. . . . If on the other hand you are willing to give ground and help us out of this morass, it could mean lots of good things."[54] The "good things" included increased Western trade and a reduction in the expensive arms race.

To take full advantage of the Soviet Union's cooperation, however, the Nixon administration realized it must prevent the further erosion of public support for the war. Negotiations could go on for years, and Nixon officials warned, "The major problem we have now is to get domestic support during the period of settlement."[55] In mid-1969, therefore, Nixon began the phased withdrawal of American combat troops and shifted the military burden to the RVN.[56] He hoped that the troop reduction would ease public pressures. He also believed that the Soviets would see the withdrawal as a good-faith gesture and pressure Hanoi into making concessions.

Ironically, the phased withdrawal of American troops—what the West has called "Vietnamization"—brought the Soviet Union and the NLF closer together. Lao Dong strategists correctly predicted in early 1969 that to forestall a domestic political crisis Nixon would assign more of the burden of fighting to South Vietnamese troops.[57] The Communists had seen this tactic before. During the First Indochina War, the French had implemented a policy called *jaunissement* (yellowing), which had involved the greater use of indigenous forces to portray the war as a civil conflict.[58] The Nixon administration, according to Lao Dong leaders, hoped to disarm opponents of the war and at the same time maintain military pressure against strategic targets and supply routes and provide combat support. The Lao Dong's Military Commission worried that the phased withdrawal of American troops would bring renewed air attacks against North Viet Nam and supply routes along the Ho Chi Minh Trail.[59]

In a series of meetings in Moscow, Paris, and Hanoi, NLF officials met with their Soviet and DRV counterparts to devise a strategy to counter Nixon's plan.[60] The Communists decided to continue to fight a protracted war, and Hanoi even suggested that it would withdraw some of its troops across the Demilitarized Zone.[61] This defensive strategy had worked in the past, and the Party had concluded that international and domestic public opinion would eventually force Nixon to withdraw from Viet Nam.[62] The goal, therefore, was to stimulate opposition to the war and initiate an international movement favoring meaningful negotiations. The crux of this offensive was the formation of a provisional government in the South that had the legitimacy to negotiate with the Saigon regime. The creation of a provisional administration might also win over many southerners who otherwise would have opposed continued reliance on the protracted war strategy. With an interim government, southern Communists felt assured that they could influence the political future of the southern zone. In this respect, Hanoi's endorsement of the Provisional Revolutionary Government (PRG) avoided the conflict that had troubled the Party previously.

As early as February 1969, Tran Buu Kiem of the NLF and Victor Zorin, the Soviet ambassador to France, had discussed the creation of a "peace cabinet." According to Kiem, a majority of South Vietnamese considered "the Thieu regime as a war government, capable only of serving war." Kiem proposed a coalition of forces comprising all those who favored negotiations with the NLF. He insisted that the Front need not dominate the cabinet and that the primary purpose of such a group would be the peaceful transition of power in Saigon. He added that "the main task is for a national union of different strata of the population to be created in this Cabinet of Peace."[63] Later the South Vietnamese people would create a provisional government based on the NLF's political platform.

Nguyen Thi Binh foreshadowed the creation of the provisional government in a 1967 interview. Madame Binh explained to a reporter that "before setting up a government of broad national unity, there must be a provisional government." Any government formed in wartime had its limits, so "it is necessary to have a provisional government."[64] By the spring of 1969, the NLF had seen the diplomatic advantage of the immediate formation of the interim administration. Soviet leaders suggested an all-out propaganda campaign to gain formal international recognition of the provisional association.[65] Perhaps Moscow thought it could encourage the peace process by promoting the formation of the temporary government even though it risked alienating the United States with its public support of the scheme. Some Western experts have speculated that the Soviets would have been the winners in Viet Nam, whatever the outcome, as long as the fighting stopped.[66] In any event, the Soviet Union supported the NLF's diplomatic maneuver from the beginning.

On May 8, 1969, the NLF released from Paris a statement concerning the peace process and took preliminary steps toward formating the provisional government.[67] The ten-point resolution described two categories of obstacles to peace: "problems between the U.S. imperialists and the anti-imperialist Vietnamese people" and "problems among the Vietnamese people."[68] The withdrawal of U.S. troops belonged to the first type of problem. To end the war, the manifesto maintained, the United States must withdraw its troops from South Viet Nam without preconditions.

The matter of Vietnamese troops in the South fell into the second category.[69] As Tran Buu Kiem explained during a Paris press conference, "the U.S. position that both sides withdraw their forces places the aggressors on a par with the victims of aggression," and therefore was unacceptable.[70] Kiem concluded that the right of the South Vietnamese to handle their own affairs belonged to the second category, so the United States had no reason to be involved in such negotiations. Kiem advocated "the formation of a provisional coalition government to enable the people of the South to exercise their right of self-determination through a free, democratic election without foreign intervention."[71] Predictably, the

United States ignored the NLF's Ten-Point Program for Peace and dismissed the proposal for an interim government as an illegal fraud.[72]

On June 6, hundreds of Vietnamese dissidents gathered in Tay Ninh province for the organizing congress of the provisional government. The Front's Central Committee had selected this date to upstage the Nixon-Thieu meeting on Midway Island scheduled for June 8, at which the United States would announce its "Vietnamization" plan.[73] After three days of meetings, the congress approved a resolution establishing the Provisional Revolutionary Government of the Republic of South Viet Nam (PRG).[74] As the PRG's slate of ministers and cabinet officials came forward for election, Liberation Studios filmed the event for future propaganda use. On June 8, delegates voted in the new government unanimously. Within days, videotape and press reports chronicling the birth of the PRG had been released throughout the world.

The first government to recognize the PRG officially was North Viet Nam's. President Ho Chi Minh and Premier Pham Van Dong sent a congratulatory telegram praising the PRG as "the legal government and the true representative of the people of South Vietnam."[75] In short order, all of the Communist bloc countries granted the PRG full diplomatic recognition at the embassy level.[76] The most important was the Soviet Union. On June 13, Minister of Foreign Affairs Andrei Gromyko cabled Nguyen Thi Binh, the PRG's foreign minister and representative at the Paris talks, pledging Moscow's support for the PRG and acknowledging the new government as the "official representative of the people of South Viet Nam at the Paris conference."[77] Gromyko confirmed on June 13 that the permanent delegation of the NLF in Moscow had become the embassy of the Provisional Revolutionary Government of the Republic of South Viet Nam.[78]

Immediate Soviet recognition was extremely important to the PRG because it understood the pressures Moscow had endured. Nixon had hoped to use the Soviet Union to persuade Hanoi to make concessions and thereby end the diplomatic impasse. He earnestly believed he could achieve a quick settlement on American terms through coercion. He told Moscow from the beginning that future agreements between the United States and the Soviet Union, such as a strategic arms limitation treaty, were tied to its ability to influence events in Hanoi. Nixon also linked Soviet cooperation in Viet Nam to events throughout the world. If Moscow desired American cooperation on other important issues, "it must deliver Hanoi."[79] Several policy makers in Washington doubted, however, that Moscow would sell out its Vietnamese friends and warned that dependence on the Soviet Union was risky.[80] Despite these warnings, the Nixon White House remained convinced that the Soviet Union would pressure Hanoi.

In many ways, therefore, recognition of the PRG was a message to the new administration that Moscow favored negotiations and a political settlement to the conflict, but would not betray its Vietnamese allies. In NLF circles, Soviet recognition solidified southern support for the diplomatic struggle. The NLF was never static on the issue of negotiations, and by 1969 powerful southerners were supporting this move. Nguyen Thi Binh heralded Moscow's favor as "the crucial turning point in our international strategy."[81] Another long-time NLF diplomat later observed that "the summer of 1969 represented a dramatic change in fortune for those of us who had supported a political settlement to the war. With international support for the PRG growing daily, led by the Soviet Union, most of us believed that Nixon would have to negotiate peace because of severe international pressure."[82] *Nhan Dan*, the official Lao Dong daily newspaper, editorialized that Soviet recognition of the PRG represented "the greatest embarrassment and setback" in Washington's plans to divide Viet Nam from its fraternal ally.[83]

Also damaging to the Nixon administration was the support for the PRG offered by nonaligned nations. In mid-June, Cambodia, Algeria, Syria, Sudan, Mali, and Congo-Brazzaville officially recognized the PRG.[84] Algeria and Syria elevated the NLF's missions to the embassy level, and Cambodia accepted the credentials of Nguyen Van Hieu, the former Front diplomat stationed in Phnom Penh.[85] On June 16, President Gamal Abdel Nasser announced that Egypt had decided to recognize the PRG.[86] Even India, a member of the International Control Commission in Viet Nam, considered recognition of the PRG. Two weeks before Nixon traveled to New Delhi, Foreign Minister Dinesh Singh told a group of Western reporters that his government favored a coalition government in South Viet Nam and that the PRG represented a move in that direction.[87] Eventually India waffled and made a vague commitment to recognize the PRG when talks in Paris produced tangible results.[88]

By the end of July, the PRG had scored a significant diplomatic victory over the United States. A quick settlement on American terms was all but impossible because the Soviet Union had supported Hanoi and the NLF in the face of Nixon's harsh threats. Even when the president made good on his promise to reescalate the war to a level never seen during the Johnson years, the PRG continued its diplomatic offensive.

In a broadcast over Liberation Radio at the end of the month, the PRG announced plans to increase its recognition among important overseas Vietnamese.[89] Ties between Viet nationals living abroad and the southern revolution had always been strong. NLF diplomats in the key European cities held information sessions to explain the goals of the PRG and encouraged Viet nationals to join the interim government. Especially important in these meetings was the support given the PRG by the Alliance of National, Democratic, and Peace Forces. The Alliance was a group of southern urban intellectuals and professionals headed by Trinh Dinh Thao. It had been organized in May 1968, for two reasons: to counteract the North's growing domination of the NLF and to promote a coalition government in the South at the Front's request. Le Ngoc Lan had first organized the Alliance in the spring of 1967, to mobilize business leaders and intellectuals in Saigon against the Thieu-Ky elections, but after his arrest and subsequent assassination, the Alliance changed direction.[90] According to one NLF member, the Alliance "would add a substantial new counterweight to the Communist overbalance, and among the uncommitted it would help restore the NLF's eclipsed coalition-based orientation."[91] One year later, Thao presided over the organizing conference of the PRG. His support gave the provisional government the aura of autonomy and independence that the Front had tried to achieve in its early years.

With the support of the Alliance and its strong nationalist figures, the NLF's diplomats persuaded hundreds of noncommunist Viets to pledge their allegiance to the PRG. The most significant endorsements came from Viet Nam's political past. Late in the summer of 1969, Tran Van Huu, the premier of the Bao Dai regime, gave the PRG his blessing. Huu sent the PRG's president, Huynh Tan Phat, a congratulatory telegram applauding the formation of the interim government and declaring his belief that the PRG was working toward "the ardent aspiration of the entire South Vietnamese people, which is peace and independence."[92] Two weeks later, Liberation Radio announced that more than a hundred former Saigon officials had signed a petition supporting the PRG.[93] Among the signatories were three former cabinet officials of the Diem regime now living in Paris and two ministers from the Khanh government.[94] The PRG also received significant support from the organized overseas Buddhists.[95]

The Thieu regime tried to counteract the PRG's diplomatic offensive by launching its own propaganda campaign to demonstrate that it had significant international support.[96] With the help of the United States Information Service and the American embassy in Saigon, the government filled the pages of the Western press with reports of its international backing.[97] Saigon also tried to recast its international image as a government broadly representative of Vietnamese society. In late August, the Thieu regime sponsored several ethnic and religious celebrations to promote an aura of diversity. The RVN even tried to reconcile with the Buddhists by releasing several activists from prison.[98] This effort was cut short, however, by the death of Ho Chi Minh in September, and events in Hanoi quickly replaced Saigon's publicity crusade as front-page news.

Ho's death also had a dramatic impact on the NLF's international strategy. For over forty years, Ho had been the symbol of Vietnamese independence and nationalism. His charismatic personality had held the Party together during its turbulent development, and his vision of Viet Nam's future had been the blueprint for the revolution. Northerners and southerners saw in Ho the Vietnamese ideal. With his death, no single figure would ever again dominate the collective psyche of Viets. The loss was particularly harsh for southern Communists, because Ho had been a truly national figure. His death left a void in the relationship between the Lao Dong and the southern revolution. Le Duan simply did not have the universal support or the charisma of "Uncle Ho." Premier Pham Van Dong and General Vo Nguyen Giap did not enjoy the admiration of many southerners, and in fact had been criticized in the past for their antisouthern policies.[99] Neither had fully responded to southern demands for armed violence in the 1950s, and many concluded that they were out of touch with southern aspirations.

Not surprisingly, therefore, the new symbol of national identity for many southerners was a member of the PRG. During its organizing congress, the PRG had selected Nguyen Thi Binh as its foreign minister. Her background was legendary in revolutionary Viet Nam. After serving the Party in a variety of functions, she joined the NLF's Foreign Relations Commission in 1962 and served as a roving ambassador, promoting the Front's neutralist platform.[100] Everyone knew that her grandfather was the patriot Phan Chu Trinh. When the Paris talks officially opened in 1968, she was sent to the French capital, along with Tran Buu Kiem, to represent the NLF. When the PRG named her its foreign minister in June 1969, she assumed the full responsibility for managing negotiations.[101]

With Ho's death, Binh was easily recognized as the Communists' leading international figure by members of the European press and the peace movement in the United States. Thanks in part to a publicity campaign organized by the Soviets in the fall of 1969, Madame Binh came to represent the broad-based, nationalist PRG movement. In a series of interviews with the European press, she conveyed a sense of pragmatism that had been lacking in previous revolutionary discourses. She gave, as one reporter suggested, "a human face to the sufferings of the Vietnamese people without being bitter or ideological."[102]

Perhaps more important was the attitude toward Madame Binh in the growing peace movement in the United States. The Lao Dong and the NLF had predicted that domestic pressure would eventually force the Nixon administration to withdraw from Viet Nam. In the fall of 1969, several American cities hosted two national moratoriums to end the war. Unlike many previous antiwar demonstrations, especially the police riots in Chicago, the fall marches were peaceful and infused with "a new respectability."[103] Huge crowds gathered in Washington, Boston, New York, Miami, Detroit, and smaller towns to listen to a wide range of speakers protesting American involvement in Viet Nam. Among the more prominent discussants were Dr. Benjamin Spock; David Dellinger, a long-time peace and justice activist; the former Supreme Court justice Arthur Goldberg; and the former ambassador W. Averell Harriman. Church bells rang, mock funerals were held for the American and Vietnamese war dead, and millions joined in the singing of John Lennon's "Give Peace a Chance." At each of these protests, NLF flags could be seen waving above the crowd and the familiar chant of "Ho, Ho, Ho Chi Minh—the NLF is going to win" was replaced by "Ho, Ho, Ho Chi Minh—the NLF and Madame Binh." Indeed, the aura of Madame Binh had permeated the American peace movement. Two of the antiwar movement's most prominent spokespeople, David Dellinger and Abbie Hoffman, later commented that Nguyen Thi Binh was the incarnation of the Vietnamese revolution. "She was everything the Saigon government was not," Hoffman explained. "She came from a family of patriots, was honest, desired peace, was pragmatic, and caused Nixon fits."[104] Dellinger concurred. "Nguyen Thi Binh was too formidable an opponent for the Nixon administration and the Saigon regime. She was extremely competent and enjoyed the overwhelming support of the Vietnamese people. For the peace movement, she represented a leader we could hang our hopes on."[105]

Despite the massive outpouring of protest, Nixon claimed "under no circumstances will I be affected," adding that policy "made in the streets is equal to anarchy." On the day of the first moratorium, he ordered his staff to "put out the word that he had been conducting business as usual."[106] Privately, however, Nixon feared that the domestic protest was having a negative impact on his plan to end the war. His attempt to coerce the Soviet Union had failed, and Hanoi had ignored his many ultimatums.

Now the NLF had launched a diplomatic offensive that had created the impression that it was a legitimate political entity through the skillful manipulation of Madame Binh's public image. By the end of October, Nixon found himself relying on Vietnamization once again.

In a major speech on November 3, the president spelled out his plan to end the war, and at the same time tried to isolate his critics. Nixon explained to a television audience that the United States could not pull out of Viet Nam, as the protesters demanded, because a withdrawal would produce a bloodbath in South Viet Nam. Vietnamization, he argued, would reduce American casualties and terminate American involvement in a noble fashion. Relying partly on the advice of a British counterinsurgency expert, Sir Robert Thompson, Nixon believed that with continued American military and economic support, the Saigon government could stand on its own within a few short years. When Hanoi saw that the United States would not abandon Thieu and would continue to supply the RVN with needed armaments, Nixon reasoned, the Communists would come to terms.

Within one year of his election, therefore, Nixon's new plan to end the war was the old one he had inherited from Lyndon Johnson. Washington would rely on Vietnamization to bring Hanoi to the bargaining table because efforts to use the Soviet Union to pressure the Vietnamese had failed. Moscow had proved to be a faithful ally. By the end of 1969, the NLF had successfully promoted its government-in-waiting, the PRG, as a legitimate political entity with a stake in Viet Nam's future. The PRG stood on equal ground with the Thieu regime, and the Vietnamese Communists had destroyed the "our side, your side" strategy of the Johnson and Nixon administrations. The Front had used its diplomatic activities, with Hanoi's constant supervision, to drive a wedge between the United States and the RVN and had undermined Washington's negotiating position and forced it to make concessions. Despite Nixon's desire to end the war in quick fashion, the Lao Dong had managed to force a diplomatic stalemate in Paris as part of its protracted war strategy, and the United States could not force Hanoi's hand.

The Lao Dong's diplomatic victories had come at a high price, however, and by the end of 1969 the Party was showing signs of internal strife. The high death rates of 1968 and 1969, the highest in the war's long history, had caused many Party officials to question the efficacy of the protracted war strategy. Indeed, Nixon's revitalized air war over South Viet Nam and Laos had exacted an enormous human toll. According to most official estimates from Hanoi, nearly 15,000 southern Communists died in the bombing campaigns of 1969.[107] Truong Nhu Tang, an NLF member and the PRG's minister of justice, described life under the bombs this way: "We lived like hunted animals . . . wariness and tension were the companions of every waking moment, creating stresses that were to take an increasing toll on our equanimity as the American bombers closed in on our bases and sanctuaries in late 1969."[108]

In addition, noncommunists in the NLF feared that the Party was gaining too much control of the southern revolution. The Party had depended on the neutrals and noncommunists to help precipitate a political and diplomatic crisis in the South. Most noncommunists understood the relationship between the Party and the Front, but believed they could always influence events in the South. "We sincerely thought we had as much influence on the NLF as the Communists," a noncommunist member of the Front later reported.[109] As more and more PAVN regulars reached the southern battlefield in the year after Tet, however, noncommunists grew anxious about their future and the southern revolution. Once the Paris peace talks officially opened, the conflict between southern and northern Communists intensified over regional negotiating needs, and the noncommunists in the NLF began to move away from the movement, making it more difficult to pressure the Saigon regime. The Lao Dong never again used the NLF as its vanguard in international affairs, and southern influence over events in Hanoi waned. A southerner later explained, "The year 1969, despite our victories over the Nixon-Kissinger clique, was the beginning of the end of the united revolution, and the Paris talks highlighted this fact."[110]

6

FIGHTING WHILE NEGOTIATING, 1970–1973

"After defeating a greater bulk of the puppet army and an important part of the American troops," General Nguyen Van Vinh declared in 1966, "we can push the Americans out of South Viet Nam by coordinating the political struggle with diplomacy." General Vinh, a veteran of the southern resistance, explained that the warfare would continue in Viet Nam "until the emergence of a situation where both sides are fighting indecisively. Then a situation where fighting and negotiations are conducted simultaneously may emerge."[1] By January 1970, Vinh's prediction had come true. The Tet Offensive had forced Washington to the bargaining table, and the Nixon administration relied on Vietnamization to facilitate an honorable withdrawal. Still, the Communists were not strong enough militarily to defeat the United States on the battlefield. For the next three years, therefore, Hanoi and the NLF adhered to the strategy of fighting while negotiating to achieve final victory.

Ironically, the negotiations to end the war created another rift between the Political Bureau in Hanoi and the NLF. After two years of fighting while negotiating, Vietnamese revolutionaries decided that diplomatic and political conditions were ideal to launch a frontal assault by main force units. The result was the first serious steps toward a negotiated settlement.

Once again, however, competing northern and southern interests within the Communist camp threatened the success of the fighting-while-negotiating strategy. During the 1972 discussions, the Political Bureau in Hanoi failed to keep the NLF informed of its changing negotiating positions. Southerners therefore objected to several main provisions in a draft peace proposal, and as a result, the bombings over the DRV intensified. Hanoi paid a serious price for the delay and many northern Lao Dong officials condemned the NLF for its actions. When the peace finally came in January 1973, the Communist Party claimed victory, but the cost had been substantial.

The Vietnamese concept of fighting while negotiating had long historic roots. In the tenth century, Dinh Bo Linh ruled over what is present-day Viet Nam by paying annual tribute to the Chinese and maintaining a strong army to repel the intruders' attacks. In 1287, Tran Hung Dao defeated the invading Mongol Kublai Khan by combining three successive battlefield victories with skillful negotiations. From 1426 to 1428, the Vietnamese emperor Le Loi embraced a strategy that subordinated military action to the political and moral struggle. He combined negotiations with Ming invaders with strategic attacks against the enemy's superior forces. Eventually China recognized Vietnam's independence, and Le Loi agreed to pay annual tribute to the Ming emperor as insurance.[2]

During Viet Nam's modern revolution, the political leadership in Hanoi had used this strategy to gain time and preserve its military advantage. The Communists had evaded a premature outbreak of war in 1946 by engaging Paris in negotiations, while at the same time mobilizing popular support for their cause.[3] In November 1953, just months before the decisive battle at Dien Bien Phu, Ho Chi Minh proposed an armistice and negotiations "to solve the Viet Nam problem by peaceful means."[4] Within a year, France formally surrendered political control over its former colony. Fighting while negotiating, according to one NLF member, "was a traditional Vietnamese approach to warfare, a technique refined over centuries of confrontation with invaders more powerful than ourselves."[5]

In the Year of the Dog, 1970, as the American war entered its third decade, the NLF's diplomats placed their distinctive southern brand on the protracted war strategy. Following the recommendations of the Eighteenth Plenum of the Lao Dong's Central Committee in January 1970, the Front sought to exploit the growing tensions between Washington and Saigon and take advantage of domestic opinion in the United States.[6] In early 1970, under the direction of the Political Bureau, the NLF launched a diplomatic offensive to portray Nguyen Van Thieu's government as the main obstacle to a political settlement. Front leaders insisted that the Thieu regime favored a military resolution of the conflict and suggested that peace could come about only through the creation of a "peace cabinet" comprising all strata of Vietnamese society.[7] The southern Communists intended to use U.S.-sponsored elections scheduled for September 1971 as the main impetus for a change in government.

The NLF introduced the first phase of its new initiative in the spring of 1970. Nguyen Thi Binh, the PRG's foreign minister, announced at a press conference that Thieu's removal was an essential precondition to any peace agreement and that a majority of his own government favored his dismissal. She further insisted that the diplomatic impasse in Paris would not end "until the Thieu-Ky-Khiem clique relinquished power."[8] Binh reiterated the PRG's Ten-Point Program for Peace, first issued on May 8, 1969, and highlighted its call for the "formation of a provisional coalition government, which would include all persons, no matter what their political beliefs and their past might be, provided they stand for peace, independence, and neutrality."[9] There were some strong anticommunists in Saigon, according to Binh, who were acceptable leaders in this coalition government. In a further effort to alienate Thieu from his urban power base, she suggested Duong Van Minh (Big Minh) as a suitable replacement.[10]

Big Minh and Thieu had become estranged in 1964 when General Thieu had provided the military support to oust Minh. Minh had been the beneficiary of the 1963 coup against Diem, but had promulgated an independent course that angered American officials in Washington and Saigon. On January 30, 1964, forces under the control of General Nguyen Khanh had arrested Minh and stripped him of power.[11] After his incarceration, Minh returned to Saigon and was active in several pro-democracy groups. As the former chief of state of South Viet Nam, Big Minh was an attractive candidate for a formal alliance with the NLF. He had survived the 1964 purge and had maintained a degree of respectability among Saigon's political elite. For the NLF, he had two important qualities. First, Big Minh had enough popular support to cause Thieu some discomfort. Many southerners had grown war-weary and believed that a political settlement was possible if the United States and Thieu stepped aside. Minh therefore was a legitimate alternative among that small group of anticommunists whom the United States might allow a voice at this point in the war. Second, the NLF had successfully infiltrated Minh's camp and had considerable influence with him.[12]

To harass the Thieu regime further, the NLF announced on September

17 a specific proposal for the makeup of a coalition government. There should be one representative from the Front, one from the anticommunists in Saigon (excluding Thieu, Ky, and Prime Minister Tran Thien Khiem), and one from among the neutralists living abroad.[13] Although the United States remained faithful to Thieu and routinely rejected such proposals, Le Duc Tho's reports from his secret meetings with Henry Kissinger in Paris suggested that Washington was becoming more flexible in its responses to a noncommunist government in Saigon. Nixon's famous "four no's"—no coalition government, no participation of Communists in any government, no neutralism, and no loss of territory—were not, according to Tho, set in concrete.[14]

In mid-September, with the Political Bureau's support, the Front's diplomats launched a propaganda blitz promoting Minh and the tripartite coalition. Nguyen Thi Binh addressed the conference of nonaligned nations in Moscow, highlighting the specifics of a shared power arrangement in South Viet Nam.[15] "There are several noncommunist, progressive leaders inside and outside of the Saigon regime who could help bring peace to our nation. Duong Van Minh has been working toward a coalition for many years now," Binh explained, "and would be acceptable in an interim government."[16] Nguyen Van Hieu, the NLF's special diplomatic envoy, traveled throughout East Asia that fall discussing South Vietnamese neutralism.[17] Hieu had been the first director of the NLF's Foreign Relations Commission and the first to promote neutralism abroad.[18] In the last years of the war, he found new popularity within the Party for his unique ability to discuss with a variety of audiences the complexities of shared power in South Viet Nam. He spent much of October advancing what became known in NLF circles as the "Big Minh theory."[19] Hoang Bich Son, another of the Front's skilled young diplomats, toured Europe in October waving the Big Minh banner.[20]

With constitutionally scheduled elections less than a year away, the Thieu regime grew anxious over the NLF's promotion of Big Minh as a political contender. To counter the Front's overture, Vice President Nguyen Cao Ky and Thieu secretly met to discuss the possibility of postponing the elections and "reworking the present system of government." Ky conveyed these secret plans to President Nixon in a meeting at the White House on November 15, 1970. Nixon was furious and urged Ky not to do anything to upset South Viet Nam's political stability. If the elections were not held, Nixon warned, "it would simply make support of Vietnam an impossibility."[21] Ky assured Nixon that the elections would go smoothly.

Although the NLF had thought of Big Minh as a coalition leader, it had not seen him as a presidential candidate before Ky's trip to Washington. Through its agents in the presidential palace in Saigon, the Front learned of the secret negotiations taking place at the highest levels to ensure a Thieu presidency.[22] NLF strategists concluded that they could exploit the situation in Saigon further by urging Minh to announce his intention to oppose Thieu.[23] In early June, Minh declared his candidacy and promised, if elected, to end the war through an immediate political settlement.[24] Thieu tried to keep Minh from the race by pressuring the newly elected National Assembly to require all candidates to meet certain requirements. In an election law passed on June 22, the Thieu-controlled Assembly mandated that any presidential candidate must obtain signatures from forty members of the National Assembly or one hundred members of the provisional councils.[25] The paranoid Thieu believed that this new law would keep Big Minh from running, but within three weeks Minh had gathered the signatures and began his campaign with the support of much of Saigon's political elite and, secretly, the NLF. Whereas the Front had officially boycotted the 1967 election, this time it urged the South Vietnamese people to participate and defeat Thieu.[26]

Simultaneously the Front published a seven-point statement calling on the Nixon administration to "stop all maneuvers, including election tricks, aimed at maintaining the puppet Nguyen Van Thieu."[27] The document urged Washington to consider free and open elections as a way of letting the South Vietnamese people themselves replace the corrupt Thieu. As a carrot, the NLF was willing to discuss, for the first time, specific concessions on the safety and welfare of American troops and prisoners of war: in exchange for an agreed-upon terminal date for the withdrawal of American troops from Viet Nam and a bilateral cease-fire, the Communists would provide for the safety of American troops during withdrawal and release all war prisoners.[28] If this agreement was to work, however, the Nixon administration must "stop propping up Thieu in defiance of the opposing majority of South Vietnamese opinion."[29]

Party strategists correctly believed that they could influence events in the United States by making this overture. By linking Thieu's removal with the release of American prisoners and withdrawal of troops, the NLF created what it called "an uncomfortable contradiction in the Nixon camp."[30] If Nixon refused to respond to its latest offer, doves in the United States Congress and antiwar forces would make it difficult for Washington to manage the domestic crisis. Furthermore, the NLF timed its July 1 offer so that if the Nixon administration accepted and allowed an open election, the new government would still be in place for Nixon's reelection bid in November 1972. The Front concluded that Washington might find this package attractive since it made it possible for Nixon to keep his oft-repeated pledge of self-determination for the South Vietnamese people and allowed the Vietnamese to "rid Washington of its pesky ally themselves."[31] Ellsworth Bunker, the U.S. ambassador in Saigon, was particularly sensitive to the election issue, believing that the future of South Viet Nam depended on at least the appearance of a free and open election.[32]

Even though the White House remained committed to Thieu and rejected the NLF's proposal, the Front's diplomatic initiative produced the desired results. Nixon faced growing opposition from powerful members of Congress, who twice voted to set a specific deadline for the removal of all U.S. troops pending the release of American prisoners of war.[33] Although Congress later rescinded its actions, NLF strategists declared that "the U.S. Senate has supported our latest proposal for peace."[34] Throughout the summer, representatives of the Vietnam Elections Project, a U.S. quasi-governmental organization with strong ties to the *New York Times*, testified before Congress in support of honest elections.[35] In addition, several antiwar groups seized upon the election issue as evidence of the hypocrisy of Washington's Viet Nam policy. "We were supposed to be in Viet Nam building a democracy," one activist later commented, "but we would not support fair elections in return for meaningful peace negotiations."[36] In August, peace activists heralded the Front's seven-point plan as another missed opportunity for peace and condemned the Nixon administration's handling of negotiations in street demonstrations in Washington, Boston, New York, and San Francisco.[37] By the end of the month, Nixon's popularity had dropped to an all-time low and nearly two-thirds of Americans polled agreed that the United States had made a mistake by sending troops to Viet Nam.[38]

Nixon's domestic crisis worsened when the NLF persuaded Big Minh not to run in the rigged election. By mid-August, the Front had grown convinced that the Nixon administration was not going to "give up on Thieu."[39] The DRV and NLF delegations in Paris correctly concluded that Nixon and Kissinger prized what they perceived to be political stability in Saigon above an open election.[40] As Frances FitzGerald has written, the United States "judged a change in men too dangerous at that moment in history."[41] The Communists therefore concluded that Minh had no chance of combating the substantial resources the Central Intelligence Agency could throw behind Thieu's campaign. They decided that Minh would be more valuable now if he withdrew from the presidential race.

The one-person election would confirm the Saigon regime's corrupt and dictatorial nature.[42] On August 22, at the NLF's urging, Big Minh withdrew.[43]

The Front moved quickly to capitalize on Minh's departure. During the first week of September, it announced that the United States had squandered a golden opportunity for peace.[44] Nguyen Thi Binh condemned the upcoming election and declared that "the United States wants to maintain the status quo in South Viet Nam despite the popular support for a negotiated settlement. The only obstacle to peace in Viet Nam today remains the corrupt Thieu clique."[45] Binh's remarks sparked more protests across the United States from antiwar forces, who had grown increasingly frustrated by the Nixon administration's handling of the war. Shortly after Thieu's election on October 3, several U.S. senators spoke out against the political process in Viet Nam and Nixon's apparent unwillingness to negotiate. "It is beyond me why the White House would surrender a chance for discussions on Thieu," an angry George Aiken reported to his constituents in Vermont. "We have been down this road before and it can only lead to disaster."[46]

Indeed, the fallout from the Thieu election debacle was swift and heavy. The NLF and Hanoi refused to meet with Kissinger in Paris for the remainder of 1971, adding credibility to their claims that Washington had missed an opportunity for peace. In late October, in a keynote speech before a meeting of nonaligned nations in Algiers, Madame Binh denounced Thieu's corrupt election campaign and noted "the golden occasion for peace presented by our seven-point proposal."[47] Several international leaders condemned the United States "for supporting a one-man election in a supposed democracy" and argued that the Nixon administration "has no plans for peace, only for war."[48] Even Washington's most trusted allies in Western Europe could not understand the Thieu election scandal. "A candidate for president has just received 94 percent of the vote in South Viet Nam," one British spokesperson announced. "Surely this is no democracy."[49]

While the Nixon administration was busy propping up the newly elected South Vietnamese president and trying to manage its own domestic crisis, the Communists were planning a major military offensive for the next spring. Shortly after Thieu's reelection, the Lao Dong's Military Commission decided that the political and diplomatic climate was ideal for a decisive offensive that would ultimately lead to victory.[50] For three years the Communists had believed that the military and diplomatic stalemate would be broken by a major engagement with South Vietnamese forces.[51] The stalemate had ensued shortly after the 1968 Tet Offensive, when the Military Commission decided to curtail its military activity in the South and withdraw some of its troops back across the seventeenth parallel. Party strategists were convinced that American public opinion would eventually force Nixon to withdraw from Viet Nam, and Hanoi would wait for that eventuality. By the spring of 1971, however, Nixon's blatant disregard for domestic sympathies caused a change of heart in Hanoi. Accordingly, a resolution passed by the Military Commission in early May concluded that "the Americans could be forced to negotiate an end to the war from a position of defeat" if the Communists attacked in the South.[52]

In mid-October, American intelligence experts first learned of a Communist military buildup, but policy makers in Washington appeared to be more interested in Nixon's upcoming trips to the Soviet Union and China.[53] By January, however, the White House was deeply alarmed by the Communists' military preparations and their unwillingness to resume secret talks in Paris. On January 25, Nixon decided to admit that Kissinger had met with representatives of the DRV for several months in private and that the White House had made a bold peace proposal on October 11.[54] Washington insiders believed that disclosure of these facts deprived the DRV and NLF of the diplomatic advantage created by the Thieu affair and quieted domestic critics who had charged that the administration had no interest in negotiations.[55] In reality, the damage had already been done. Nixon continued to be attacked in Congress, and the Front maintained the upper hand in propaganda.

Nixon's speech in January had unforeseen results, however, as it supported the Lao Dong's fighting-while-negotiating strategy. For the next several weeks, while the combined forces of the DRV and the NLF prepared for the spring offensive, the United States and the Communists debated the merits of the various peace proposals. On February 5, Xuan Thuy, one of the DRV's chief negotiators, called the May 31 plan "a meaningless proposal" and denied that the United States had offered to set a deadline for an American troop withdrawal.[56] Nguyen Thi Binh denounced the May 31 and August 16 proposals as "a cruel hoax" and suggested that the United States had no serious desire to end the war.[57] Two weeks later, however, on February 14, Thuy informed Kissinger that the Vietnamese would agree to secret talks again after March 15.[58]

With this agreement in hand, Nixon prepared for his February trip to China. The journalist Stanley Karnow has suggested that the U.S.-Chinese agreements on major issues, such as the reduction of the American military presence on Taiwan, signaled that Washington was once again trying to use the superpowers to pressure Hanoi and the NLF into a negotiated settlement.[59] Even postwar studies from Hanoi have suggested that "leaders of the Lao Dong feared a Chinese sell-out."[60] Despite these efforts, neither the Chinese nor the Soviets ever pressured Hanoi to accept anything less than the most favorable conditions. If Peking had made such a move, a Hanoi diplomat later revealed, it would have fallen "on deaf ears because we could not be fooled by the Chinese twice."[61] In addition, in late 1971, for the first time in several years, Chinese military aid to the DRV and NLF increased substantially to balance the growing Soviet influence in Viet Nam and to reassure Hanoi that the summit with Nixon meant nothing.[62] The Soviet Union also increased its military shipments to the DRV, and eventually Russian-made tanks played an important role in the Communists' success.[63]

Nixon's preoccupation with superpower diplomacy perhaps shielded Washington from the significance of the military buildup taking place along the DMZ. Just four weeks after his return from China, Nixon learned of the coordinated DRV/NLF offensive. On March 30, 1972, 120,00 North Vietnamese troops crossed the DMZ and launched an attack in Quang Tri province. One week later, northern troops liberated Loc Ninh, Bu Dop, and Thien Ngo provinces and occupied the city of Loc An, just sixty miles from Saigon. Of major importance was the Communists' ability to control Route 13, the main highway west of Saigon. In the Central Highlands, DRV forces occupied much of the territory west of the Po Co River. By the end of April, the Communists threatened Hue and Com Tum City, the most strategically important towns north of Saigon. While the DRV forces launched conventional assaults with main force units, NLF elite local guerrilla units attacked the major urban areas in the South. The Front's military forces, the People's Liberation Armed Forces (PLAF), scored significant victories in several delta towns and along the border with Cambodia. By late spring, the NLF controlled most of the territory west and south of Saigon.[64]

The Nixon administration responded quickly to the Communist offensive by approving one of the most intensive air campaigns of the war. The president authorized B-52 strikes along the DMZ and ordered raids on the fuel depots along the Haiphong shoreline and near Hanoi. From April 6 to April 15, the Red River Delta from Hanoi to Haiphong was the site of daily bombing assaults.[65] The White House warned Hanoi that the raids would continue until the offensive stopped.[66] While the B-52 attacks went on, Nixon also tried to coerce Hanoi through diplomatic pressure.

On April 20, Kissinger met with Soviet Premier Leonid Brezhnev in Moscow. He told the Soviet leader that the United States held the Russians accountable for the Vietnamese offensive and warned that the administration was willing to take "whatever steps are necessary" to prevent a Communist military victory. During the last of his four-day meetings with the premier, Kissinger added, for the first time, that the United States would accept a cease-fire in exchange for the withdrawal of DRV troops that had entered the South since the offensive began.[67] According to conservative estimates, this proposal would allow nearly 100,000 DRV forces to remain below the DMZ.[68] Kissinger was confident that the Soviets would react positively to this new initiative, fearing that an escalation of the war would threaten détente.[69] On May 1, 1972, Moscow informed Hanoi of Kissinger's offer.[70]

Kissinger left Washington on the evening of May 1 to meet secretly with Le Duc Tho in Paris to discuss the latest peace proposal. After four hours of discussions, Tho flatly rejected the new initiative, dismissing it as "simply old wine in new bottles."[71] Perhaps Tho had left Hanoi with explicit instructions not to negotiate at all because the spring offensive was still in full operation. Combined DRV and NLF forces threatened to capture Hue and had liberated Quang Tri.[72] Kissinger left Paris convinced that the time had come for more severe military action, since the DRV showed no signs of weakening under diplomatic pressure.[73]

On May 8, the president met with his National Security Council staff and concluded that intensified bombing raids over Hanoi and the mining of Haiphong Harbor were needed to offset the DRV's intransigence. Some members of his administration warned that the Soviets might respond negatively, but Nixon correctly predicted that Moscow was more interested in good relations with the United States than in the war in Viet Nam.[74] Likewise, China had undergone a dramatic shift in its public opposition to American actions in Indochina.[75] In late May, therefore, with little opposition from the Communist powers, the United States launched its new military reprisal, code-named LINEBACKER. During the next several weeks, it dropped over 200,000 tons of bombs on Viet Nam and mined Haiphong's ocean harbor.[76]

Although the American escalation caused tremendous destruction in Viet Nam, it did little to break the diplomatic and military stalemates. Traveling constantly between Washington, Moscow, Peking, and Paris, Kissinger concluded in midsummer that the Nixon administration could not "let the Vietnam issue plague us for four more years."[77] When Le Duc Tho therefore hinted that Hanoi would accept anyone but Thieu in a tripartite government, Kissinger saw the possibility of a settlement.[78] On September 11, the NLF announced a new proposal for a government of national concord, initiating a series of negotiations that moved discussions away from a coalition government and toward a tripartite electoral commission. It would also set off the most intense debate within the Party since the secret negotiations of 1965.

The NLF's new declaration promoted a government in the South with three equal parts: the NLF, the neutralists, and the Saigon regime. Following up on Le Duc Tho's previous announcement, the Front implied that Saigon could select anyone except Thieu as its representative.[79] The American delegation in Paris flatly rejected the NLF's new initiative and declared that it was "nothing more than an undisguised attempt to put the Viet Cong in power in South Viet Nam without an election."[80] Nixon's policy had been to reject summarily any talk of a coalition government. For Washington, therefore, the only acceptable tripartite arrangement would be a joint commission that would oversee national elections in South Viet Nam. During a meeting with Le Duc Tho on September 15, Kissinger reiterated the United States' opposition to a coalition government of any kind.

By the third week of September, Hanoi was convinced that the United States would never agree to the NLF's tripartite solution. In a desperate move, Le Duc Tho dropped the demand for a coalition government and Thieu's ouster. According to the historian Gareth Porter, the DRV realized that it needed to concede on these issues because Nixon had successfully "reestablished public confidence in his Vietnam policy" and because the military offensive had not "achieved as much as it needed in order to force more concessions from Nixon."[81] American bombing raids had caused increased hardship in the North, and the loss of life was a significant factor in the Party's thinking. Vietnamese-language sources in Hanoi suggest that the Political Bureau was eager to reach a settlement before the 1972 election and thought that the coalition government was not as important as recognition by the United States that Thieu did not have exclusive sovereignty over South Viet Nam.[82] The Nixon White House was happy to concede this point in exchange for Hanoi's compromise. DRV officials later commented that "the matter of a coalition government and Thieu's removal were minor points" and that "we gave nothing away to the Americans."[83]

Tho's new proposal came as a complete surprise to NLF leaders, however. Since negotiations had started in Paris in 1968, the Political Bureau in Hanoi had directed the Party's overall negotiating strategy. Once the

Political Bureau approved a policy line, it informed its negotiators in Paris. How the NLF was left out of this major change in policy is unclear. What is clear is that the DRV's proposal was not made known to the NLF until October 8, when Le Duc Tho presented Kissinger with a detailed draft of a peace agreement.[84] The document offered an immediate cease-fire, a complete U.S. withdrawal, the return of all prisoners of war within sixty days, and an administrative structure that would oversee national elections to be held within six months. In addition, Viet Nam would be reunified step by step through peaceful means and without foreign interference.[85] The key political section of the treaty called for the Thieu regime to hold power alongside the oversight commission until national elections were held.[86] After three days of hard negotiations, Kissinger and Le Duc Tho concluded they had an agreement that "could possibly lead to peace."[87] Still, they left two substantial issues unresolved: the release of civilian prisoners in South Viet Nam and the cessation of all military aid by the United States to its Saigon ally and by Hanoi to the NLF. Kissinger presented the joint peace draft to the Nixon cabinet on October 11 and informed the president that the DRV had set a deadline for signing of October 31. The White House accepted the spirit of the agreement, but added that some provisions "had to be tightened."[88] With no apparent obstacles, a settlement seemed possible.

Kissinger, the White House, and Le Duc Tho had seriously underestimated the response of the two southern protagonists. On October 19, Thieu rejected outright the Tho-Kissinger draft.[89] Ostensibly, he opposed it because it did not provide for an immediate withdrawal of DRV troops and forced an American evacuation from South Viet Nam. The NLF, in contrast, objected to the lack of a guarantee that civilian prisoners would be released and to the fact that Thieu would be left in control of the political apparatus in Saigon.[90] While the NLF had been informed of the general policy line approved by the Political Bureau in Hanoi, it had never been apprised of the change regarding southern detainees. On October 13, shortly after it had learned of Hanoi's new initiative, the NLF formally protested to several Lao Dong officials. In Paris, Nguyen Thi Binh met with Le Duc Tho and Xuan Thuy to clarify the DRV draft. The northerners assured Madame Binh that the freedom of American POWs was tied to the liberation of civilians in the South and that Thieu would be only a figurehead until elections were held.[91] In Hanoi, Huynh Tan Phat, the NLF's secretary general, received guarantees from several high-ranking Party officials that Thieu's ouster was only a matter of time. One Party member later recalled, "We told Phat that in the time between the signing of the peace agreement and national elections, Thieu would be powerless."[92] Nguyen Van Tien, the NLF's diplomatic representative in Hanoi, spent hours trying to persuade members of the Political Bureau that the Front would lose considerable political prestige if "our southern brothers and sisters were not freed from Thieu's prisons with any peace agreement."[93]

Indeed, the issue of political prisoners was particularly important to southern cadres because Thieu held the keys to the jails. Beginning in 1965, it had been American policy to place all civilian prisoners in the RVN's custody. This meant, of course, that the Saigon regime could use terror as a weapon against the population of South Viet Nam. Almost every member of the NLF's Central Committee and many of its diplomats, including Madame Binh, had spent time in prison. "The only power Thieu held was that he could throw thousands of us into jail," reported one NLF member, "and he used this fear to his political advantage."[94] Hanoi seemed insensitive to this issue, despite its promises "to see to it that all Vietnamese are freed from bondage."[95]

Not swayed by Hanoi's promises that its interests were always considered in negotiations, the NLF approached the Soviet Union to intervene. In Moscow, Dang Quang Minh, the Front's diplomat, met with several high-ranking Soviet officials to clarify the NLF's objections to the October 11 Kissinger-Tho peace proposal. The Soviets assured Minh that any agreement would consider "conditions in the South" and that "these are minor points that can be cleared up during implementation of the agreement."[96] The NLF was in no mood to compromise, however, and Madame Binh continued her protest in Paris.

Meanwhile, Kissinger had flown back to France to meet with Le Duc Tho to clear up two remaining issues: the replacement of war matériel and the release of prisoners. The first issue was a technical problem and, both sides concluded, could probably be overcome.[97] The second was a major stumbling block. Although Tho and Xuan Thuy were eager to get an agreement before the United States held its presidential election in November, they were sensitive to NLF demands. For two days the Vietnamese negotiators insisted that the final agreement link the release of American POWs to the emancipation of civilian detainees. The United States was unwilling to commit itself to such a bargain, however, and flatly rejected the proposal. On October 16, Thuy caved in and agreed that the accord could separate American prisoners from southern arrestees. He demanded guarantees from Washington and Saigon, however, that Thieu would release all political prisoners within ninety days. Again the United

States backed off and offered a vaguely worded substitute: "The two South Vietnamese parties will do their utmost to resolve the questions within ninety days after the cease-fire comes into effect."[98] Despite anxious warnings from Madame Binh not to embrace such a faulty arrangement, the DRV accepted the American resolution on October 17.[99]

On October 19, Kissinger presented Thieu with the draft he and the North Vietnamese had negotiated. Kissinger did not realize at the time that Thieu had already learned of the accord through documents captured in Quang Tin province. After reading these documents, Thieu later reported, he knew for the first time "what was being negotiated over my head. The Americans told me the negotiations were still going on and that nothing was fixed, but the other side already had all the information." An outraged Thieu met with Kissinger privately in the presidential palace. As Kissinger explained the major provisions of the treaty he and Nixon endorsed, Thieu sat silently thinking, "I want to punch Kissinger in the mouth."[100] The next day, Thieu questioned Kissinger about specifics of the agreement. He was particularly outraged that it called for a public signing ceremony in Hanoi in only a few days. In any event, he rejected most of its major provisions. The most important problem was the absence of a mutual withdrawal clause that would force North Viet Nam out of the South when the Americans left. Kissinger explained that an American withdrawal was inevitable and that the United States was trying to provide the RVN with a decent interval between the cease-fire and that retreat.[101] Thieu totally opposed the draft, and after three days of negotiations in Saigon Kissinger left for Washington disappointed that "America's own ally had blocked the peace."[102]

In Washington, Nixon had informed Hanoi that negotiations had been stalled in Saigon and that signing on October 31 was now impossible.[103] Hanoi correctly concluded that the Nixon administration was using the October negotiations as a way of undermining the presidential campaign of the peace candidate, George McGovern, and the antiwar constituency at home.[104] "Nixon had no interest in peace," explained one Lao Dong official, "only in getting reelected."[105] Indeed, the Nixon administration had calculated that a brief delay in the negotiations would allow the United States to secure Thieu's support, improve the ARVN's military position, and negotiate with a huge electoral mandate and thus from a position of strength.[106] The Lao Dong saw through this stalling tactic, however, and on October 26 published a statement outlining the Kissinger-Tho document and the October negotiations. In addition, the DRV insisted that the Nixon administration was using Thieu's objections as cover "for its diabolical plans to prolong the war and to sabotage all peaceful settlement of the Viet Nam problem."[107]

The DRV's action caused consternation in Washington. Kissinger held a news conference at noon on October 26 to clarify the situation. He assured the press and the American people that "peace was at hand" and that a final agreement required only a few more meetings with the North Vietnamese in Paris.[108] His comments calmed fears in the United States but produced outrage in Hanoi and in the NLF. Lao Dong officials correctly concluded that "the Nixon administration will not sign the October 11 agreement and will change its negotiating position after Nixon's reelection."[109] Privately, NLF officials complained bitterly that Hanoi's hastiness had elevated Thieu's status. "By trying to secure a peace agreement by the November election, Hanoi sacrificed many principles that we in the South held dear," reported one NLF diplomat. "Our northern brothers were duped by the Nixon administration, and Washington used Saigon to achieve its deceitful objectives. In the process, however, Nixon granted the Thieu regime a veto power over negotiations that it had not previously enjoyed." In addition, Phat and others severely criticized Xuan Thuy's decoupling of the American POW issue from the release of southern political prisoners.[110] Another NLF official later commented, "Hanoi's message was clear. It cared more about the American prisoners of war, those who had fought against us, than it did for its southern comrades."[111]

Indeed, the political differences between northern and southern Communists were highlighted during the peace negotiations. Many NLF leaders believed that Hanoi was willing "to sacrifice southern revolutionaries for northern peace." Most southerners simply could not understand the Lao Dong's haste. "By early spring 1972, Hanoi was committed to an agreement with the United States before the American presidential election," one NLF diplomat later commented, "and we could not understand why."[112] In addition, those noncommunists who made up a significant portion of the NLF and the PRG had undergone some harsh ideological training at Hanoi's hands. Truong Nhu Tang, a founding member of the NLF and the PRG's minister of justice, has explained, "At the same time that Xuan Thuy was entertaining the United States with chimerical peace proposals in Paris, other Party experts . . . were preparing to educate South Vietnam's revolutionary bourgeoisie to the truths of dialectical materialism . . . in striking contrast to the careful solicitude the Lao Dong had always shown to non-Party southern leadership."[113] From the founding of the NLF, southern Communists had depended on noncommunist elements to strengthen the Front and help it achieve its goals. This was the nature of united fronts in Viet Nam's revolutionary history, but many southern Communists rejected the idea that these allies could be simply thrown away as the war progressed and deeply resented the Lao Dong's attempts to do just that.

Many southerners, Communists and noncommunists alike, simply could not understand the Lao Dong's haste to reach an agreement or its policies toward the south. Some suggested that although the spring offensive had stalled, DRV and NLF forces still controlled more territory than before, so they should not rush to make major concessions in Paris.[114] Perhaps, as Tad Szulc has suggested, Lao Dong leaders feared that "after the election the President's position might harden and the agreement . . . might become unhinged."[115] Gareth Porter argues that Hanoi was ready to end the conflict in 1972 because "the North itself badly needed a respite from the war . . . to devote its resources fully to production and economic development." The Lao Dong was willing to make serious concessions in 1972, Porter concludes, "provided the agreement still represented a net gain for the struggle."[116] George Herring writes that Hanoi had "suffered terribly from the latest round of American bombings" and that the northerners were "anxious for peace" if they could achieve it "without sacrificing [their] long-range goals."[117] Military leaders in Hanoi claimed they had crushed the ARVN, so "the time was right for an end to the war."[118] Henry Kissinger commented that the North Vietnamese fought for a peace agreement in 1972 "almost as maniacally as they fought the war."[119]

While Herring and Porter are indeed right, it seems clear that some war-weary northerners, fearing that the noncommunists in the NLF were once again becoming a problem, hoped to extract a settlement while their control of the Front was unquestioned.[120] Throughout the 1972 military campaign and subsequent negotiations in Paris, some NLF leaders had reasserted autonomous impulses that made several Lao Dong officials nervous. "We knew that our southern brothers would react according to their own interests," one Party official later revealed, "and we feared that they might jeopardize all that we had worked for." Several northern leaders had predicted continued southern "obstinance" in 1972 and therefore urged the Party to move ahead swiftly.[121]

Truong Nhu Tang's account of this period confirms the validity of Hanoi's fears. By the end of 1971, many noncommunists in the Front, angered by the forced reeducation seminars and Hanoi's increasing control over events in the South, made plans to form a "third force" that would harness popular southern support for an alternative. "If a coalition was to result from the bloodletting and mutual exhaustion that were likely to follow the American withdrawal," Tang writes, "political power would inevitably gravitate toward the middle."[122] Apparently Hanoi's concerns about its noncommunist allies were legitimate. By the end of October, therefore, because of problems in Washington and within its own Front, most Lao Dong leaders understood that no settlement would be forthcoming.

In early November, Nguyen Van Tien, the NLF's representative in Hanoi, suggested that the DRV/NLF negotiating team prepare for postelection discussions in which "the Americans will reverse themselves on almost every point."[123] On November 27, *Nhan Dan*, the Party's daily newspaper, declared that "if the United States is intent on going back on the points agreed upon, our people are determined to fight on until total victory." The paper was responding to a November 2 speech in which Nixon stated that central points still needed clarification.[124] Angrily the DRV delegation prepared for Kissinger's return to Paris on November 20. After weeks of heated negotiations, Hanoi and Washington had returned to their October positions. Throughout these talks, Kissinger had threatened to use "savage" force against Hanoi if the Communists did not make some concessions and accept a modified peace settlement.[125] Hanoi was willing to concede several points to the United States, but it could not retreat on the issue of civilian prisoners in the South.

Xuan Thuy had accepted a vaguely worded provision of the October draft that expressed a desire to have all political prisoners released within ninety days of an agreement. After the NLF's objections, however, Hanoi's diplomats returned to Paris in November with the demand that civilian prisoners be freed within sixty days.[126] Nguyen Thi Binh underscored this point in Paris on December 8 when she demanded that southern political prisoners be released at the same time as American prisoners of war.[127] In a press conference that day Madame Binh declared that no American prisoners would be released in the South unless Thieu emptied his jails as well. "There is no reason why we should free American prisoners while our compatriots remain in jail." When asked about the Kissinger-Tho draft and the release of prisoners, she said that the Americans had misinterpreted the agreement and that naturally the release of American POWs was linked with that of Vietnamese civilians. She quickly added, however, that some Vietnamese might have misinterpreted that clause too.[128]

Despite the differences that separated Washington and Hanoi in early December, many Lao Dong officials still believe that the NLF's intransigence destroyed a chance for peace. "We had come very close to reaching an agreement," one Party member later commented, "when southerners sabotaged the entire plan."[129] Another Lao Dong leader complained, "The southerners put their own interests above the revolution's needs."[130] Their bitterness stemmed from the events that took place after the failed December meetings.

On December 16, Kissinger left Paris declaring that another impasse had been reached because Hanoi was raising "one frivolous issue after another."[131] In reality, the White House was planning the most intensive bombing raids of the war. Intent upon punishing Hanoi for its perceived intransigence and weakening the Communists' military capabilities, the Nixon administration unleashed a relentless bombing campaign against North Viet Nam. The B-52 attacks, code-named LINEBACKER II, produced devastating results. Nearly two thousand civilians died under American bombs and much of the Kham Thien district of Hanoi was destroyed.[132] The Christmas bombings, as they became known in the West, also hit targets in the heavily populated Bach Mai district, including the region's largest hospital.[133] In all, American war planes dropped more than 36,000 tons of bombs.[134]

Despite U.S. claims to the contrary, the bombings did not force the Communists back to the negotiating table.[135] Negotiations resumed on January 8, 1973, because Hanoi and the NLF had concluded that international public opinion and the U.S. Congress now demanded that the Nixon administration produce a final settlement.[136] Indeed, several friendly governments severely criticized the Christmas bombings, and even Pope Paul condemned the "sudden resumption of harsh and massive war actions" in Viet Nam.[137] In Moscow, Brezhnev cursed the bombing raids and stressed that the future of Soviet-American relations depended on "the question of ending the Vietnam War."[138] On December 29, the Chinese Communist Party responded to the bombings by organizing the largest anti-American demonstration to be held in Peking during the war.[139] In the U.S. Congress, senators voted overwhelmingly to condemn the bombings and to end American involvement in Viet Nam through legislation.[140] Many of Nixon's long-time supporters abandoned him, and his popularity rating plummeted to an all-time low.[141] On December 30, a White House aide announced that "negotiations between presidential adviser Dr. Kissinger and special adviser Le Duc Tho and Minister Xuan Thuy will be resumed in Paris on January 8."[142]

In Hanoi, the Communists claimed a diplomatic and military victory. The White House had threatened to continue the bombing raids until the Vietnamese caved in. The air raids stopped after twelve days, however, and domestic and international pressure forced Nixon to resume talks. In

Paris, Washington quickly surrendered most of its previous objections. The final peace accord, signed on January 23, reflected practically all of the Communists' demands. The PRG was officially recognized in the preamble, North Vietnamese troops were allowed to remain in the South, the agreement restricted no civilian movement across the DMZ, and the National Council of Reconciliation and Accord remained relatively intact.[143]

Peace had come at a high price, however. Besides the tremendous loss of human life and environmental destruction, relations between northern and southern Communists had once again deteriorated, and this time the divisions were hard to repair. Despite Le Duc Tho's claim that the bombings of December 1972 "deepened the Vietnamese people's hatred of Nixon and tightened the bonds of unity," some northerners would not forget southern objections to the Kissinger-Tho draft and the price that Hanoi had to pay for the delay.[144] Southerners, for their part, remembered how casually northerners had dealt with civilian prisoners. In the last two years of the war, 1973 through 1975, these memories stirred up repressed regionalist feelings and threatened to destroy much of what the revolution had gained.

7

THE CEASELESS FIRE, 1973–1975

The Paris agreements did little to stop the war in Viet Nam. Neither of the southern protagonists was willing to abandon its objectives, and by mid-1974 the Thieu regime had declared the opening of the "Third Indochina War."[1] During the last two years of the conflict, the NLF skillfully combined its military and diplomatic struggle movements to precipitate a political crisis in Saigon. The political crisis and southern pressure led the Party to use military force to bring down the Saigon regime. Postwar studies emanating from Hanoi, however, have emphasized the North's role in the final victory of the southern revolution.[2] In 1988, for example, Le Duc Tho, the DRV's chief negotiator at the Paris talks and one of the Political Bureau's most powerful members, explained that the liberation of Saigon was made possible by large contingents of regular forces from the DRV army.[3] As PAVN tanks rolled south, however, they carried NLF flags, a gesture not soon forgotten by southerners after the war. In reality, there was considerable conflict within the Lao Dong concerning the use of revolutionary violence to end the war. As in the debate that had preceded the formation of the Front, some northern officials worried that armed force in the South threatened northern objectives.

This conflict began when NLF diplomats walked out of negotiations with the Saigon regime at La Celle St-Cloud, a French estate outside of Paris. On March 19, 1973, the two southern adversaries met in direct discussions for the first time in an attempt to settle the political issues of the Paris peace accord. Article 12 had called on the parties to reach agreement on the "internal matters of South Viet Nam as soon as possible and to do their utmost to accomplish this within ninety days after the cease-fire went into effect."[4] The Front's representative, a revived Nguyen Van Hieu, hoped to secure a standstill cease-fire that would stop the RVN's southern offensives. Thieu, for his part, had viewed the Paris peace agreement not as an end to the war but, according to Gareth Porter, as "the start of a new war under ground rules which he hoped would be advantageous to Saigon."[5] Indeed, the Saigon regime used new shipments of American war matériel to launch major territory-grabbing campaigns in early 1973. In Long Khanh, Tay Ninh, and Hau Nghia provinces, the RVN relied on air power to retake key hamlets after the cease-fire.[6] The cost in civilian lives was tremendous, but the RVN justified the attacks on the ground that it was recapturing territory illegally gained by the NLF just before the cease-fire went into effect.[7]

The NLF sincerely believed that it could force the Thieu regime to abide by the Paris agreement, and Hieu hoped he could use these direct negotiations to end the fighting. "I think we can show the Saigon government that the world wants peace," Hieu explained before leaving for Paris, "but we are also prepared to defend ourselves should Thieu continue to violate the Paris agreement."[8] For its part, the RVN sent Nguyen Luu Vien as its delegate and suggested an extended agenda for the first round of discussions. These items included the election of a national president, the makeup of the Council of National Reconciliation, and the removal of all foreign troops (including North Vietnamese) from the South.[9] The NLF countered with its own agenda, proposing to discuss a cease-fire, the return of all political prisoners, and civil freedoms for opposition candidates.[10] The Front also included the need to discuss the character and nature of the Council of National Reconciliation. The council was supposed to supervise national elections and oversee the implementation of all political agreements between the two parties. The proposed agendas, then, differed in substantial ways, with the makeup of the reconciliation council the only agreed-upon topic. This impasse represented the limited impact of the Paris agreement on events on the ground in the South.

In a lengthy press conference on April 20, Hieu criticized the Saigon government's agenda, claiming that it was premature to discuss elections while the war dragged on. "The house is burning, threatening everything inside," he explained. "We propose to extinguish the fire. The other side pretends not to see the fire, and suggests that we discuss how to decorate the living room."[11] The Thieu regime, he reported, wanted the NLF to make significant sacrifices without surrendering any of its own political control. "The Thieu government has used terror to crush all democratic opposition," Hieu complained. "It now wants to use the peace process to ensure this stranglehold on the people of South Viet Nam."[12] He vowed not to return to the negotiating table until the Saigon regime altered its agenda.

Hieu informed Hanoi of the deadlock and threatened to walk out of the talks unless the Saigon regime ended its military offensives. He urged the Military Commission of the Lao Dong's Political Bureau to consider an all-out military campaign to overthrow the RVN.[13] Party leaders warned, however, that "opposition to the enemy will not win victory unless there is a change in the ratio of military forces between us and the enemy."[14] The only way to accomplish this shift, Hanoi insisted, was to attack Thieu politically. The Communists hoped to use the talks "to exploit the growing contradiction between the Thieu regime and the southern Vietnamese people."[15] The Political Bureau in Hanoi ordered Hieu back to the negotiating table and urged him to exploit the enemy's political weakness. Hieu complied, but confided to friends privately that the Political Bureau's decision perhaps delayed an end to the war.[16]

On April 25, the NLF and RVN presented their formal peace proposals. The Saigon regime submitted a ten-point plan that outlined, in the broadest terms, its conditions for a settlement. They included the election of an "organ representing the people of South Viet Nam" within four months.[17] From the very beginning, Saigon had wanted an early election date to take advantage of a DRV withdrawal from South Viet Nam and to limit the opposition's ability to organize. Thieu correctly assumed that the DRV would be incapable of mobilizing troops for a southern campaign (or unwilling to do so) after they had crossed the DMZ. The RVN planned to loosen its restrictions on civil freedoms only months before the election, making it impossible for the opposition to organize a nationwide crusade. Furthermore, Thieu's proposal included no guarantees that he would release political prisoners before the election.[18]

The Thieu regime was under no illusion that the NLF would accept such a proposal; its hope was that its offer of a quick election and its promise of political reform would put the Communists in an awkward position.[19] The Front would refuse to accept the conditions for elections, Saigon officials predicted, and then Thieu could exploit the NLF's recalcitrance in the West. "The United States Congress was eager for us to settle the conflict through political elections," one Saigon official later commented. "We knew that the Communists would never agree to an open election, so we pressed the issue immediately for our advantage."[20] The Thieu government also believed that few people would actually read the detailed provisions of its proposal, so that it would appear more acceptable than it actually was.

To counter Saigon's election ploy, the NLF released its own six-point program for peace.[21] The Front proposed that the two sides settle each of the political issues separately and that the negotiators not move forward to the next item on the list until the last had been satisfactorily resolved and the solution implemented. Only after the settlement of all of the political considerations would the NLF agree to elections, and only for a national constituent assembly, not the presidency, as the RVN had proposed. NLF strategists correctly feared that the Saigon regime would continue to use American military support to prolong the war unless each issue was settled individually. After careful consideration, each side rejected the other's proposal.

As the talks at La Celle St-Cloud continued with no apparent results in the spring of 1973, an impatient NLF began to urge the Lao Dong's Political Bureau to revise its postwar strategy. Shortly after signing the Paris agreement, the Military Commission and the Political Bureau met in Hanoi and approved a policy that granted primacy to the political struggle. Many northern Lao Dong leaders feared that the renewal of main force warfare would give the Nixon administration an excuse to resume bombing North Viet Nam. In early 1973, Hanoi therefore decided to consolidate its gains and force Thieu from power by applying tremendous political pressure. "We wanted a strict interpretation of the Paris agreement," a Lao Dong leader explained, "because we correctly believed that the Saigon regime would never allow a fair election and that its failure to do so would erode its base of support throughout the South and promote a universal movement against Thieu."[22] Shortly after signing the January 1973 compact, Party leaders in Hanoi issued a directive that outlined the new phase of the southern struggle: "Cadres are to mobilize the masses to create basic conditions to guarantee the implementation of the agreements, maintain peace, and enable the revolution to continue its march forward."[23] Some southerners have also suggested that Hanoi believed it could secure American reconstruction aid if it did not violate the spirit of the accord.[24]

The Lao Dong's defensive posture angered many southerners, who remembered too well Diem's anticommunist sweeps from 1954 to 1959. "Hanoi was asking us to return to the pre-NLF days," one angry NLF cadre later commented, "when we were told to avoid the use of armed force altogether. That policy led to disaster, and only the formation of the Front and the reliance on the military struggle saved southerners from complete annihilation."[25] The Front's diplomatic corps once again drew parallels to Geneva. One former NLF cadre insisted that the key to lasting peace in the South rested with a battlefield victory over the RVN.[26] Another NLF leader complained, "We were making the same mistakes all over again. We left the enemy in the field and in control in Saigon and retreated to a defensive posture."[27] Even General Tran Van Tra, the military commander in Nam Bo, the southernmost region of Viet Nam, argued later, "We sincerely did not want a recurrence of the grievous naiveté of the 1954–1959 period."[28] "Hanoi's policy was based on the knowledge that the puppet government in Saigon would not negotiate in good faith," complained one cadre. "It was as if we were used for bait."[29]

Several southern Lao Dong officials supported the NLF's calls for a more aggressive military policy and the Front's intransigence at La Celle St-Cloud. Beginning in April, Le Duan, the Party's secretary general, argued that Hanoi's protracted war strategy and its defensive posture must give way to tactics more sensitive to southern revolutionary requirements. He understood the demoralizing impact of the Saigon regime's military offensives and worried that southern cadres thought that "the enemy was stronger than we were, that the balance of forces on the battlefield had changed in favor of the enemy, and that the revolution was in danger."[30] In an emotional speech before the Political Bureau, Le Duan read a letter from a southern cadre who criticized the Party's defensive posture: "How could we sink any lower?"[31] The secretary general had always been one of the most flexible Lao Dong leaders, willing to change overall policy as long as it led to victory and reunification with the South.[32]

In mid-April, at a secret meeting of the Central Committee, Le Duan asked Lao Dong officials to consider several points for discussion at the regular Central Committee meeting the following week. The Paris peace agreement had been a victory, he said, but the enemy "still had a large army with a full complement of equipment." He asked if the southern revolution had shifted to a new phase with new requirements and how the Party might build up the local armies in the South. Clearly, Le Duan was preparing the Lao Dong for more aggressive action in the South. When the Central Committee reconvened the following week, on April 19, it had concluded that the "possibility of American intervention had diminished" and that the time had come "to build up our military forces . . . because only with a powerful punch by the main force could we launch our general counteroffensive."[33]

On May 24, 1973, the Political Bureau met to discuss the Central Committee's conclusions. Representing the South was Tran Huu Duc, from Tri-Thien province; Vo Chi Cong and Chu Huy Man, from the Fifth Military Zone; the southern Party leaders Nguyen Van Linh, Senior General Tran Van Tra, Tran Nam Truong, Vo Van Kiet, and Nguyen Minh Duong; and General Hoang Van Thai. Le Duan presided over the conference and carefully outlined the Central Committee's thinking on the future of the southern revolution. The secretary declared that "now that the U.S. and its agents were blatantly sabotaging the Paris Agreement and obviously committed to continuing the war, there was no alternative in South Viet Nam but to use revolutionary violence to oppose them." Premier Pham Van Dong concurred, adding, "If we want to force the enemy to de-escalate, we must use violence, to strike them repeatedly, wearing them out in order to defeat them step by step." On June 1, after several weeks of discussion, Le Duan reported, "The heated debate and its results underline the complete unanimity of views among the leadership on many crucial questions. It reflects another step in the maturing of our Party through the realities of struggle."[34]

Despite Le Duan's optimistic remarks about Party unity, tactics and strategy in the South were still subjects of debate. Throughout the summer, therefore, the Military Commission and the Political Bureau met to "determine the direction and policies with regard to fulfilling the people's democratic national revolution, liberating the South, and unifying the homeland."[35] One participant described the meetings as "animated" and "very tense," and reported that "there was a clashing of many different opinions and interpretations regarding the developments on the battlefields."[36] The main protagonists once again were Le Duan and Truong Chinh. The two were old rivals, and Chinh still harbored great bitterness over the fact that Le Duan had replaced him as Party secretary. During the first few weeks of discussion, Truong Chinh, the leader of the DRV's National Assembly, reminded Lao Dong leaders that the Americans could unleash a bombing campaign at any minute and that the revolution had always had twin objectives: "building socialism in the North and carrying out a national democratic revolution in the South. We cannot sacrifice one goal for the other . . . we must continue to attend to our economic policies in the North."[37] In an interview with a reporter from the *Far Eastern Economic Review* in July, Chinh revealed the nature of the conflict within the Party when he emphasized the need to "strictly respect and scrupulously implement the Paris Agreement on Vietnam."[38]

Although Le Duan had significant support within the military, most political leaders accepted Chinh's argument. "If we use our forces to smash the Saigon army it would open the possibility of a renewed war with the United States," cautioned Hoang Tung, a Lao Dong Central Committee official. "That is why our efforts are to try to keep the war on a small scale and to force the other side to implement the Paris Agreement and have real peace."[39] Another Party strategist had explained earlier in the Lao Dong's theoretical journal, "We cannot exterminate imperialism at one time and in a single battle; we drive it back step by step and destroy it part by part."[40]

With the debate raging in Hanoi, NLF diplomats left for Algiers and the conference of nonaligned nations. Front strategists correctly predicted that they could use these meetings to influence the Party's deliberations.[41] "We understood that international support and recognition of the PRG were very important to future strategy considerations concerning the South," one NLF official later explained. "If we wanted to have any impact in Hanoi, we had to show that the progressive peoples of the world supported our right to exist and to fight back."[42] On August 31, Nguyen Thi Binh and Nguyen Huu Tho left for Algiers to launch the Front's new diplomatic initiative. On the first day of the conference, the delegates of the seventy-five represented nations approved a motion offered by Algeria to grant the NLF full status as the third Vietnamese state.[43] Despite an angry protest from the Thieu regime, all but three nations voted to approve the resolution.[44]

The conference also provided Tho with the first opportunity to express NLF goals and aspirations in the post-Paris period. "We ask you to assist in the application of the Paris cease-fire agreement," Tho said, "but we also need your support should the Saigon government refuse to end the war through negotiations and national elections."[45] Since talks between Nguyen Van Hieu and the RVN representatives had already stalled and the prospects of a political settlement appeared dim, Tho was warning the Saigon regime that the NLF intended to launch a counteroffensive soon. He also hoped that support from the nonaligned nations would shift Hanoi toward a more forceful policy.

The NLF's official report to the Lao Dong's Central Committee arrived in Hanoi on September 10, as the Party was preparing resolutions discussed at the Twenty-first Plenum, in June. Tho apparently authored the summary, which reported that the nonaligned nations supported the

Communists' wish to abide by the conditions of the Paris agreement, but clearly understood that further military action might be needed to "force the enemy to strictly implement them." The report also said that the Saigon regime's land-grabbing offensives in the spring were a direct violation of the peace compact and that the Front therefore had "the right to punish the enemy."[46] The NLF's report seems to have had an impact on the resolutions approved in October.

Indeed, the Lao Dong passed a resolution, number 21, confirming the use of military force to keep Saigon off balance and deter truce violations; it also confirmed that "the path of the revolution in the South is the path of revolutionary violence." The manifesto concluded that "whatever the situation, we must maintain the offensive strategy line."[47] Le Duan and Tran Van Tra were instrumental in forcing the policy shift. As southerners, they were no doubt sympathetic to conditions in the region and were perhaps influenced by the NLF's report from Algiers. Records from the plenum indicate a dramatic shift in thinking among policy elites when Duan said that southern forces were stronger now than they had been at any time since 1954.[48] This had not been the feeling among a majority of the northern officials when the Military Commission first met in the late spring. Also, as Le Duc Tho noted in 1988, "southern cadres fought back, in spite of orders to the contrary by northern cadres," and as a result, "the Central Committee was forced to meet in October 1973 and authorized the revolutionary fighters in the South to strike back against encroachments by Saigon."[49]

Resolution 21 had an immediate impact on the conduct and outcome of the war in the South. The shift in military policy allowed NLF main force units to attack RVN rear base units and other selected targets.[50] The main emphasis of the counteroffensives was the destruction of the Saigon regime's pacification program and the liberation of previously held territory. Within weeks of its passage, Resolution 21 had shifted the balance of the war. The Front regained significant territory and sent the message that it would no longer be a passive actor in South Viet Nam's future. More important, the ability to launch counterattacks made the NLF's diplomatic and political struggle movements more effective. "The combination of military, political, and diplomatic pressure made it possible to exploit the internal contradictions within the Saigon regime," one NLF official reported, "and this is what caused its eventual collapse."[51]

The Saigon regime used the NLF counterattacks approved in Resolution 21 to move another step toward the complete rejection of the Paris agreement and total reliance on a military solution. Declaring that the

"Third Indochina War" had begun, Thieu urged his troops to forget about the peace accord and carry out operations "in areas where their army is now stationed." He warned, "As far as the armed forces are concerned, I can tell you the war has restarted."[52] The Saigon government had expected all along that the United States would continue to support the war in Indochina. Thieu hoped that these new attacks against NLF territory would provoke a severe Communist reaction and force the United States to accept Saigon's rejection of the Paris agreement. Thieu had long feared that direct negotiations with the NLF at La Celle St-Cloud gave the Communists added prestige and created the perception that there were indeed two southern governments. By launching new attacks, he believed, he could end the negotiations and renew the war.

Thieu had not been a good student of events in the United States, however, and the NLF quickly exploited the political situation. In July 1973, the U.S. Congress had passed a resolution to end all bombing in Indochina and prohibit any future military action there without prior congressional approval.[53] In November, it approved the War Powers Act, requiring the president to notify the appropriate congressional committees within forty-eight hours of the deployment of American troops abroad and obligating him to withdraw them within sixty days unless Congress specified otherwise.[54] Furthermore, the Watergate scandal was now front-page news and the Nixon administration was under siege. By February 1974, the NLF realized that the United States would not reenter the war and that any further aggressive action by the Saigon regime opened it to the possibility of a complete political collapse. "We understood clearly that Saigon wanted to do away with the Paris agreement and settle the conflict on the battlefield," commented one Vietnamese general, "but the balance of forces was shifting in our favor because of our superior political and moral position."[55]

By March 1974, the NLF recognized that it could maintain enough military pressure on the Saigon government to cause a complete political collapse. "The Thieu regime had relied on military strength and technological superiority to hide its political weakness," explained a former military official in 1995, "but by March 1974 we had taken away that advantage and left the Saigon administration open for political attack from within."[56] Front strategists correctly predicted that internal political pressure was mounting against Thieu and that only fear and terror had kept it from exploding before 1974. The goal, therefore, was to combine military campaigns with political agitation to foster the domestic dissent.

The result of the combined domestic political and military struggle was total chaos in Saigon. The absence of the Americans left the southern economy in a shambles. During the war, neither the United States nor Saigon had concentrated on developing a commercial foundation for the South's urban areas. The influx of refugees had turned the cities into powder kegs ready to blow as more and more of them failed to find employment. At the same time, the worldwide inflation caused by the Middle East oil embargo had a tremendous negative impact on the southern economy. By midsummer, more than 90 percent of the RVN's forces claimed that their pay was not enough to support their families.[57] Desertion rates increased dramatically and former soldiers began to blame their commanding officers for the economic crisis. According to one Western journalist, "Corruption was now exceeding all bounds as commanders robbed payrolls and embezzled other funds."[58]

In the spring of 1974, Thieu urged his armed forces to do their utmost to enforce a blockade to defeat the NLF by "starving them out."[59] This blockade, labeled the "rice war" by several Western reporters, restricted the transportation of rice from one village to the next, prohibited the milling of rice except in government-run facilities, and outlawed the sale of rice to anyone other than an approved government buyer.[60] The result was widespread starvation. In Thua Thien province alone, over 20,000 people died of hunger as a result of Thieu's blockade.[61]

By mid-July 1974, Thieu's economic blockade had created a major economic depression and had contributed significantly to the political unrest in the South's cities. Demonstrators demanding jobs and food filled the streets daily, and even conservative Saigon newspapers condemned Thieu's policies.[62] By the end of August, veterans' groups threatened to take over several towns to protest the lack of food and jobs. On September 21, workers in Cholon walked off their jobs, demanding food and temporary economic relief.[63] The blockade had caused suffering in Saigon as well, where only a quarter of the population had enough to eat. According to several Saigon newspapers, most families could afford only one meal of steamed rice a day.[64]

By late summer, the Thieu regime faced opposition from every quarter, including the United States. In late August, Tran Huu Thanh, a Catholic priest and former lecturer at the RVN's military command school, began an anticorruption campaign that led many former Thieu supporters to call for his ouster.[65] Thanh had the support of the U.S. Central Intelligence Agency, and by early September the American embassy in Saigon called for a coalition of conservative forces to replace Thieu.[66] Ironically, several members of Thieu's own National Assembly supported Thanh, and throughout the fall they abandoned the president. Eventually the American embassy, aware of the damage caused by its own actions, issued a statement denying that it had supported any opposition group and renewing its commitment to Thieu.[67] By that time, however, the damage had been done.

By late September, the Lao Dong realized that the Thieu regime could no longer resist a major military offensive. During a policy review meeting of the Political Bureau, the Party discussed the impact of the political, diplomatic, and military struggle movements in the South. Party leaders concluded that "the present opportunity is most favorable" to liberate the South militarily.[68] This decision, known as COSVN Directive 08 in the West, committed the Lao Dong to a major military action within the next several months.[69] From September 30 until October 8, the General Staff of the Military Commission prepared for a strategic offensive. On October 8, the Political Bureau unanimously approved the General Staff's plan to liberate the South in 1975 and 1976 with a campaign to begin in the Central Highlands. The two-year, two-step crusade called for main force units to mount continuous attacks in 1975, paving the way for a general offensive and uprising in 1976. Military leaders warned the Political Bureau not to expect an uprising until the ARVN "had been smashed. Only then could favorable conditions be created for uprisings by the urban masses."[70] Le Duan heralded the Political Bureau's decisions. "This is an event of paramount importance, a very courageous decision. This decision is the outcome of the collective wisdom of the Politburo, and the result of a long weighing up process based on the experience of several decades of fighting, on the implementation of revolution on the battlefield, on the balance of forces in our country and throughout the world."[71]

Naturally, the NLF's diplomats fired the first shot in the Party's new military campaign. On the same day that the Lao Dong approved the two-year offensive, Madame Binh announced that the Front was breaking off all negotiations with the Saigon regime until Thieu was removed from office.[72] Conditions in the South had deteriorated so rapidly that even Thieu's supporters urged him to reach a political settlement. The only hope of attaining this goal, of course, lay in a continued dialogue with the Front. When the NLF called off the talks, therefore, it precipitated a political crisis in Saigon. Several conservative newspapers called for Thieu to step down immediately to avoid an all-out war.[73] "We can no longer match the Communists with U.S. aid so unpredictable," one paper editorialized in late October, "and new enemy divisions have crossed the border into South Viet Nam."[74] Although the press was wrong on both counts, the NLF's action had created the proper conditions for the military offensive.[75]

When the campaign began in early January, even the most optimistic Lao Dong cadre could not have foreseen the events of the next four months. In its initial plan, the General Staff in Hanoi envisioned a three-phased offensive. The first phase was to begin in January and end in late February, with main force units confining their attacks to the western portion of the B-2 theater, the southernmost region of Viet Nam. The next phase was to extend from March until June and encompass the entire country. Beginning in July, the military strategy shifted to small-scale encounters to prepare the urban areas for the general uprisings and the grand offensive.[76] With the first attacks on ARVN forces in Phuoc Long province, northeast of Saigon, it appeared as if the Party might have to speed up its timetable.[77]

On January 9, officials of the Lao Dong's Military Commission and General Staff met with the COSVN commander, Vo Chi Cong, to select the first target in the Central Highlands offensive.[78] The generals finally concluded that the seizure of Ban Me Thuot would isolate the ARVN from the other principal cities in the highlands (Play Ku and Kontom) and would make it difficult for the Saigon forces to control movement in the region.[79] On March 10, combined NLF and DRV forces attacked the city and within twenty-four hours it was in Communist hands.[80] Spurred on by their relatively easy victory, revolutionary forces pursued ARVN troops as they retreated to Play Ku. After two weeks of fierce fighting, the ARVN commander, Pham Van Phu, ordered a complete withdrawal from the highlands.[81]

On March 16, after inflicting several costly defeats on the ARVN, Van Tien Dung, the commander in charge of the final southern offensive, sent a report to the Political Bureau "reviewing the situation and proposing follow-up action to win decisive victory in this current dry season." The report recommended that the Lao Dong consolidate its victories in the Central Highlands by launching a two-pronged military offensive. The first group of attacks would be eastward and the second into the Fifth Military Zone, northeast of Saigon. Senior General Vo Nguyen Giap and the Military Commission accepted Dung's proposals and urged the armed forces "not to let the enemy withdraw safely and conserve their forces. You have to move right away and cut the enemy's retreat along Highway 1. . . . "[82] When Le Duan read Dung's report, he predicted that victory was at hand.[83]

With the highlands secured, Communist forces attacked the coastal cities of Quang Tri and Hue. Using Soviet-made tanks and taking advantage of the lack of U.S. air support, DRV and NLF forces routed the ARVN's elite First Division. Within weeks the Communists had isolated Da Nang, the second largest city in the South. President Thieu had ordered his troops to hold on to the city at all costs, but the flood of refugees from the highlands, reportedly a million strong, made it impossible to defend.[84] On March 29, three DRV divisions entered the city unopposed.[85]

In just three weeks, Communist forces had captured twelve provinces and the ARVN had lost nearly half of its troop strength.[86] Optimistic Saigon generals predicted that the Communists would be incapable of sustaining the offensive and urged their troops to remain in the field.[87] By the end of March, however, hundreds of officers had left their commands and thousands of troops had abandoned their units. NLF flags prominently displayed in the majority of homes along National Highway 1 welcomed the combined regular force units as they marched south toward the RVN's capital city.

In early April, the Political Bureau met to assess the results of the military campaign. It concluded that "with regard to both strategy and political-military forces, we have sufficient strength to overwhelm the enemy troops. The U.S. has proved to be completely impotent, and even if it increases its aid, it cannot save the puppets from collapse."[88] The decision was therefore made to grasp the strategic opportunity and end the war by May 1, 1975. Responding to the Political Bureau's resolution, Communist forces rushed toward Saigon. It was only a matter of days before the city was completely surrounded by NLF and DRV troops.

On April 19, Vo Dong Giang, speaking for the NLF, warned the RVN that if Thieu were not removed immediately, the Communists would take the city by force. Two days later, under pressure from Ambassador Graham Martin, Thieu resigned.[89] In a television speech on April 22, Thieu blamed the Ford administration for refusing to rescue its ally, as it had promised to do. Thieu escaped to Taiwan, apparently with a substantial amount of the RVN treasury, and named Vice President Tran Van Huong as his replacement. The NLF rejected Huong, however, and demanded that Saigon accept a leader who would support the Paris agreement.[90] On April 28, the National Assembly turned power over to Big Minh. Two days later, at 11:30 A.M., Minh ordered RVN troops to abide by a cease-fire and urged the Communists to accept a peaceful transfer of power to avoid further bloodshed.[91] With Minh's surrender on April 30, the Second Indochina War had finally come to an end.

EPILOGUE

On May 15, 1975, two weeks after the fall of Saigon, hundreds of thousands of people gathered in the former RVN capital to celebrate the end of the Second Indochina War. Bands played, students and business leaders spoke of reconciliation, and Lao Dong officials claimed that "all Vietnamese are victorious."[1] Later that day, the Party sponsored a victory parade, pointing with pride to the endless PAVN regular units that marched by the reviewing stand. Truong Nhu Tang, a founder of the NLF and the PRG's minister of justice, noticed, however, that there were no PLAF units. "Where are our divisions?" Tang asked PAVN General Van Tien Dung. The general replied, "The army has already been unified."[2]

Despite assurances to the contrary, the Lao Dong had moved quickly to unite Viet Nam under the socialist banner. Within a matter of months, all front organizations that the Party had created to wage war against the RVN were either dissolved or merged with existing Lao Dong associations. COSVN, the Lao Dong's central office in the South, and the People's Revolutionary Party were immediately eliminated. The Alliance of National, Democratic, and Peace Forces, the Youth League, the Federation of Trade Unions, and the Women's Union merged with their northern counterparts. The NLF was quickly absorbed into the National United

Front, a recruitment arm of the Lao Dong. The Provisional Revolutionary Government, which many southerners had long thought of as a government-in-waiting, was replaced by military management committees in key cities and district towns. In Saigon, for example, the Party issued the following communiqué:

> In order quickly to stabilize order and security in the city, to build a new revolutionary order, to consolidate and develop the people's sovereign right, and rapidly to restore and stabilize the normal life of the various strata of all compatriots in Saigon/Gia Dinh, in accordance with a decision made by the PRG, we wish to make public the following list of members of the Saigon/Gia Dinh City Military Management Committee:
>
> 1. Col. Gen. Tran Van Tra.
> 2. Vo Van Kiet, deputy.
> 3. Mai Chi Tho, deputy.
> 4. Maj. Gen. Hoang Cam.
> 5. Maj. Gen. Tran Van Danh.
> 6. Cao Dang Tien, deputy.
> 7. Sr. Col. Bui Thanh Khiet.
> 8. Dr. Nguyen Van Thu.
> 9. Vong Ky Thuat.
> 10. Vo Thanh Van.
> 11. Phan Minh Thanh.[3]

It is unclear whether the PRG actually issued such an order; it is doubtful, however, inasmuch as no official PRG member appeared on the list. Only Vo Van Kiet had served officially with the NLF, and of course there were no noncommunists from the Alliance or other sympathetic southern front organizations.

During the war, most southerners believed that reunification would come as the result of negotiations between the NLF and the Lao Dong. This assumption had been a rallying point for many noncommunists in the Front and had helped create the political crisis that led to military victory. Reunification came swiftly, however, and noncommunists in the NLF were not allowed to participate. On November 15, 1975, representatives of the North and South met in Saigon for a "Consultative Conference on National Reunification."[4] In just six days, Communist officials settled all issues of reunification. Pham Hung, who had assumed the leadership of COSVN after the death of Nguyen Chi Thanh in 1967, represented the South. He was soon to take a place in Premier Pham Van Dong's cabinet, and many southern Communists have since complained that "he seemed eager to get on the train to Hanoi."[5] On the opposite side of the table sat Truong Chinh, former Lao Dong secretary general and now president of the National Assembly, who had long favored northern interests over southern liberation. Naturally, the two Party leaders reached consensus on reunification.

In a brief communiqué released shortly after the conference ended, the Communist leaders reported: "The conference was unanimous on the method of the country's unification. . . . A general election over the entire territory of Viet Nam must be held soon to elect a common National Assembly. This National Assembly . . . will determine the structure of the state, elect the leading organs of the state, and prescribe the new constitution of a unified Viet Nam."[6]

The editor of *Nhan Dan*, the Party's daily newspaper, was quick to point out, however, that "the elections . . . to be held on April 25, 1976 . . . were not to decide the nature of the regime. . . . That has been decided during the struggle."[7] Hundreds of noncommunists in the NLF understood the fragility of their relationship with the power structure in Hanoi too late. "I guess we were naive," an Alliance member later commented. "We always believed there would be a place for us in a new government of reconciliation."[8] Perhaps noncommunists in the NLF did not fully understand the united front strategy. The Party had always made temporary alliances with noncommunists to meet its objectives, but once those objectives were met, the alliance was quickly dissolved. Few noncommunists in the Front would enjoy political power after the war.

According to the November conference agreements, only candidates approved by the Lao Dong could run for election, and many noncommunists and neutrals in the South found themselves ineligible. Former Communist leaders of the NLF fared much better. Of the 492 seats in the National Assembly, southern Communists or those sympathetic to the Party controlled 243. Most of those seats were filled by former NLF members. Nguyen Thi Binh became the minister of education before assuming the vice presidency of Viet Nam in 1992. Nguyen Huu Tho, the former NLF president, was made vice president of the unified Viet Nam. Huynh Tan Phat, the former NLF secretary general and PRG premier, was appointed vice premier of the new government. Other leading southern military leaders were given positions of leadership in the unified army.

Nguyen Van Hieu, the NLF's leading diplomat, was offered a ministry position, as were Vo Chi Cong and Tram Nam Trung. Hoang Bich Son joined Hanoi's Foreign Ministry.[9]

The Lao Dong faced serious problems with rapid reunification. Hanoi's swift integration of the South into a Communist unified whole confirmed the worst fears of many foreign leaders. For over three decades, Western leaders had charged that the Communists wanted to take Viet Nam by force. For American officials, Hanoi's immediate postwar actions were proof enough that they had been right all along. Ironically, several high-profile antiwar activists, such as Joan Baez and Staughton Lynd, condemned Hanoi's postwar actions, particularly their policy of reprisals against southerners.[10] Many Southeast Asian leaders also interpreted the Lao Dong's swift actions in the South as a sign that Hanoi had thoughts of expanding its influence elsewhere. "We feared that the Communists in Viet Nam were indeed interested in regional hegemony," complained one Cambodian Communist after the war.[11] Why, then, in view of the risks involved, did the Lao Dong move so swiftly to unite the country?

According to William Duiker, the Lao Dong had little choice. Duiker sees three essential reasons for the swiftness of Hanoi's actions. The long and costly war had so seriously depleted the number of trained and dedicated cadres in the South that Hanoi would have to send replacements from the North. For a variety of obvious reasons, this was far easier to do in a united Viet Nam. The economy, now in a shambles because of the war, would have to be nursed back to health, and the economy was easier to manage by mechanisms already established in Hanoi. Party leaders, therefore, saw expeditious reunification as an economic imperative. Finally, northern Party leaders correctly feared what southern dissidents might do. According to Duiker, Lao Dong officials had concluded by mid-1975 that "the longer the delay in unification, the more potential obstacles could be expected to rise."[12] Duiker is no doubt correct in his analysis. There may be other reasons, however, for the decisive action taken by the Central Committee.

Throughout the war, the Lao Dong and the NLF shared a strategic culture. That is, the Front and the Central Committee shared some basic assumptions about the nature of the anti-American conflict. Once that conflict was over, however, the strategic preferences that had joined Communist and noncommunist were altered. Since the Party's objectives had been met, the preferences shifted. The temporary nature of alliances in the united front guaranteed such a shift, and southern Viets should not have been surprised that the Central Committee controlled the future of the Party. The shared strategic culture had allowed the Lao Dong to sweep aside cultural and regional differences to create a modern revolutionary movement with ties to a glorious national past. Lao Dong leaders stressed strategic and cultural unity, therefore, and downplayed regional sentiments.

The Lao Dong's effort to create a unified strategy shared by all Party members was largely successful until the 1954 political division. Before the Geneva decisions, Party members tended to have common ideas and attitudes about the nature of their struggle, the character of the enemy, and the inevitability of conflict in human affairs. When the temporary political division forced the Party to accept twin revolutionary goals—to build socialism in the North and liberate the South—the shared strategic values came into question for the first time. From 1954 until 1975, there were serious differences of opinion within the Party over the efficacy of violence and the role of negotiations in the modern revolution. This conflict came to light after the Lao Dong had tried to use the NLF's able diplomats as the first wave of its diplomatic struggle initiatives.

Despite these serious setbacks, the NLF enhanced the Party's ability to mobilize southern dissidents and world opinion in support of Hanoi's claims against the Saigon regime. Over time, the Lao Dong learned how to use southern passions and interests to the revolution's advantage, scoring significant diplomatic victories and frustrating the war effort of the United States. Diplomacy had always played an important role in Viet Nam's long history, and the Front's diplomatic leaders understood its importance to the modern revolution. Some postwar histories issued in Hanoi have downplayed the NLF's role in the Lao Dong victory, but we have seen that the Front's diplomatic accomplishments were critical to the revolution's success.

CHRONOLOGY, 1954–1975

1954

June 16 Bao Dai selects Ngo Dinh Diem as prime minister.

July 7 Ngo Dinh Diem returns to Saigon after five-year absence.

July 15–18 Sixth Plenum of Lao Dong's First Central Committee.

July 20 Geneva Accords signed.

September 5–7 Lao Dong's Political Bureau resolves to stress political struggle in South.

September 8 Southeast Asia Treaty Organization (SEATO) formed.

1955

March 3–12 Seventh Plenum of Lao Dong's First Central Committee.

April Ngo Dinh Diem crushes Binh Xuyen sect.

June 27 Vo Nguyen Giap travels secretly to Peking to discuss reconstruction of DRV army and military plans.

July Ho Chi Minh travels to Moscow to secure Soviet aid. Lao Dong negotiates support from People's Republic of China.

August 13–20 Eighth Plenum of Lao Dong's First Central Committee.

September 10 Formation of Fatherland Front.

October 23 Ngo Dinh Diem defeats Bao Dai in national referendum to become chief of state.

October 26 Ngo Dinh Diem declares himself president of Republic of Viet Nam (RVN).

1956

April Prince Norodom Sihanouk, Cambodia's prime minister, announces his country's neutralist policy. Deputy Premier Chen Yun of People's Republic of China visits Hanoi to discuss DRV's socialist economic plan.

April 19–24 Ninth Plenum of Lao Dong's First Central Committee. Lao Dong reaffirms its commitment to unification through political means alone. Truong Chinh, Party's secretary general, criticizes those "who do not yet believe in the correctness of this political program and in the policy of peaceful reunification of the country."

June 8–9 Lao Dong's Political Bureau meets to discuss southern revolution.

August Le Duan travels to Nam Bo [South].

September Tenth Plenum of Lao Dong's First Central Committee. Truong Chinh forced to resign as Lao Dong secretary general; is temporarily replaced by Ho Chi Minh.

November Chou En-lai, premier of People's Republic of China, visits Hanoi to discuss economic and political matters.

December Plenum of Nam Bo [Southern] Interzone Party Committee determines to "use violent general uprising to win power" in South. At Eleventh Plenum of First Central Committee, Lao Dong struggles with dual problem of building socialism in North and waging war for national liberation in South. Le Duan presents "Revolutionary Line," theoretical justification for armed violence in South.

1957

January Soviet Union suggests that DRV and RVN be admitted to United Nations as separate states.

March Twelfth Plenum of Lao Dong's First Central Committee decides to build up national army and consolidate national defenses. Le Duan asked to join Political Bureau.

May 8 Ngo Dinh Diem visits United States.

October Formation of Unit 250, first battalion-sized unit in South. Nam Bo Interzone Party Committee adopts political and military struggle strategy for southern revolution.

December Thirteenth Plenum of Lao Dong's First Central Committee. Le Duan reports on enlisting support from socialist camp, especially financial aid from Soviet Union.

1958

July 22 Prince Souvanna Phouma of Laos dissolves neutralist government. United States supports formation of anticommunist state under Phoui Sananikone.

November Fourteenth Plenum of Lao Dong's First Central Committee. Three-year economic plan approved and sent to National Assembly for ratification. Again primacy is granted to socialist construction in North, but Le Duan is sent south on secret mission to be reported at next Central Committee meeting.

December At Phu Loi Prison, detention center for many Lao Dong leaders in Thu Dau Mot province, 33 kilometers from Saigon, over 1,000 die of food poisoning and gunshot wounds. Massacre becomes emotional rallying point for southern cadres.

1959

January Fifteenth Plenum of Lao Dong's First Central Committee. Party adopts Resolution 15, based on Le Duan's report, approving development of revolutionary armed forces in South and use of armed violence to accompany political struggle.

March Lao Dong's Political Bureau approves creation of revolutionary base in Central Highlands; makes broad appeal to ethnic minorities to join national struggle.

May Lao Dong's Political Bureau decides time is right to implement Resolution 15, often called "Great Leap Forward" of southern revolution. Military Commission of Central Committee establishes Group 559, or Truong Son troops, responsible for transporting revolutionary supplies from North to South.

August Ngo Dinh Diem authorizes severe repression of suspected Communists.

October Formation of PAVN's first armored tank division.

1960

January 1 First National Assembly passes and Ho Chi Minh approves first socialist constitution.

January 17 Ben Tre uprisings, first massive uprising under Lao Dong's policy of armed violence in South.

January 26 First large-scale battle of southern revolutionary forces against ARVN at Tua Hai.

April Promulgation of Military Obligation Law; first draft.

April 11–15 Twelfth session of First National Assembly.

May 8 Election of Second National Assembly of Democratic Republic of

Viet Nam (DRV): president, Ho Chi Minh; vice president, Tan Duc Thang; chairman of Standing Committee, Truong Chinh; premier, Pham Van Dong.

May 9 Chinese delegation led by Prime Minister Chou En-lai visits Viet Nam.

August Coup in Laos brings Souvanna Phouma back to power.

September 5–10 Third National Congress of Lao Dong (First Party Congress, March 1935; Second Party Congress, February 1951) elects new Central Committee with Ho Chi Minh as president and Le Duan as first secretary; also elects new Political Bureau with eleven regular members and Central Committee Secretariat with seven regular members. (New Central Committee and Political Bureau account for changes in numbers of Party plenums, etc.) Lao Dong approves formation of united front in South.

September 11 More than 1,000 professors, students, and parents march in Saigon to demand use of Viet language in colleges and universities.

October 4 10,000 people in Sa Dec demonstrate for three days against Saigon regime.

October 15 10,000 people protest rule of Ngo Dinh Diem in Ben Tre.

October 20 Uprisings in Tay Nguyen in Central Highlands.

November 8 John F. Kennedy elected president of United States.

November 11 Phan Quang Dan leads coup attempt against Ngo Dinh Diem. Over 5,000 people in Saigon demonstrate in support of coup. Secret police quickly smash the protest, killing more than twenty demonstrators.

December 20 Formation of National Front for Liberation of South Viet Nam (NLF, derogatorily called Viet Cong by its enemies) as approved by Lao Dong at Third National Congress, Resolution 15 at 15th Party Plenum in January 1959, and Political Bureau directive of May 1959.

1961

January 31 Lao Dong's Political Bureau issues directive making armed struggle as important as political struggle.

February 1 Liberation News Agency, NLF's propaganda arm, is formed.

February 15 Formation of People's Liberation Armed Forces (PLAF), NLF's military arm.

March 5 Over 10,000 protesters against Diem regime in Sa Dec are attacked by secret police.

March 8 Women's Union for Liberation of South Viet Nam is formed.

March 12 Over 20,000 people of Long Xuyen and Chau Doc provinces meet to demonstrate against shipments of American arms from Malaya to South Viet Nam.

March 31 Patriotic Group of Workers and Businessmen of South Viet Nam is formed.

April 2 Workers' Liberation Association of South Viet Nam is formed.

April 8 Luc Hoa Buddhist Association is formed.

April 24 Farmers' Liberation Association of South Viet Nam is formed.

May Vice President Lyndon Johnson visits South Viet Nam.

May 10 More than 40,000 people from Tan An and Cho Lon provinces demonstrate against Saigon regime.

May 15 More than 20,000 people in Ben Tre province march against American intervention in Viet Nam.

May 16 Conference on political future of Laos opens in Geneva.

May 17 More than 200 NLF delegates meet to discuss military guidelines.

June Premier Pham Van Dong visits Peking to discuss military situation in Viet Nam. Mao expresses support for armed struggle through "people's war" strategy.

June 4 John F. Kennedy meets Soviet Prime Minster Nikita Khrushchev in Vienna.

July 1 Progressive Socialist Party of South Viet Nam is formed.

July 1 Former Resistance Fighters' Association declares its support of NLF.

July 15 Liberation Literature and Arts Association of South Viet Nam is formed.

July 20 Asian-African Unity Committee is formed.

September 17–18 Battle of Phuoc Thanh.

October Delegates to First Plenum of NLF's Central Committee discuss new line and tasks for revolution in South Viet Nam.

October 18 General Maxwell Taylor and Walt Whitman Rostow arrive in Saigon to assess U.S. military and political objectives.

November 11 Association of Patriotic and Democratic Journalists of South Viet Nam is formed.

November 22 White House issues NSAM 111, spelling out new U.S. policy toward Viet Nam.

December Asian-African United Council accepts NLF as member with full standing.

December 8 State Department releases white paper, "North Viet Nam's Effort to Conquer South Viet Nam."

1962

January 1 South Viet Nam's Communist Party is renamed People's Revolutionary Party of South Viet Nam. This is the one openly Communist mass association of the NLF.

January Honolulu Conference. Kennedy administration decides to replace Military Assistance and Advisory Group (MAAG) with Military Assistance Command–Viet Nam (MACV).

January 1 Revolutionary People's Youth Group is formed.

February Lao Dong's Political Bureau meets to discuss response to increased American presence in South.

February 1 NLF's Liberation Radio begins operations.

February 16–March 3 NLF's First Congress.

February 27 RVN pilots attack Ngo Dinh Diem's palace.

April 6 PLAF attacks Tra Bong.

June Nguyen Van Hieu mission begins.

June 24 International Peace-Keeping Committee of South Viet Nam sends delegation to international conference in Moscow. Vietnamese delegation is led by Nguyen Van Hieu.

June–July Ho Chi Minh and Nguyen Chi Thanh travel to Peking to discuss military matters. Lao Dong expresses concern about possibility of American invasion of DRV.

July 23 Geneva agreement on Laos signed.

July 25 NLF sends its first representative to Cuba.

August 10 NLF's Central Committee officially declares neutrality policy; issues Fourteen-Point Statement on neutralization.

September Nguyen Van Hieu mission in China.

October 19 NLF delegation led by Nguyen Van Hieu visits Hanoi.

1963

January 2 Lao Dong calls battle at Ap Bac a victory, says it "signified the coming of the new revolutionary armed forces in the South."

January 3 Executive Committee of International Labor Union in Prague accepts Liberation Workers' Association of South Viet Nam as official member.

February NLF sends its first representative to Algeria.

February 4 African-Asian United Association selects Asian-African United Committee of South Viet Nam as full member with seat on Standing Secretariat.

February 15 NLF's Central Committee condemns use of chemical weapons in Viet Nam.

April Eighth Plenum of Lao Dong's Second Central Committee discusses development of socialism in North, debates allocation of resources to southern battlefield.

April 21 Battle of Bien Nhi.

May Liu Shaoqi, chair of People's Republic of China's Communist Party, travels to Hanoi and tells Ho Chi Minh that Viets can "regard China as your rear" in military matters.

May 8 ARVN and Diem's secret police attack Buddhists during demonstration in Hue.

May 14 NLF's Central Committee denounces Diem's attacks on Buddhists.

June 11 Bonze Superior Thich Quang Duc burns himself to death on busy Saigon street to protest oppressive policies of Diem regime.

June 16 500,000 Buddhists march to Xa Loi, where Thich Quang Duc's body is memorialized.

July 4 ARVN general Tran Van Don informs CIA agent Lucien Conein that South Vietnamese officers are plotting to overthrow Diem.

July 5 Battle of Giong Trom in Ben Tre province.

July 20 Battle of Quang Long–Cho Gao.

August 21 Saigon regime imposes curfew and raids Buddhist pagodas.

August 23 French president Charles de Gaulle pledges support for neutral Viet Nam.

September 1 In message to international leaders NLF president Nguyen Huu Tho condemns Diem's attacks against Buddhists and declares NLF's neutrality.

September 9–10 Battle of Soc Trang Airport.

September 13 UN secretary general U Thant condemns Saigon regime, calls for withdrawal of U.S. troops and international conference to end hostilities.

October NLF establishes diplomatic office in Czechoslovakia.

October 9 Battle of Loc Ninh; second attack on Ap Bac.

November 1 Ngo Dinh Diem and Ngo Dinh Nhu assassinated by officers of their own army.

November 7–8 NLF's Central Committee holds special session to discuss situation in South Viet Nam after the successful coup against Ngo Dinh Diem.

November 22 John F. Kennedy assassinated.

December Ninth Plenum of Lao Dong's Second Central Committee analyzes revolution to date and assesses situation in South after Diem's assassination.

1964

January 1 NLF's Second Plenum elects new Central Committee of forty-five members.

January 16 President Johnson approves OPLAN-34-A, provocative actions against North Viet Nam that lead to Gulf of Tonkin incident.

January NLF establishes liaison office in Indonesia.

January 17 Battle of Thach Phu.

January 30 Nguyen Khanh wrests power from Duong Van Minh in bloodless coup in Saigon.

February 8 NLF president Nguyen Huu Tho issues statement on new government of Nguyen Khanh, declaring that neutrality holds key to peace in South Viet Nam.

March 3 Battle of Thuong Phuc.

March 27 Special Lao Dong political conference deals with Sino-Soviet dispute and increased presence of Americans. Ho proclaims, "Everyone must do the work of two for the sake of our compatriots in the South."

April 11–14 Battle of Vinh Thuan.

May 23 NLF president Nguyen Huu Tho predicts escalation of war by United States.

June 2 Honolulu conference on increased American aid for RVN.

June 18 J. Blair Seaborn, Canadian representative to International Control Commission, meets secretly with Pham Van Dong in Hanoi.

July 5 Chou En-lai, prime minister of People's Republic of China, leads Chinese delegation to Hanoi to discuss situation with Pathet Lao in Laos.

July 30 RVN naval forces operating under OPLAN 34-A guidelines raid islands of Hon Me and Hon Niem, hoping to destroy DRV radar and radio facilities.

August 2–4 Gulf of Tonkin incident.

August 7 Gulf of Tonkin Resolution passes Congress, 88–2 in Senate and 416–0 in House.

August 30 NLF's Central Committee holds special plenum to discuss Gulf of Tonkin incident.

September Formation of Central Highlands front. NLF sends permanent representative to People's Republic of China.

September 21 More than 200,000 students and workers launch general strike in Saigon, seeking political and religious freedoms and an end to the curfew.

October 1 First issue of *People's Newspaper* is published.

October People's Republic of China explodes its first atomic bomb.

October 14 Nikita Khrushchev ousted; replaced by Leonid Brezhnev and Aleksei Kosygin.

November 3 Lyndon Johnson elected president of United States.

November 23 NLF delegation led by Tran Van Thanh visits Hanoi.

December First issue of *Liberation Newspaper* is published.

December 5–March 8 Binh Gia Campaign.

December 7–8 Battle of An Lao.

December 24 American military billet attacked in Saigon.

1965

January NLF sends its first official representative to Soviet Union. Aleksei Kosygin, chair of Soviet Union's Council of Ministers, visits Hanoi.

February 4 McGeorge Bundy, U.S. national security adviser, arrives in Saigon.

February 7 PLAF attacks U.S. Army installation at Play Ku.

February 10 PLAF attacks U.S. Army installation at Quy Nhon.

February 19 Johnson approves sustained bombing of DRV.

March 2 Operation ROLLING THUNDER begins.

March 8 First U.S. combat troops arrive in Viet Nam.

March 22 NLF announces Five-Point Peace Plan.

March 25–27 Eleventh Plenum of Lao Dong's Second Central Committee resolves to send aid to South and to "win a decisive victory . . . in a relatively short period of time."

March 30 NLF sappers attack U.S. embassy in Saigon.

April 7 Lyndon Johnson pledges $1 billion in development aid to Viet Nam and his preparedness to undertake unconditional discussions to end hostilities.

April 7–23 Lao Dong delegation led by Le Duan visits Soviet Union and People's Republic of China to discuss economic and military aid.

April 8 Premier Pham Van Dong announces DRV's Four-Point Plan for Peace.

May 7 Ho Chi Minh pays secret visit to Mao in Changsha, asks for aid in repairing and building roads and bridges in DRV.

May 10–11 Battle of Song Be.

May 12 Operation MAYFLOWER launched.

May 18 Secret discussions between Mai Van Bo and Edmund Gullion begin.

May 29–31 Battle of Ba Gia.

June PAVN general Van Tien Dung visits Peking to discuss China's military plans in Viet Nam.

June 8 Battle of O Mon.

June 9–12 Battle of Dong Xoai.

June 16 PLAF attacks Tan Son Nhut, Saigon's airport.

June 29–July 3 Battle of Thuan Man.

August 18 Battle of Van Tuong.

August 23 PLAF attacks Bien Hoa airport.

September Lao Dong's Political Bureau meets in special session. Mao Tse-tung proclaims Great Proletarian Cultural Revolution.

September 3 More than 10,000 people march in My Tho province to protest Saigon's forced conscription laws.

October 28 PLAF attacks airport at Chu Lai.

November 8 Battle of Dat Cuoc.

November 12 Battle of Bau Bang.

November 14–19 Battle of Ia Drang Valley.

November 16 NLF sends delegation of highly decorated PLAF soldiers to Hanoi for special recognition by Party.

December Harriman peace mission launched. Twelfth Plenum of Lao Dong's Second Central Committee approves Resolution 12, protracted war strategy, escalating controversy between hard-line southerners and northern doves who want to limit hostilities to South to protect nascent northern industries from American bombs.

December 25 Johnson announces pause in bombing of North Viet Nam.

1966

January Operation PINTA.

January 3 Dean Rusk announces Fourteen Points, comprehensive statement of the U.S. negotiating position on Viet Nam.

January 8 Battle of Cu Chi.

January 19–February 10 Battle of Phu Yen.

January 31 Johnson resumes bombing.

February 2 PLAF attacks Phu Cat airport.

February 8–12 Battle of Rach Gia.

February 17 PLAF attacks headquarters of U.S. command staff near Tan Son Nhut airport.

March–June Ronning mission.

March 22–25 Le Duan visits People's Republic of China.

March 26–April 16 Le Duan visits Soviet Union.

March 31 25,000 people march in Hue against new government of Nguyen Van Thieu.

April–June Tri-Thien Military Region formed.

April 2 Second round of demonstrations in Hue.

April 5 Battle of Gia Dinh.

April 8 Street demonstrations in Cho Lon, Tan An.

April 10 Demonstrations in My Tho province.

April 12 PLAF attacks Tan Son Nhut airport.

April 16–22 Third session of Third National Assembly meets in Hanoi.

May 16 Nationwide labor strike in South Viet Nam.

May 18 Battle of Ba Ria.

June 8 Battle of Cau Dam.

June 29 First American air attacks against Hanoi and Haiphong.

July Lao Dong issues Limited Mobilization Decree, calls up reserves and noncommissioned officers under broadened draft guidelines.

July 15 Battle of Quang Tri.

August 17 Battle of Da Nang.

August 28 PLAF attacks military airport in Vinh Long.

September 2 More than 100 ARVN troops revolt against their commanding officers.

September 22 Battle of Nui Mo.

October 18 Battle of Go Quao.

October 19 Medical students at Saigon University strike for classes in Vietnamese.

October 23–25 Manila conference.

October 28 Battle of Long Binh.

October 28–November 25 Battle of Tay Ninh.

November 10 Battle of Dau Tieng.

December 4 PLAF attacks Tan Son Nhut airport.

December 6 U.S. military headquarters at Kontum attacked. Operation MARIGOLD begins.

December 12 NLF delegation led by Nguyen Van Tien visits Hanoi.

December 15 Street demonstrations in Saigon.

December 26 Demonstrations close Port of Saigon.

1967

January 23–26 Thirteenth Plenum of Lao Dong's Second Central Committee calls for new emphasis on diplomatic struggle. Ho's proclamation that "the military is the bell, but diplomacy is the sound of the bell" suggests that Lao Dong is relying increasingly on USSR, which supports negotiations—a strategy that Peking denounces as dangerous revisionism.

February 6 Operation SUNFLOWER begins.

February 15 In a letter to Lyndon Johnson, Ho Chi Minh declares that "the people of Viet Nam are determined not to surrender under the threats of bombing."

March Huynh Tan Phat replaces Nguyen Huu Tho as chair of NLF Central Committee.

March 20 Rallies held all over Viet Nam in support of anti-aircraft batteries that have shot down American planes.

March 21 Lyndon Johnson, Nguyen Cao Ky, and Nguyen Van Thieu meet in Guam.

June 5 Fourth session of Third National Assembly.

June 25 Johnson meets Kosygin in Glassboro, N.J.

July–September: Operation PENNSYLVANIA.

July 6 Nguyen Chi Thanh, director of COSVN, dies of "serious heart attack" in Hanoi at age 53.

August Stokely Carmichael is greeted by Premier Pham Van Dong. Defense Secretary Robert S. McNamara, testifying before Congress, declares American bombing raids ineffective.

September 1 Special NFLSV congress plans for increased military struggle.

September 3 Nguyen Van Thieu elected president and Nguyen Cao Ky vice president of RVN.

September 29 Johnson announces "San Antonio formula": bombing halt in exchange for meaningful discussions and slowed infiltration.

October 20–22 Special enlarged plenum of NLF's Central Committee meets to assess battlefield situation, probably holds first discussions of Tet Offensive with Lao Dong leaders.

December Party debates after death of Nguyen Chi Thanh; decision on Tet Offensive probably finalized.

December 30 DRV foreign minister Nguyen Duy Trinh announces that peace talks "will" begin once U.S. halts its bombings.

1968

January 30–March 31 First stage of Tet Offensive.

February 11–12 Special NLF plenum discusses success of offensive.

April 21 Formation of Alliance of National, Democratic, and Peace Forces, another southern front with broad support in Saigon, especially among intellectuals and some Buddhists. Lao Dong looms large in this organization.

April 24 Political Bureau convenes to assess success of first stage of Tet Offensive.

May 3 DRV announces representatives to Paris peace talks.

May 13 Paris peace talks open.

May 19–22 Fourth session of Third National Assembly discusses strategy at Paris peace talks.

May 30 Le Duc Tho leaves for Paris to serve as special adviser to Xuan Thuy.

May 4–August 17 Second and third phases of Tet Offensive launched.

October 4 NLF holds Fourth Plenum on guerrilla warfare; Nguyen Thi Dinh reads special report.

November 3 NLF Central Committee announces Five-Point Political Plan for end to hostilities in South Viet Nam.

1969

January 25 Four-party conference on Viet Nam opens in Paris.

March 18 Newly elected president Richard Nixon begins secret bombing of Cambodia.

April Lao Dong's Political Bureau meets to discuss new military offensives in Central Highlands.

May 8 NFLSV offers ten-point plan to solve political and military stalemate. Two points: (1) withdrawal of all U.S. troops; (2) ARVN, PAVN, and PLAF negotiate withdrawal of their troops. Open call for all-Vietnamese solution has some support among ARVN and RVN National Assembly.

June 6–8 Provisional Revolutionary Government (PRG) formed: Huynh Tan Phat, architect, president; Nguyen Doa, Phung Van Cung, and Nguyen Van Kiet, vice presidents; Nguyen Huu Tho, president of advisory board; Trinh Dinh Thao, vice president of advisory board.

June 10 First Session of PRG.

June 13 Soviets officially recognize PRG.

August Henry Kissinger meets secretly with Xuan Thuy in Paris.

September 3 Ho Chi Minh dies.

September 9 Ho Chi Minh's funeral in Ba Dinh Square, Hanoi.

September 22–23 Fifth Session of Third National Assembly elects Ton Duc Thang president and Nguyen Luong Bang vice president.

September 27–October 26 Pham Van Dong visits Soviet Union, East Germany, and People's Republic of China.

November 3 Nixon delivers "silent majority" speech.

November 15 Moratorium against war held in Washington, D.C.

November 16 My Lai massacre of 1968 uncovered.

1970

January Eighteenth Plenum of Lao Dong's Second Central Committee, Third National Assembly, places renewed emphasis on political and diplomatic struggle movements.

February Le Duan publishes theoretical piece outlining twin goals of constructing socialism and national liberation.

February 20 Henry Kissinger begins secret discussions with Le Duc Tho in Paris.

March 18 Prince Norodom Sihanouk overthrown by Lon Nol in Cambodia.

April 30 Nixon announces Cambodian raids.

May National Guard kills student demonstrators at Kent State University in Ohio and Jackson State University in Mississippi.

June 19 Lao Dong's Political Bureau pledges military support for Laos and Cambodia.

September 17 Nguyen Thi Binh, PRG's foreign minister, announces Seven-Point Peace Plan in Paris.

December 10 Nguyen Thi Binh proposes comprehensive cease-fire based on Seven-Point Peace Plan.

1971

February Nineteenth Plenum of Lao Dong's Second Central Committee focuses on economic consolidation in North.

February 9 Planning for Route 9 offensive undertaken by Military Commission.

February–March ARVN offensives launched.

May Lao Dong's Political Bureau and Military Commission meet to discuss 1972 strategic military offensive.

June 13 *New York Times* begins to publish *Pentagon Papers.*

October 3 Nguyen Van Thieu reelected president of RVN.

1972

January 25 Nixon reveals that Kissinger has been negotiating secretly with DRV.

March 11 Military Commission issues resolution on 1972 offensive focusing on Thi Thieu battlefield.

April 4 Twentieth Plenum of Lao Dong's Second Central Committee reviews Easter offensive.

April 15 Nixon authorizes bombing of Hanoi and Haiphong.

April 20 Kissinger goes to Moscow to prepare for Nixon's summit meeting with Brezhnev on May 20.

May 1 PAVN captures Quang Tri City.

May 8 Nixon announces mining of Haiphong Harbor and intensification of bombing raids over Hanoi.

August 10 Foreign ministers of nonaligned nations, meeting in Georgetown, Guyana, recognize PRG.

October 17–22 Kissinger-Tho meetings produce peace draft. RVN and PRG reject key provisions.

November 7 Nixon reelected.

November 20 Kissinger resumes talks with Le Duc Tho, presents 69 new amendments to October peace draft.

December 15 Paris peace talks break down.

December 21 Christmas bombings of Hanoi and Haiphong.

1973

January 8 Paris peace talks resume.

January 23 Paris peace agreement initialed.

January 27 Cease-fire signed.

February 18–21 National Assembly ratifies Paris Peace Agreement.

June Military Commission meets to discuss future operations in South.

September COSVN holds its twelfth conference to discuss future operations in South.

October Twenty-first Plenum of Lao Dong's Second Central Committee considers two options stemming from June Military Commission meetings: (1) gradually force United States and RVN to carry out Paris agreement; (2) wage intense offensive in South. Decision: option 2.

1974

January Nguyen Van Thieu declares beginning of new Viet Nam War.

March Military Commission supervises formation of main force corps for final offensive.

September 30–October 8 Political Bureau meets to decide South's fate; Party adopts two-year plan for military victory.

1975

January Lao Dong's Political Bureau decides on major offensive under Senior General Van Tien Dung.

January 6 PAVN and PLAF capture Phuoc Long province.

February 5 General Van Tien Dung assumes command of southern offensive.

March 11 Le Duan, Political Bureau, and Military Commission decide to launch full-scale offensive.

March 30 PAVN captures Da Nang.

April 1 Lao Dong's Political Bureau decides to complete general offensive by end of April, much sooner than anticipated.

April 14 Political Bureau approves Ho Chi Minh campaign to liberate Saigon/Gia Dinh.

April 17 Phnom Penh falls to Khmer Rouge.

April 21 PAVN and PLAF capture Xuan Loc.

April 25 President Nguyen Van Thieu leaves Viet Nam for Taiwan; power is transferred to General Duong Van Minh.

April 30 PAVN armored tank division and PLAF forces take control of Independence Palace in Saigon; General Duong Van Minh surrenders.

NOTES

1. The Maquis: Origins of the NLF and Its Diplomatic Front

[1] Interview with Le Thi Hai, former NLF cadre, Ho Chi Minh City, July 1989.

[2] "A Threat to Peace: North Viet Nam's Effort to Conquer South Viet Nam," Department of State, 1961, 23, in Douglas Pike Collection, NLF Documents, document no. 000358, Indochina Archive, University of California at Berkeley.

[3] George McT. Kahin and John Lewis, *The United States in Viet Nam* (New York: Dial, 1967), 119.

[4] Philippe Devillers, "The Struggle for Unification in Vietnam," *China Quarterly* 9 (January–March 1962): 19.

[5] Nguyen Van Hieu, *Ban be tap khap nam chau* [Our friends around the world] (Hanoi: Nha Xuat Ban Van Hoc, 1963), 46.

[6] Truong Nhu Tang, *A Viet Cong Memoir: An Inside Account of the Vietnam War and Its Aftermath* (New York: Vintage, 1985), 65.

[7] Marvin Gettlemen, "Against Cartesianism: Three Generations of Vietnam Scholarship," in Douglas Allen and Ngo Vinh Long, eds., *Coming to Terms: Indochina, the United States, and the War* (Boulder: Westview, 1991), 235.

[8] William Conrad Gibbons, *The U.S. Government and the Vietnam War: Executive and Legislative Roles and Relationships*, vol. 1 (Princeton: Princeton University Press, 1986), 56.

[9] "How the Dien Bien Phu Battle Was Won," *Vietnamese Studies* 8 (March 1965): 68–69.

[10] Ho Chi Minh, *Nhung chang duong lich su ve van* [Glorious historic episodes] (Hanoi: Nha Xuat Ban Quan Doi Nhan Dan, 1973), 83–84.

[11] G. F. Hudson, Richard Lowenthal, and Roderick MacFaquhar, *The Sino-Soviet Dispute* (New York: Praeger, 1961), 43.

[12] Chen Jian, "China and the First Indochina War," *China Quarterly* 133 (March 1993): 107.

[13] General Vo Nguyen Giap, *People's War, People's Army* (Hanoi: Foreign Languages Publishing House, 1961), 29–30.

[14] Huynh Kim Khanh, *Vietnamese Communism, 1925–1945* (Ithaca: Cornell University Press, 1982), 265.

[15] Interview with Nguyen Dinh Ngo, vice president of the Fatherland Front, Thua-Thien-Hue province, Hue, July 1989.

[16] Carlyle A. Thayer, *War by Other Means: National Liberation and Revolution in Viet-Nam, 1954–1960* (Sydney/Boston: Allen & Unwin, 1989), 16.

[17] "How the Dien Bien Phu Battle Was Won," *Vietnamese Studies* 8 (March 1965): 56.

[18] *Tu Do* (Saigon daily newspaper), March 3, 1961.

[19] Dang Tran Xa, *Les reformes de sa majesté Bao Dai en Annam* (Paris: Domat-Montchrestien, 1939), 22.

[20] Bruce Lockhart, *The End of the Vietnamese Monarchy*, Lac Viet series 15 (New Haven: Council on Southeast Asian Studies, 1993), 78–86.

[21] Interview with Nguyen Xuan Oanh, economist and former RVN official, Ho Chi Minh City, July 1989.

[22] Stanley Karnow, *Vietnam: A History* (New York: Penguin, 1983), 218.

[23] National Security Council, "Review of U.S. Policy in the Far East" (August 1954), in *United States–Vietnam Relations*, vol. 10 (Washington, D.C.: Government Printing Office, 1971), 737.

[24] *Department of State Bulletin*, November 7, 1955.

[25] Karnow, *Vietnam*, 227.

[26] Thayer, *War by Other Means*, 57.

[27] Interview with Le Thi Hai, Ho Chi Minh City, July 1989.

[28] *Nhan Dan*, April 27, 1956.

[29] Ibid., April 28, 1956.

[30] "Report of the Eighth Session of the National Assembly, April 16–29, 1958," Viet Nam News Agency, April 17, 1958. Radio transcripts, Trung Tam Luu Tru Quoc Gia-1 (hereafter National Archives Center 1, Hanoi).

[31] Quang Tri province extends southward from the seventeenth parallel.

[32] Le Duan to Le Thi Hai, September 1939. The letter was shown to me by Le Thi Hai in Ho Chi Minh City, July 1989.

[33] Danny J. Whitfield, *Historical and Cultural Dictionary of Vietnam* (Metuchen, N.J.: Scarecrow Press, 1976), 141.

[34] *Nhan Dan*, October 30, 1956.

[35] Ibid.

[36] Le Duan, "Duong loi cach mang mien Nam" [The revolutionary path in the South], ca. 1956, National Archives Center 1, Hanoi.

[37] *Cuoc khang chien chong My, cuu nuoc, 1954–1975: Nhung su kien quan su* [The anti-U.S. resistance war for national salvation of the fatherland, 1954–1975: Military events] (Hanoi: Nha Xuat Ban Quan Doi Nhan Dan, 1988), 20.

[38] Interview with Nguyen Van Vinh, former NLF cadre, Hanoi, November 1995.

[39] Thayer, *War by Other Means*, 111.

[40] Le Duan, *Thu vao Nam* [Letters to the South] (Hanoi: Nha Xuat Ban Su That, 1986), 52.

[41] *Tinh hinh phong trao dau tranh chinh tri o Nam Bo tu hoa binh lap lai den hien nay* [The situation of the political struggle movement in Nam Bo from the restoration of peace to the present], Party document, ca. 1960, 19, National Archives Center 1, Hanoi.

[42] Ta Xuan Linh, "Armed Uprisings," *Vietnam Courier*, October 1974, 18–19.

[43] "Tinh hinh va nhiem vu 59" [The situation and tasks for 1959], Party document, ca. 1959, 7, National Archives Center 1, Hanoi.

[44] Jeffrey Race, *War Comes to Long An: Revolutionary Conflict in a Vietnamese Province* (Berkeley: University of California Press, 1972), 19.

[45] Nguyen Thi Dinh, *Khong con duong nao khac* [No other road to take] (Hanoi: Nha Xuat Ban Phu Nu, 1968), 58.

[46] As quoted in Jeffrey Race, "The Origins of the Second Indochina War," *Asian Survey* 10 (May 1969): 376.

[47] George McT. Kahin, *Intervention: How America Became Involved in Vietnam* (New York: Doubleday/Anchor, 1986), 110.

[48] *An Outline History of the Vietnam Workers' Party* (Hanoi: Foreign Languages Publishing House, 1970), 110–11.

[49] *Cuoc khang chien chong My*, 30.

[50] Ta Xuan Linh, "Armed Uprisings," *Vietnam Courier*, October 1974, 20.

[51] Le Duan, "Political Report of the Central Committee of the Lao Dong," in *Third National Congress of the Viet Nam Workers' Party: Documents*, vol. 1 (Hanoi: Foreign Languages Publishing House, 1961), 62–63.

[52] Khanh, *Vietnamese Communism*, 138.

[53] Tang, *Viet Cong Memoir*, 78–79.

[54] Interview with Le Thi Hai, Ho Chi Minh City, July 1989.

[55] Tang, *Viet Cong Memoir*, 85.

[56] Remarks by Nguyen Co Thach, former foreign minister of the Socialist Republic of Viet Nam, Hanoi, November 1995, in Critical Oral History Project transcripts, Watson Institute for International Studies, Brown University and Institute for International Relations, Hanoi.

[57] Douglas Pike, *Viet Cong: The Organization and Techniques of the National Liberation Front of South Vietnam* (Cambridge: MIT Press, 1966), 92–93.

[58] Ibid., 97.

[59] Race, *War Comes to Long An*, 150.

[60] Gerald Hickey, *Village in Vietnam* (New Haven: Yale University Press, 1964).

[61] Interview with Ngoc Quang Huynh, former resident of My Tho, Bennington, Vt., April 1989.

[62] Pike, *Viet Cong*, 99.

[63] Anthony Bouscaren, *The Last of the Mandarins: Diem of Vietnam* (Pittsburgh: University of Pittsburgh Press, 1965).

[64] *The Pentagon Papers: The Defense Department History of United States Deci-*

sionmaking on Vietnam, Senator Gravel ed., 4vols. (Boston: Beacon, 1971–72), 2:60.

[65] John F. Kennedy, "State of the Union Address, January 30, 1961," in *John F. Kennedy: The Public Papers of the President, 1961* (Washington, D.C.: Government Printing Office, 1962), 27.

[66] George C. Herring, *America's Longest War: The United States and Vietnam, 1950–1975*, 3d ed. (New York: McGraw-Hill, 1996), 85.

[67] Robert S. McNamara, personal communication, New York, August 1995.

[68] Maxwell Taylor, *Swords into Plowshares* (New York: Harper & Row, 1972), 241.

[69] Herring, *America's Longest War*, 91.

[70] Gibbons, *U.S. Government and the Vietnam War*, 2:82.

[71] Herring, *America's Longest War*, 91.

[72] William Bundy, "Reflections on Some Possible Outcomes of U.S. Intervention in South Vietnam, November 7, 1961," National Security Files, Vietnam, John F. Kennedy Presidential Library.

[73] General Bruce Palmer Jr., *The 25-Year War: America's Military Role in Vietnam* (Lexington: University of Kentucky Press, 1984), 30–31.

[74] Herring, *America's Longest War*, 95.

[75] *Cuoc khang chien chong My*, 47–48.

[76] Commission for Foreign Relations of the South Vietnam National Front for Liberation, *Personalities of the South Vietnam Liberation Movement* (Hanoi, 1965).

[77] Carlyle A. Thayer, "Southern Vietnamese Revolutionary Organizations and the Vietnam Workers' Party: Continuity and Change," in Joseph Zasloff and MacAlister Brown, eds., *Communism in Indochina* (Lexington, Mass.: D. C. Heath, 1975), 51.

[78] Interview with Le Thi Hai, Ho Chi Minh City, July 1989.

[79] Commission for Foreign Relations, *Personalities of the South Vietnam Liberation Movement*, 5.

[80] The August Revolution was the seizure of power by Ho Chi Minh's Communists at the time of the Japanese surrender in 1945. On September 2, 1945, Ho delivered Viet Nam's declaration of independence.

[81] Commission for Foreign Relations, *Personalities of the South Vietnam Liberation Movement*, 10.

[82] Ibid., 21.

[83] Pike, *Viet Cong*, 216.

[84] Tang, *Viet Cong Memoir*, 87.

[85] *Nhan Dan*, April 21, 1961.

[86] Sun Tzu, *The Art of War*, trans. Samuel B. Griffith (London: Oxford University Press, 1963).

[87] Interview with Le Thi Hai, Ho Chi Minh City, July 1989.

[88] Remarks by Nguyen Co Thach, November 1995, in Critical Oral History Project transcripts, Watson Institute for International Studies, Brown University and Institute for International Relations, Hanoi.

2. Our Friends Around the World: The NLF's Neutralist Platform

[1] Nguyen Van Hieu, *Ban be ta khap nam chau* [Our friends around the world] (Hanoi: Nha Xuat Ban Van Hoc, 1963), 11.

[2] Interview with Nguyen Van Tinh, former Lao Dong official, Hanoi, March 1996.

[3] Remarks by Nguyen Co Thach, former foreign minister of the Socialist Republic of Viet Nam, Hanoi, November 1995, in Critical Oral History Project transcripts, Watson Institute for International Studies, Brown University and the Institute for International Relations, Hanoi.

[4] "Resolution of the Third National Congress of the Viet Nam Workers' Party on the Tasks and Line of the Party in the New Stage," in *Third National Congress of the Viet Nam Workers' Party*, vol. 1 (Hanoi: Foreign Languages Publishing House, 1961).

[5] The goals enumerated in the NLF's Ten-Point Manifesto:

1. To overthrow the disguised colonial regime of the U.S. imperialists and the dictatorial Ngo Dinh Diem administration-lackey of the United States and to form a national democratic coalition administration.
2. To bring into being a broad and progressive democracy and to promulgate freedom of expression, of the press, of belief, of assembly, of association, and of movement and other democratic freedoms; to grant general amnesty to all political detainees, dissolve all concentration camps ("prosperity zones") and "resettlement centers," and abolish the fascist law 10–59 and other antidemocratic laws.
3. To abolish the economic monopoly of the United States and its henchmen, protect homemade products, encourage home industry and trade, expand agriculture, and build an independent and sovereign economy; to provide jobs for the unemployed and increase wages for workers, army personnel, and office employees; to abolish arbitrary fines and apply an equitable and rational tax system; to help displaced persons return home if that is their wish, and to provide jobs for those among them who want to remain in the South.
4. To reduce land rents, guarantee the peasants' right to till the plots of land they currently hold, redistribute communal land, and advance toward land reform.
5. To eliminate the enslaving and depraved U.S.-style culture, construct a national and progressive culture and educational system; to eliminate illiteracy, open more schools, carry out reform in the educational and examination systems.
6. To abolish the system of American military advisers, eliminate foreign military bases in Viet Nam, and build a national army for defense of the Fatherland and the people.
7. To guarantee equality between men and women and among nationalities and the autonomy of national minorities; to protect the legitimate interests of foreign residents in Viet Nam; to protect the interests of Vietnamese living abroad.
8. To carry out a foreign policy of peace and neutrality, and to establish diplo-

matic relations with all countries that respect the independence and sovereignty of Viet Nam.

9. To establish normal relations between the two zones and to work toward the peaceful reunification of the Fatherland.

10. To oppose aggressive war and actively to defend world peace.

Tran Van Giau and Le Van Chat, *The South Viet Nam Liberation National Front* (Hanoi: Foreign Languages Publishing House, 1962), 27–29.

[6] Le Duan, *Ta nhat dinh thang, dich nhat dinh thua* [We will certainly win, the enemy will certainly be defeated] (Hanoi: Nha Xuat Ban Tien Phong, 1966), 18; and *On The Socialist Revolution in Vietnam*, vol. 1 (Hanoi: Foreign Languages Publishing House, 1965).

[7] Giau and Chat, *South Viet Nam Liberation National Front*, 31.

[8] Broadcast to Europe and East Asia, in English, February 2, 1962, 1530 GMT, Radio Hanoi; radio transcripts, Trung Tam Luu Tru Quoc Gia-1 (hereafter National Archives Center 1, Hanoi).

[9] Interview with Nguyen Van Ho, former university professor, Ho Chi Minh City, March 1996.

[10] *Mot so van kien cua Dang ve chong My, cuu nuoc* [Selected Party documents related to the anti-U.S. resistance war for national salvation of the fatherland], vol. 1, *1954–1965* (Hanoi: Nha Xuat Ban Su That, 1985), 136–56.

[11] Interview with Tran Quang Co, Viet Nam's deputy foreign minister, Hanoi, November 1995.

[12] Clandestine broadcast in Vietnamese, June 12, 1962, 1400 GMT, Liberation Radio, radio transcripts, National Archives Center 1, Hanoi.

[13] Ibid.

[14] Hieu, *Ban be ta khap nam chau*, 10–11.

[15] Broadcast in French, June 27, 1962, 1800 GMT, International Service, Radio Prague, radio transcripts, National Archives Center 1, Hanoi.

[16] Hieu, *Ban be ta khap nam chau*, 12.

[17] Ibid., 15–19, 11.

[18] *New York Times*, July 9, 1962.

[19] "Some Historic Documents," *South Viet Nam in Struggle*, February 1965, 17–18.

[20] Huong Nam, "Nhan Dan 3 nuoc Dong-Duong tang cuong doan ket chong de quoc My va bon tay sai" [The people of the three Indochina nations were united against the American imperialists and their followers], *Hoc Tap* 16 (July 1970): 51.

[21] Hieu, *Ban be ta khap nam chau*, 75–79.

[22] *Eastern Star*, September 23, 1962.

[23] Interview with Tranh Quynh Cu, historian and former NLF political writer, Hanoi, July 1992.

[24] *Eastern Star*, September 28, 1963.

[25] Walter LaFeber, *The American Age: United States Foreign Policy at Home and Abroad since 1750* (New York: Norton, 1989), 536.

[26] Department of State, Central Files, "Telegram from the Embassy in Vietnam to the Department of State," document no. 751K.00/ 4–1662 (April 16, 1962), and "Telegram from the Embassy in Vietnam to the Department of State," docu-

ment no. 158 (April 16, 1962), both in *The Foreign Relations of the United States, 1961–1963: Vietnam, 1962* (Washington, D.C.: Government Printing Office, 1990), 2:329.

[27] Douglas Pike, *Viet Cong: The Organization and Techniques of the National Liberation Front of South Vietnam* (Cambridge: MIT Press, 1966), 366.

[28] *Declaration of the First Congress of the South Viet Nam National Front for Liberation* (Hanoi: Foreign Languages Publishing House, 1962), 20–24.

[29] "Prince Sihanouk," *Far Eastern Economic Review* 37 (July 26, 1962): 158.

[30] Interview with Le Thi Hai, former NLF cadre, Ho Chi Minh City, July 1989.

[31] Richard P. Stebbins, ed., *The United States in World Affairs, 1963* (New York: Council on Foreign Relations, 1964), 182–85; and Martin Goldstein, *American Policy Toward Laos* (Rutherford, N.J.: Fairleigh Dickinson University Press, 1973), 161–273.

[32] "Memorandum of a Conversation, United States Delegation Building, Geneva, July 22, 1962," document no. 246, in *Foreign Relations of the United States, 1961–1963: Vietnam, 1962*, 2:541–43.

[33] Dean Rusk, *As I Saw It* (New York: Norton, 1990), 369.

[34] Rudy Abramson, *Spanning the Century: The Life of W. Averell Harriman* (New York: Morrow, 1992), 605–6.

[35] Robert S. McNamara with Brian VanDeMark, *In Retrospect: The Tragedy and Lessons of Vietnam* (New York: Times Books, 1995), 62.

[36] Rusk, *As I Saw It*, 370.

[37] Remarks by Senior General Vo Nguyen Giap, Hanoi, November 1995, in Critical Oral History Project transcripts, Watson Institute for International Studies, Brown University and the Institute for International Relations, Hanoi.

[38] George McT. Kahin and John W. Lewis, *The United States in Vietnam* (New York: Dial, 1967), 281. On September 2, 1962, the People's Republic of China and the coalition government of Laos established formal diplomatic relations and signed an agreement for the exchange of diplomatic representatives at the ambassadorial level. See Peter Cheng, ed., *A Chronology of the People's Republic of China* (Totowa, N.J.: Littlefield, Adams, 1972), 149.

[39] Hieu, *Ban be ta khap nam chau*, 110.

[40] Ibid., 111, 112, 106.

[41] *Nhan Dan*, October 20, 1962.

[42] Pike, *Viet Cong*, 313.

[43] *Nhan Dan*, October 20, 1962.

[44] *Cuoc khang chien chong My, cuu nuoc, 1954–1975: Nhung su kien quan su* [The anti-U.S. resistance war for national salvation of the fatherland, 1954–1975: Military events] (Hanoi: Nha Xuat Ban Quan Doi Nhan Dan, 1988), 54.

[45] Remarks by Nguyen Co Thach, Hanoi, November 1995, in Critical Oral History Project transcripts, Watson Institute for International Studies, Brown University and the Institute for International Relations, Hanoi.

[46] Interview with Nguyen Thi Hai, former NLF cadre, Ho Chi Minh City, July 1989.

[47] Stanley Karnow, *Vietnam: A History* (New York: Penguin, 1983), 285.

[48] Interview with Tran Quynh Cu, Hanoi, July 1992.

[49] *New York Times*, September 13, 1963.

[50] Ibid., August 30, 1963.

[51] Fredrik Logevall, "De Gaulle, Neutralization, and American Involvement in Vietnam, 1963–1964," *Pacific Historical Review* 61 (February 1992): 69–102.

[52] Interview with a former NLF Central Committee member who requested anonymity, Hanoi, March 1996.

[53] Stebbins, *United States in World Affairs*, 119.

[54] "Memorandum of a Conference with the President, White House, Washington, August 28, 1963," document no. 1, in *Foreign Relations of the United States, 1961–1963: August–December, 1963* (Washington, D.C.: Government Printing Office, 1991), 4:5.

[55] "Memorandum from the Secretary of State (Rusk) to the President, January 8, 1964," document no. 8, in *The Foreign Relations of the United States, 1964–1968: Vietnam, 1964* (Washington, D.C.: Government Printing Office, 1992), 1: 9–10.

[56] Interview with Douglas Pike, former official with the U.S. Information Service in Saigon, Berkeley, October 1992.

[57] "Memorandum for the President, April 14, 1962," document no. 156, in *Foreign Relations of the United States, 1961–1963: Vietnam, 1962*, 2:327.

[58] Department of State, "Secretary's Memoranda of Conversation, United States Delegation Building, Geneva, July 22, 1962," document no. 65D 330, and "Memorandum of a Conversation, Barrington's Suite, Hotel Suisse, Geneva, July 22, 1962," document no. 247, both ibid., 541–46.

[59] Interview with Hue Phuc Le, former university professor, Ho Chi Minh City, March 1996.

[60] Interview with a former NLF Central Committee member who requested anonymity, Hanoi, March 1996.

[61] Interview with a former Lao Dong official who requested anonymity, Hanoi, November 1995.

[62] *New York Times*, September 23, 1963.

[63] "Diplomatic and Psychological Offensive of the National Liberation Front," in Douglas Pike Collection, NLF Documents, document no. 001485, Indochina Archive, University of California at Berkeley (hereafter Pike Collection).

[64] Chester A. Bain, "Viet Cong Propaganda Abroad," *Foreign Service Journal*, October 1968, 3.

[65] *New York Times*, September 3, 1963.

[66] Chester Cooper, personal communication, Washington, April 1997.

[67] "Memorandum from the Counselor for Public Affairs of the Embassy in Vietnam (Mecklin) to the Director of the United States Information Agency (Murrow)," document no. 81, September 10, 1963, in *Foreign Relations of the United States, 1961–1963: Vietnam, August–December 1963*, 4:152.

[68] "Memorandum Prepared by Michael V. Forrestal of the National Security Council Staff," document no. 91, September 11, 1963, ibid., 183.

[69] "Memorandum from the Director of the United States Information Agency (Murrow) to the President's Special Assistant for National Security Affairs (Bundy)," document no. 108, September 14, 1963, ibid., 210–11.

[70] "Memorandum of a Conversation by the Secretary of Defense (McNamara), Saigon, September 30, 1963," document no. 160, September 30, 1963, ibid., 324.

[71] Interview with Douglas Pike, Berkeley, October 1992.

[72] "Interview with the President, Hyannis Port, Massachusetts, September 2, 1963," document no. 50, in *Foreign Relations of the United States, Vietnam, 1961–1963: August–December, 1963*, 4:93–94.

[73] Michael Forrestal oral history interview, Lyndon Baines Johnson Presidential Library, Austin, Tex.

[74] "Secretary of State Dean Rusk to Ambassador Bohlen, November 25, 1963," National Security Files, Country File Vietnam, Box 169, ibid.

[75] "Memorandum from the Chairperson of the Policy Planning Council (Rostow) to the Secretary of State (Rusk)," document no. 9, January 10, 1964, in *Foreign Relations of the United States, Vietnam, 1964–1968: Vietnam, 1964*, 1:15.

[76] Clandestine broadcast in Vietnamese, November 30, 1964, 1400 GMT, Liberation Radio, radio transcripts, National Archives Center 1, Hanoi.

[77] Ibid., December 28, 1964.

[78] *The Pentagon Papers: The Defense Department History of United States Decisionmaking on Vietnam*, Senator Gravel ed., 4 vols. (Boston: Beacon, 1971–72), 2:193–94.

[79] Karnow, *Vietnam*, 326–27.

[80] McGeorge Bundy to President Johnson, February 1, 1964, in National Security Files, Box 2, Lyndon Johnson Papers, Lyndon Baines Johnson Presidential Library.

[81] *New York Times*, November 10, 1963.

[82] Henry Cabot Lodge to Dean Rusk, December 18, 1963, in National Security Files, Country File Vietnam, Box 169, Lyndon Baines Johnson Presidential Library.

[83] *Pentagon Papers*, 2:193.

[84] Interview with Douglas Pike, Berkeley, October 1992.

[85] *Pentagon Papers*, 3:37–39.

[86] "Telegram from the Central Intelligence Agency Station in Saigon to the Agency," document no. 18, January 28, 1964, in *Foreign Relations of the United States, Vietnam, 1964–1968: Vietnam, 1964*, 1:36.

[87] "Telegram from the Embassy in Vietnam to the Department of State," document no. 19, January 29, 1964, ibid., 38–39.

[88] *Pentagon Papers*, 3:37–39.

[89] Logevall, "De Gaulle, Neutralization, and American Involvement," 87.

[90] Charles Bohlen to Dean Rusk, March 9, 1964, in National Security Files, Country File Vietnam, Box 169, Lyndon Baines Johnson Presidential Library.

[91] George Ball to Johnson and Rusk, June 5, 1964, in Box 170, ibid.

[92] See, e.g., Fredrik Logevall, "The Swedish-American Conflict over Vietnam," *Diplomatic History* 17 (Summer 1993): 421–45.

[93] *New York Times*, July 9, 1964.

[94] Marcus G. Raskin and Bernard B. Fall, eds., *The Vietnam Reader: Articles and Documents on American Foreign Policy and the Vietnam Crisis* (New York: Vintage, 1967), 270–71.

[95] Hanoi later withdrew its support.

[96] Clandestine broadcast in Vietnamese, July 28, 1964, 1400 GMT, Liberation Radio, radio transcripts, National Archives Center 1, Hanoi.

[97] *New York Times*, July 25, 1964.

[98] *Pentagon Papers,* 3:173.

[99] George McT. Kahin, *Intervention: How America Became Involved in Vietnam* (New York: Doubleday/Anchor, 1986), 236–86.

[100] The Gulf of Tonkin Resolution, which was passed by the U.S. Senate with only two dissenting votes, gave the president the authority to respond to "hostile action against the United States" without the congressional deliberations called for by the U.S. Constitution.

[101] *Nhan Dan,* August 18, 1964.

[102] Tuyet-Nguyet Makbreiter, "Interview with Thich Tri Quang," *Far Eastern Economic Review* 47 (March 12, 1965): 436–37; and P. H. M. Jones, "The Holy Alliance," ibid. 48 (April 1, 1965): 48–49. The Self-Determination Movement (Phong Trao Dan Toc Tu Quyet Mien Nam Viet Nam), formed in 1964 under the direction of several members of the NLF, comprised various professional, intellectual, and business leaders in Saigon.

[103] Kahin, *Intervention,* 232–33.

[104] Central Intelligence Agency, "The Situation in South Vietnam," *Weekly Reports,* August 20–27, 1964.

[105] "Telegram from the Embassy in Vietnam to the Department of State," document no. 337, September 2, 1964, in *Foreign Relations of the United States, Vietnam, 1964–1968: Vietnam, 1964,* 1:727.

[106] Interview with Buddhist leaders, Ho Chi Minh City, July 1989. George Kahin's interviews with Buddhist leaders coincide with this conclusion. See his *Intervention,* 510–11n.

[107] Tran Van Don, *Our Endless War Inside Vietnam* (San Rafeal: Presidio Press, 1978), 167. Khanh confirmed this contact during a January 1975 press conference in France.

[108] Ibid., 139.

[109] Huynh Tan Phat to Nguyen Khanh, January 28, 1965, mimeographed and distributed by Khanh to scholars and the press on January 26, 1975.

[110] Truong Nhu Tang, *A Viet Cong Memoir: An Inside Account of the Vietnam War and Its Aftermath* (New York: Vintage, 1985), 96–97.

[111] Interview with Le Mau Han, historian, Hanoi, July 1992.

[112] Clandestine broadcast in Vietnamese, February 28, 1965, 0539 GMT, Liberation Radio, radio transcripts, National Archives Center 1, Hanoi.

[113] "Report on Propaganda and Foreign Affairs," in Pike Collection.

[114] Interview with a Lao Dong official who requested anonymity, Hanoi, November 1995. Several former northern Party officials interviewed in July 1992 revealed the same lack of understanding of the NLF's overseas diplomatic mission.

[115] For a summary of events at the Ninth Party Plenum, see *Mot so van kien cua Dang ve chong My,* 1:154–210; Le Duan, *Some Questions Concerning the International Tasks of Our Party: Speech at the Ninth Plenum of the Third Central Committee of the Viet Nam Workers' Party, December 1963* (Peking: Foreign Languages Press, 1964); *Communist Strategy as Reflected in Lao Dong Party and COSVN Resolutions* (Saigon: U.S. Military Assistance Command, 1964); and "The Viet-Nam Workers' Party's 1963 Decision to Escalate the War in the South," *Viet-Nam Documents and Research Notes,* document no. 96, July 1971.

[116] Liberation Radio announced the change on February 24, 1964, in a clandes-

tine broadcast in Vietnamese, 1400 GMT, radio transcripts, National Archives Center 1, Hanoi.

[117] Le Duan, *Thu vao Nam* [Letters to the South] (Hanoi: Nha Xuat Ban Su That, 1986), 74.

[118] See, e.g., Thomas Latimer, "Hanoi's Leaders and Their South Vietnam Policies, 1954–1968" (Ph.D. diss., Georgetown University, 1972), 128–31; Donald Zagoria, *Vietnam Triangle* (New York: Pegasus, 1967), 108.

[119] William J. Duiker, "Waging Revolutionary War: The Evolution of Hanoi's Strategy in the South, 1959–1965," in Jayne S. Werner and Luu Doan Huynh, eds., *The Vietnam War: Vietnamese and American Perspectives* (Armonk, N.Y.: M. E. Sharpe, 1993), 34.

[120] Interview with a Lao Dong official who requested anonymity, Hanoi, November 1995.

3. Haunted by Geneva: The Bombing Pauses of 1965

[1] Clandestine broadcast in Vietnamese, August 14, 1965, 1430 GMT, Liberation Radio, radio transcripts, Trung Tam Luu Tru Quoc Gia-1 (hereafter National Archives Center 1, Hanoi).

[2] Interview with a former NLF official who requested anonymity, Ho Chi Minh City, July 1989.

[3] Interview with Le Thi Hai, former NLF cadre, My Tho, July 1989.

[4] Carlyle A. Thayer, *War by Other Means: National Liberation and Revolution in Viet-Nam, 1954–1960* (Sydney/Boston: Allen & Unwin, 1989).

[5] Chester Cooper oral history interview, Lyndon Baines Johnson Presidential Library, Austin, Tex., 10.

[6] *The Pentagon Papers: The Defense Department History of the United States Decisionmaking on Vietnam*, Senator Gravel ed., 4 vols. (Boston: Beacon, 1971–72), 3:418.

[7] Neil Sheehan, Hedrick Smith, E.W. Kenworthy, and Fox Butterfield, eds., *The Pentagon Papers as Published by the New York Times* (New York: Bantam, 1971), 412.

[8] George C. Herring, *America's Longest War: The United States and Vietnam, 1950–1975*, 2d ed. (New York: Knopf, 1986), 139.

[9] Pham Van Dong announced Hanoi's Four-Point Plan for Peace on April 7, 1965. The four points:

1. Recognition of the basic national rights of the Vietnamese people—peace, independence, sovereignty, unity, territorial integrity. In accordance with the Geneva Accords, the U.S. government must withdraw its troops, military personnel, and weapons of all kinds from South Viet Nam, dismantle all U.S. military bases there, and cancel its military alliance with South Viet Nam. It must end its policy of intervention and aggression in South Viet Nam, stop its acts of war against North Viet Nam, and completely cease all encroachments on the territory and sovereignty of the DRV.
2. Pending the peaceful reunification of Viet Nam, while Viet Nam is still temporarily divided into two zones, the military provisions of the 1954 Geneva Accords on Viet Nam must be strictly respected. The two zones must refrain

from entering into any military alliance with foreign countries and there must be no foreign military bases, troops, or military personnel in either territory.

3. The internal affairs of South Viet Nam must be settled by the Vietnamese people themselves in accordance with the program of the National Front for the Liberation of South Viet Nam, with no foreign interference.
4. The peaceful reunification of Viet Nam is to be settled by the Vietnamese people in both zones, with no foreign interference.

Broadcast to Europe and East Asia, in English, April 13, 1965, 0539 GMT, Radio Hanoi, radio transcripts, National Archives Center 1, Hanoi. For the importance of the Four Points in the Lao Dong's diplomatic strategy, see Nguyen Duy Trinh, "Lap Truong Bon Diem, ngon co doc lap va hoa binh cua chung ta hien nay" [The Four-Point Stand, our banner of independence and peace at the present time], *Hoc Tap* 13 (April 1967): 10–22.

[10] "NLF's Five Points," document no. 000115, and "The Five Point Peace Plan," document no. 001478, Douglas Pike Collection, NLF Documents, Indochina Archive, University of California at Berkeley (hereafter Pike Collection).

[11] Marcus Raskin and Bernard Fall, eds., *The Viet-Nam Reader: Articles and Documents on American Foreign Policy and the Viet-Nam Crisis* (New York: Random House, 1965), 232–49; changes 249–52.

[12] Remarks by Nguyen Co Thach, Hanoi, November 1995, in Critical Oral History Project transcripts, Watson Institute for International Studies, Brown University and Institute for International Relations, Hanoi.

[13] Interview with a Lao Dong official who requested anonymity, Hanoi, July 1992.

[14] Ibid., November 1995.

[15] Interview with a former NLF official who requested anonymity, Ho Chi Minh City, July 1989.

[16] CIA, Directorate of Intelligence, "The Situation in South Vietnam, 31 March 1965–7 April 1965," document no. 000345, Pike Collection.

[17] Dean Rusk, *As I Saw It* (New York: Norton, 1990), 399.

[18] George C. Herring, ed., *The Secret Diplomacy of the Vietnam War: The Negotiating Volumes of the Pentagon Papers* (Austin: University of Texas Press, 1983), 53, 57.

[19] Ibid., 64.

[20] Broadcast to Europe and East Asia, in English, May 15, 1965, 1400 GMT, Radio Hanoi, radio transcripts, National Archives Center 1, Hanoi.

[21] *Pentagon Papers*, 3:354–56.

[22] Chester Cooper, *The Lost Crusade*, rev. ed. (Greenwich, Conn.: Fawcett, 1972), 271–72.

[23] Wallace Thies, *When Governments Collide: Coercion and Diplomacy in the Vietnam Conflict, 1964–1968* (Berkeley: University of California Press), 95; George W. Ball, *The Past Has Another Pattern: Memoirs* (New York: Norton, 1982), 404; and David Kraslow and Stuart H. Loory, *The Secret Search for Peace in Vietnam* (New York: Random House, 1968), 123–24.

[24] "Record of the Meeting in the President's Office, May 16, 1965," Johnson Papers, Meeting Notes File, Box 1, Lyndon Baines Johnson Presidential Library.

[25] Herring, *Secret Diplomacy*, 69.

[26] Because of the time difference between Hanoi and Paris, both the resumption of the bombing and Bo's visit took place on the morning of May 18, 1965.

[27] Herring, *Secret Diplomacy*, 72. Unfortunately, Bo's memoirs make little reference to his secret contacts in 1965. See Mai Van Bo, *Hanoi-Paris: Hoi ky ngoai giao cua* [Hanoi-Paris: Personal memories of the secret diplomacy] (Ho Chi Minh City: Nha Xuat Ban Van Nghe, 1993).

[28] Herring, *Secret Diplomacy*, 73.

[29] Kraslow and Loory, *Secret Search for Peace*, 123.

[30] Luu Van Loi and Nguyen Anh Vu, *Tiep xuc bi mat Viet Nam—Hoa Ky truoc hoi nghi Pa-ri* [Secret contacts between Viet Nam and the United States before the Paris talks] (Hanoi: Vien Quan He Quoc Te, 1990), 92–98.

[31] *Pentagon Papers*, 3:467.

[32] Thies, *When Governments Collide*, 106.

[33] Loi and Vu, *Tiep xuc*, 88.

[34] Herring, *Secret Diplomacy*, 80, 82.

[35] Ibid., 85; *Le Monde*, August 13, 1965.

[36] Herring, *Secret Diplomacy*, 85, 106, 107.

[37] Ibid., 85–87.

[38] An official history from Hanoi reports, "Gullion wanted to meet again on September 7, 1965, but Mai Van Bo refused. During the four previous meetings with Mai Van Bo, Gullion kept mentioning the withdrawal of U.S. troops as a concession, but Washington continued to bring combat ground forces to South Vietnam. His activity was just part of the American scheme to cover U.S. escalation." See Loi and Vu, *Tiep xuc*, 95.

[39] Quoted in Jeffrey Race, *War Comes to Long An: Revolutionary Conflict in a Vietnamese Province* (Berkeley: University of California Press, 1972), 74.

[40] Interview with a former NLF official who requested anonymity, Hanoi, July 1992.

[41] In 1965 alone the Party's theoretical journal, *Hoc Tap*, published more than twenty essays concerning the dilemma presented by the twin revolutionary goals. Most urged Lao Dong leaders to pursue both policies at once. A few examples: Nguyen Tho Can, "Quang-ninh day manh san xuat va san sang chien dau" [Quang-ninh steps up production and combat readiness], *Hoc Tap* 11 (April 1965): 64–69; Nguyen Tu Thoan, "Quang-binh vua san xuat vua chien dau thang loi" [Quang-binh both produces and fights successfully], ibid. (June 1965): 30–35; Nguyen Duy Trinh, "Tang cuong nha nuoc dan chu nhan dan de lam tot nhiem vu vua san xuat vua chien dau" [Let us strengthen the people's democratic state to fulfill the task of production and combat], ibid. (September 1965): 24–31; and Phan Hanh, "Ket hop dau tranh chinh tri voi dau tranh vu trang la hinh thuc dau tranh sang tao cua cach mang mien Nam" [A combination of the political struggle with the armed struggle is the creative form of the revolution in the South], ibid. (July 1965): 30–38.

[42] Le Duan, *Thu vao Nam* [Letters to the South] (Hanoi: Nha Xuat Ban Su That, 1986), 97–162; and *Nhan Dan*, August 6, 1965.

[43] Le Thanh Nghi, "Phat huy cao do chu nghia anh hung cach mang, day manh cao trao thi dua chong My, cuu nuoc, quyet tam danh thang giac My xam luc"

[Promote revolutionary heroism, enhance the anti-U.S. resistance movement for national salvation, determine to defeat U.S. aggressors], *Hoc Tap* 13 (January 1967): 21–45.

[44] *Chu Tich Ho Chi Minh voi cong tac ngoai giao* [President Ho Chi Minh and the diplomatic works] (Hanoi: Nha Xuan Ban Su That, 1990), 199–212.

[45] *Nhan Dan*, August 6, 1965.

[46] *Hoc Tap* published a summary of Tho's comments: Le Duc Tho, "Chuyen huong va tang cuong cong tac xay dung Dang de bao dam hoan thanh thang loi su nghiep chong My, cuu nuoc" [Change direction and build up the Party to complete the victory in the anti-U.S. resistance war for national salvation of the fatherland], *Hoc Tap* 12 (February 1966): 14.

[47] Ibid., 15, and P. J. Honey, "North Vietnam Quarterly Survey, no. 20," *China News Analysis* 604 (March 18, 1966): 4.

[48] Nguyen Chi Thanh, "Cang thuoc tu tuong cong viec giua luc luong vu trang va nhan dan o mien Nam va 1965–66 kho mua thang loi" [The ideological task among the armed forces and people of our South and the 1965–66 dry season victories], *Hoc Tap* 12 (July 1966): 1–10.

[49] Nguyen Chi Thanh, *Who Will Win in South Viet Nam?* (Peking: Foreign Languages Press, 1963), 8–9.

[50] Truong Chinh first raised this problem during the Lao Dong's Ninth Enlarged Session of the Central Committee: "Bao Cao cua Dong chi Truong Chinh o Hoi Nghi Trung Uong Lan Thu 9 mo rong, 20.4.56" [Report by Comrade Truong Chinh at the 9th Enlarged Session of the Central Committee, 4/20/.56], *Nhan Dan*, April 28, 1956. He repeated this theme in several essays, including "De thau suot nghi quyet cua dai hoi toan quoc lan thu III cua Dang" [To thoroughly understand the resolution of the Third Party Congress], *Hoc Tap* 7 (April 1961): 10–36, and "Nam vung moi quan he giua chien tranh va cach mang o Viet Nam de hoan thanh thang loi su nghiep chong My, cuu nuoc" [Let us fully understand the relationship between war and revolution in our anti-U.S. resistance war for national salvation of the fatherland], *Hoc Tap* 11 (September 1965): 18–23.

[51] Ha Van Lu, "That bai va khung hoang tram tong cua de quoc My va be lu tay sai o mien Nam" [Serious failure of the U.S. imperialists and their henchmen in the South], *Hoc Tap* 10 (October 1964): 58–65, and "Van de giai phong dan toc trong thoi dai hien nay" [The question of national liberation in the present era], ibid. (March 1964): 1–12.

[52] *Cuoc khang chien chong My, cuu nuoc, 1954–1975: Nhang su kien quan su* [The anti-U.S. resistance war for national salvation of the fatherland, 1954–1975: Military events] (Hanoi: Nha Xuat Ban Quan Doi Nhan Dan, 1988), 85.

[53] Le Duan, *Thu vao Nam*, 124–30, and "Cuu nuoc la nghia vu thieng lieng cua ca dan toc ta" [National salvation is the sacred mission of our people], *Hoc Tap* 12 (December 1966): 7–13.

[54] General Nguyen Van Vinh, *Address before the Fourth Congress of the Directorate of the Central Committee–Mien Nam [southern region of Viet Nam]* (Ben Tre: Victory Publishing House, 1966).

[55] Duan, *Thu vao Nam*, 127.

[56] Interview with a Lao Dong official who requested anonymity, Hanoi, June 1997.

[57] Broadcast to Europe and East Asia, in English, September 2, 1965, 0540 GMT, Radio Hanoi, radio transcripts, National Archives Center 1, Hanoi.

[58] *Vietnam Courier*, September 27, 1965. The NLF had announced a five-point plan for peace shortly before Pham Van Dong's April 7 proclamation of the Lao Dong's four-point plan.

[59] *Luc luong vu trang nhan dan Tay nguyen trong khang chien chong My, cuu nuoc* [The people's armed forces of the Western Highlands during the anti-U.S. resistance war for national salvation of the fatherland] (Hanoi: Nha Xuat Ban Quan Doi Nhan Dan, 1980), 69–90.

[60] *Lich Su Quan Doi Nhan Dan Viet Nam* [History of the People's Army of Vietnam], vol. 2, bk. 1 (Hanoi: Nha Xuat Ban Quan Doi Nhan Dan, 1988), 312–15.

[61] Clandestine broadcast in Vietnamese, September 12, 1965, 1430 GMT, Liberation Radio, radio transcripts, National Archives Center 1, Hanoi.

[62] Duan, *Thu vao Nam*, 121–23.

[63] Ibid., 125, 119, 123–24.

[64] Interview with a Lao Dong official who requested anonymity, Hanoi, November 1995.

[65] Ibid., Hanoi, July 1992.

[66] "Peace in South Viet Nam," document no. 002262, Pike Collection.

[67] Broadcast in English, November 1, 1965, 1720 GMT, International Service, Viet Nam News Agency, radio transcripts, National Archives Center 1, Hanoi.

[68] Interview with a former NLF official who requested anonymity, Ho Chi Minh City, March 1996. For a good report on U.S.-Swedish relations during the war, see Fredrik Logevall, "The Swedish-American Conflict over Vietnam," *Diplomatic History* 17 (Summer 1993): 421–45.

[69] Broadcast in English, November 18, 1965, 0539 GMT, International Service, Viet Nam News Agency, radio transcripts, National Archives Center 1, Hanoi.

[70] "We Shall Win in South Viet Nam," document no. 00263, Pike Collection.

[71] *Mainichi Shimbun*, November 19, 1965.

[72] Wilfred Burchett summarizes his many interviews with NLF leaders in his *Vietnam Will Win!* (New York: Guardian Books, 1968).

[73] Clandestine broadcast in Vietnamese, December 20, 1965, 0900 GMT, Liberation Radio, radio transcripts, National Archives Center 1, Hanoi; Nguyen Huu Tho, *Speech of the President of the Presidium of the Central Committee of the South Viet Nam National Front for Liberation on the Occasion of the Fifth Founding Anniversary of the NFL* (Saigon: Liberation Editions, 1965), document no. 000095, Pike Collection; broadcast in English, December 13, 1965, 0554 GMT, International Service, Viet Nam News Agency, radio transcripts, National Archives Center 1, Hanoi; and *Discours du président Nguyen Huu Tho à l'occasion du cinquième anniversaire de la fondation du FNLSVN, 20 décembre 1965* (Saigon: Editions en Langages Etrangers, 1966).

[74] Clandestine broadcast in Vietnamese, December 12, 1965, 1530 GMT, Liberation Radio, radio transcripts, National Archives Center 1, Hanoi.

[75] Duan, *Thu vao Nam*, 97–118.

[76] Thies, *When Governments Collide*, 338.

[77] Thanh, "Cach thuoc," 1–10.

[78] *Cuoc khang chien chong My*, 83–86.

[79] "Communist Strategy as Reflected in Lao Dong Party and COSVN Resolutions," document no. SRAP 1569, United States Military Assistance Command, Saigon.

[80] Broadcast to Europe and East Asia, in English, December 22, 1965, 1600 GMT, Radio Hanoi, radio transcripts, National Archives Center 1, Hanoi.

[81] Interview with Tranh Quynh Cu, historian, Hanoi, July 1992.

[82] Robert S. McNamara with Brian VanDeMark, *In Retrospect: The Tragedy and Lessons of Vietnam* (New York: Times Books, 1995), 224.

[83] Herring, *Secret Diplomacy*, 144–45.

[84] Chester Cooper, oral history interview, Lyndon Baines Johnson Presidential Library, 22–23.

[85] Herring, *Secret Diplomacy*, 129.

[86] Broadcast to Southeast Asia, in Vietnamese, January 4, 1966, 1740 GMT, Radio Hanoi, radio transcripts, National Archives Center 1, Hanoi.

[87] *Chu Tich Ho Chi Minh voi cong tac ngoai giao*, 207, and Ho Chi Minh, *Toan Tap* [Complete works], vol. 10 (Hanoi: Nha Xuat Ban Su That, 1990), 280–85. The *New York Times* reprinted Ho's letter on January 29, 1966.

[88] Herring, *Secret Diplomacy*, 156.

[89] Associated Press release, "President's Announcement of His Intended Trip to Honolulu," February 4, 1966; "Declaration of Honolulu," *New York Times*, February 7, 1966; and National Security Files, Memos to the President, "Memorandum for the President from Walt Rostow," April 5, 1966, Box 7, Lyndon Baines Johnson Presidential Library.

[90] Nguyen Viet Phuong, *Van tai quan su chien luoc tren Duong Ho Chi Minh trong khang chien chong My* [Strategic military transport on the Ho Chi Minh Trail during the war against the Americans] (Hanoi: Tong Cuc Hau Can, Nha Xuat Ban Quan Doi Nhan Dan, 1988), 278–95; *Tong ket cong tac hau can: chien truong Nam Bo cuc Nam Trung Bo (B.2) trong khang chien chong My* [Rear services operations report: Southern Region battlefield, South Central (B-2) department, during the war against the Americans] (Hanoi: Tong Cuc Hau Can Nha Xuat Ban Quan Doi Nhan Dan, 1986), 340–75; *Su Doan Dong Bang, Su Doan 320B, Quan Doan 1* [The Delta Division, 320 B Division, 1st Corps] (Hanoi: Nha Xuat Ban Quan Doi Nhan Dan, 1983), 24–26; and Nguyen Quyet, *Quan Khu Ba, nhung nam danh My* [Military Region 3, the years of fighting the Americans] (Hanoi: Nha Xuat Ban Quan Doi Nhan Dan, 1989), 53–66.

[91] "Summary Notes of the National Security Council Meeting, January 29, 1966," in Johnson Papers, NSC Meetings, Box 2, Lyndon Baines Johnson Presidential Library.

4. Glory Days: The NLF's Diplomatic Victories of 1966–1967

[1] Interview with Senior General Hoang Minh Thao, Hanoi, November 1995.

[2] The number of sorties against the North increased from 25,000 in 1965 to 79,000 in 1967 while the tonnage of bombs increased from 63,000 to 226,000: personal communication, Robert S. McNamara, former secretary of defense, Washington, D.C., June 1996.

[3] George C. Herring, *America's Longest War: The United States and Vietnam, 1950–1975*, 2d ed. (New York: Knopf, 1986), 164.

[4] Ibid., 148.

[5] David Floyd, *Mao against Khrushchev: A Short History of the Sino-Soviet Conflict* (New York: Praeger, 1963), 68.

[6] As reported in *Nhan Dan*, December 2, 1960.

[7] Donald S. Zagoria, *Vietnam Triangle: Moscow, Peking, Hanoi* (New York: Pegasus, 1967), 57–58.

[8] Anatoly Dobrynin, *In Confidence: Moscow's Ambassador to Six Cold War Presidents* (New York: Times Books, 1995), 140, 157.

[9] Interview with Tran Huu Dinh, historian, Hanoi, July 1992.

[10] Thomas Latimer, "Hanoi's Leaders and Their South Vietnam Policies, 1954–1968" (Ph.D. diss., Georgetown University, 1972).

[11] Chen Jian, "China's Involvement in the Vietnam War, 1964–1969," *China Quarterly* 142 (June 1995): 383.

[12] Interview with a former NLF official who requested anonymity, Hanoi, July 1992.

[13] Interview with a Lao Dong official who requested anonymity, Hanoi, July 1992.

[14] Hoang Minh Thao, "Quan diem chien tranh nhan dan cua Dang ta" [Our party's view of people's war], *Hoc Tap* 12 (December 1966): 29.

[15] *Hoc Tap* 12 (September 1966): 2.

[16] Le Duan, "Cuu nuoc la nghia vu thieng lieng cua ca dan toc ta" [National salvation is the sacred mission of our people], *Hoc Tap* 12 (December 1966): 7–13.

[17] Hong Chuong, "Lanh tu va quan chung" [Leaders and the masses], *Hoc Tap* 13 (May 1967): 61–66. See also Melvin Gurtov, *Hanoi on War and Peace* (Santa Monica: Rand Corporation, 1967), 23.

[18] Foreign Relations Commission, *Personalities of the South Vietnam Liberation Movement* (Tran Phu: South Vietnam National Front for Liberation, 1965).

[19] Interview with Tran Van Do, former NLF official, Ho Chi Minh City, July 1989.

[20] Chester A. Bain, "Viet Cong Propaganda Abroad," *Foreign Service Journal*, October 1968, 7.

[21] Broadcast in English, December 19, 1966, 1600 GMT, International Service, Radio Peking, radio transcripts, Trung Tam Luu Tru Quoc Gia-1 (hereafter National Archives Center 1, Hanoi).

[22] "South Vietnam People's Delegation Welcomed in Kwangchow," document no. 002722, Douglas Pike Collection, NLF Documents, Indochina Archive, University of California at Berkeley (hereafter Pike Collection).

[23] Ibid.

[24] "China Supports the NLF," document no. 001495, Pike Collection.

[25] *People's Daily*, December 20, 1966.

[26] Interview with Tung Le, former NLF official, Ho Chi Minh City, March 1996.

[27] *New York Times*, January 5, 1967.

[28] Ibid., January 16, 1967, and clandestine broadcast in Vietnamese, January 17,

1967, 1400 GMT, Liberation Radio, radio transcripts, National Archives Center 1, Hanoi.

[29] George McT. Kahin, "The NLF's Terms for Peace," *New Republic*, October 14, 1967, 13.

[30] Interview with Douglas Pike, former American official with the U.S. Information Service–Saigon, Berkeley, Calif., October 1992.

[31] *New York Times*, January 16, 1967.

[32] "China Recognizes NLF," document no. 002734, June 16, 1967, Pike Collection.

[33] "South Vietnam National Liberation Front President Acclaims Successful Explosion of China's First Hydrogen Bomb," document no. 002736, Pike Collection.

[34] *Cuoc khang chien chong My, cuu nuoc, 1954–1975: Nhung su kien quan su* [The anti-U.S. resistance war for national salvation of the fatherland, 1954–1975: Military events] (Hanoi: Nha Xuat Ban Quan Doi Nhan Dan, 1988), 93.

[35] *Vietnam Courier*, September 7, 1967.

[36] Denis Warner, "The NLF's New Program," *Reporter*, October 1967, 23.

[37] "Text of Political Program Adopted by South Vietnam National Front for Liberation, August 1967," document no. 001506, Pike Collection.

[38] Jeffrey Race, *War Comes to Long An: Revolutionary Conflict in a Vietnamese Province* (Berkeley: University of California Press, 1972), 186.

[39] Interview with Tung Le, Ho Chi Minh City, July 1989.

[40] Lin Piao, *Long Live the Victory of the People's War* (Peking: Foreign Languages Press, 1965).

[41] Ralph T. Powell, "Maoist Military Doctrine," *Asian Survey* 8 (April 1968): 249.

[42] Mao Tse-tung, *Problems of Strategy in China's Revolutionary War* (1936; Peking: Foreign Language Press, 1967).

[43] "Political Programme of the South Viet Nam NLF," *Women of Viet Nam* 3 (suppl.) (1967): 1–8.

[44] Associated Press release in *Jakarta Times*, September 4, 1967.

[45] Viet Nam News Agency, telex, September 6, 1967, telex transcripts, National Archives Center 1, Hanoi; and "Premier Chou En Lai Receives Acting Head of South Vietnam NFL Mission," document no. 002752, Pike Collection.

[46] Broadcast in English from Peking, September 5, 1967, New China News Agency, radio transcripts, National Archives Center 1, Hanoi.

[47] Ibid., September 29, 1967, and "Premier Chou En-lai's Speech at Banquet for Vietnamese Delegations," document no. 002758, Pike Collection.

[48] Interview with Tung Le, former NLF official, Ho Chi Minh City, March 1996.

[49] "Vietnamese Comrades-in-Arms Report on Heroic Exploits in Their Resistance to U.S. Aggression," *Peking Review* 42 (October 13, 1967): 21–23.

[50] Broadcast in English from Peking, September 29, 1967, New China News Agency, radio transcripts, National Archives Center 1, Hanoi.

[51] "Vietnamese Party and Government Delegation, S. Vietnam N.F.L. Delegation in Peking," *Peking Review* 41 (October 6, 1967): 26–27.

[52] Broadcast in English from Peking, October 7, 1967, New China News

Agency, radio transcripts, National Archives Center 1, Hanoi; and "South Vietnam NLF Delegation Gives Reports to Chinese PLA," document no. 002771, Pike Collection.

[53] Broadcast in English from Peking, October 7, 1967, New China News Agency, radio transcripts, National Archives Center 1, Hanoi.

[54] Ibid., October 14, 1967, and "Shanghai Visit, Rally," document no. 001513, Pike Collection.

[55] "South Vietnam Delegation in Shanghai" and "South Vietnam Delegation Visits PLA Navy Fleet in Shanghai," document no. 002778, Pike Collection.

[56] Interview with General Hoang Minh Thao, Hanoi, November 1995.

[57] *Mau Than Saigon* [The Tet offensive in Saigon] (Ho Chi Minh City: Nha Xuat Ban Van Nghe, 1988).

[58] *Tap chi lich su quan su: So dac biet 20 nam Tet mau than* [Journal of military history: Special twentieth anniversary issue on the Tet offensive], February 1988, 2–3.

[59] Paper delivered by General Tran Van Quang, the first minister of defense, at a Ministry of Defense conference on the Tet Offensive, Ho Chi Minh City, March 1–8, 1986. The title of the conference was "Scientific Conference for an Overall Assessment of the Spring Offensive of 1968." The paper is in my possession. I confirmed this view in a conversation with General Quang in June 1997.

[60] I am indebted to the historian Ngo Vinh Long for lengthy conversations on this topic and for an advance copy of his paper "The Tet Offensive and Its Aftermath," delivered at the conference "Remembering Tet 1968: An Interdisciplinary Conference on the Vietnam War," Salisbury State University, Salisbury, Md., November 18–21, 1992.

[61] General Tran Van Tra, *A History of the Bulwark B-2 Theatre*, vol. 5, *Concluding the Thirty Years War*, in *Southeast Asia Report*, no. 1247, JPRS 82783, February 2, 1983, Foreign Broadcast Information Service.

[62] Clandestine broadcasts in Vietnamese, July 23 and September 8, 1967, 1400 GMT, Liberation Radio, radio transcripts, National Archives Center 1, Hanoi.

[63] Stanley Karnow, *Vietnam: A History* (New York: Penguin, 1983), 450.

[64] Interview with a former NLF official who requested anonymity, Ho Chi Minh City, March 1996.

[65] *Tu Do* (Saigon daily newspaper), September 23, 1967.

[66] Nguyen Cao Ky, *Twenty Years and Twenty Days* (New York: Stein & Day, 1976), 157.

[67] *Washington Post*, October 18, 1967.

[68] Truong Nhu Tang, *A Viet Cong Memoir: An Inside Account of the Vietnam War and Its Aftermath* (New York: Vintage, 1985), 110. Lan was later executed for his actions.

[69] Ibid., 119.

[70] Don Oberdorfer, *Tet!* (Garden City, N.Y.: Doubleday, 1971), 63.

[71] Ibid.

[72] Interview with Nguyen Xuan Oanh, economist and former RVN official, Ho Chi Minh City, July 1989.

[73] Interview with a former NLF official who requested anonymity, Ho Chi Minh City, July 1989.

[74] It was General Loan who was captured in that famous photograph executing a suspected NLF cadre on a street in Saigon during the Tet Offensive.

[75] *Dung Phuong* (Saigon daily newspaper), December 18, 1967.

[76] Interview with Nguyen Xuan Oanh, Ho Chi Minh City, July 1989.

[77] Interview with Nguyen Van Phung, former RVN official, Ho Chi Minh City, July 1989.

[78] Oberdorfer, *Tet!*, 64.

[79] George C. Herring, *LBJ and Vietnam: A Different Kind of War* (Austin: University of Texas Press, 1994), 145.

[80] Larry Berman, *Lyndon Johnson's War* (New York: Norton, 1989), 116.

[81] Broadcast in English, January 1, 1968, 1400 GMT, Radio Hanoi and Viet Nam News Agency, radio transcripts, National Archives Center 1, Hanoi.

[82] George C. Herring, ed., *The Secret Diplomacy of the Vietnam War: The Negotiating Volumes of the Pentagon Papers* (Austin: University of Texas Press, 1983), 384; emphasis added.

[83] Robert S. McNamara with Brian VanDeMark, *In Retrospect: The Tragedy and Lessons of Vietnam* (New York: Times Books, 1995), 302.

[84] Herring, *Secret Diplomacy*, 523, 553, 555.

[85] Interview with a former Lao Dong official who requested anonymity, Hanoi, July 1992.

5. Old Wine in New Bottles: Johnson, Nixon, and the PRG, 1968–1969

[1] Don Oberdorfer, *Tet!* (Garden City, N.Y.: Doubleday, 1971), 158.

[2] George C. Herring, *America's Longest War: The United States and Vietnam, 1950–1975*, 2d ed. (New York: Knopf, 1986), 202.

[3] Clark Clifford, "A Viet Nam Reappraisal," *Foreign Affairs* 47 (July 1969): 613. Clifford's position was hardly unique; McNamara had been advocating the same course of action for months and had sent Johnson a memo to this affect in May 1967.

[4] Eugene McCarthy, *Required Reading: A Decade of Political Wit and Wisdom* (New York: Harcourt Brace Jovanovich, 1988), 4–5.

[5] *New York Times*, March 13, 1968.

[6] George C. Herring, *LBJ and Vietnam: A Different Kind of War* (Austin: University of Texas Press, 1994), 151, 131.

[7] *The Pentagon Papers: The Defense Department History of the United States Decisionmaking on Vietnam*, Senator Gravel ed., 4 vols. (Boston: Beacon, 1971–72), 4:270.

[8] Mai Van Bo, *Hanoi-Paris: Hoi ky ngoai giao cua* [Hanoi-Paris: Personal memories of the secret diplomacy] (Ho Chi Minh City: Nha Xuat Ban Van Nghe, 1993), 123.

[9] *Chu Tich Ho Chi Minh voi cong tac ngoai giao* [President Ho Chi Minh and the diplomatic works] (Hanoi: Nha Xuat Ban Su That, 1990), 222–23.

[10] Interview with Dang Nhiem Bai, director of the American Department, Viet Nam Foreign Ministry, Hanoi, July 1989.

[11] Interview with a former NLF official who requested anonymity, Ho Chi Minh City, July 1989.

[12] Interview with Deputy Foreign Minister Dao Huy Ngoc, Hanoi, November 1995.

[13] Truong Nhu Tang, *A Viet Cong Memoir: An Inside Account of the Vietnam War and Its Aftermath* (New York: Vintage, 1985), 131. The NLF flag was a yellow star on a field half blue and half red. The DRV flag was a yellow star on a solid red field.

[14] *Cuoc khang chien chong My, cuu nuoc, 1954–1975: Nhung su kien quan su* [The anti-U.S. resistance war for national salvation of the fatherland, 1954–1975: Military events] (Hanoi: Nha Xuat Ban Quon Doi Nhan Dan, 1988), 105–8.

[15] Interview with Ba Chu, former NLF official, Hanoi, July 1992.

[16] Clandestine broadcast in Vietnamese, July 12, 1968, 1430 GMT, Liberation Radio, radio transcripts, Trung Tam Luu Tru Quoc Gia-1 (hereafter National Archives Center 1, Hanoi).

[17] Phan Chu Trinh was born in 1872 in Quang Nam province, in central Viet Nam, the son of a lower-level military officer. Like other Vietnamese patriots of his day, he received a traditional Confucian education. After passing the civil service exams with honors, he became an official in the imperial bureaucracy at Hue. In 1905 he resigned his position and traveled throughout Viet Nam to explore domestic opposition to the French. Like Phan Boi Chau, perhaps the most famous of Viet Nam's early twentieth-century patriots, Trinh traveled to Japan in the early 1900s to find answers to Viet Nam's colonial problem. Whereas Chau eventually advocated the violent overthrow of the French, Trinh believed that Viet Nam must modernize before it would be ready for complete independence from its colonial master. Trinh was arrested in 1908 and deported to France, where he spent fourteen years under house arrest. Upon his return to Viet Nam in 1925, Trinh spoke out against violence, arguing that Vietnamese patriotism was not incompatible with the French presence in Viet Nam. He died one year later. See William J. Duiker, "Hanoi Scrutinizes the Past: The Marxist Evolution of Phan Boi Chau and Phan Chu Trinh," *Southeast Asia* 3 (Summer 1971): 243–54.

[18] Foreign Relations Commission, *Personalities of the South Vietnam Liberation Movement* (Tran Phu: South Vietnam National Front for Liberation, 1965), 14, 22.

[19] "NLF Makes Claims," document no. 002325, and "NLF Is Key to Peace," document no. 001459, both in Douglas Pike Collection, NLF Documents, Indochina Archive, University of California at Berkeley (hereafter Pike Collection); and broadcast in English, July 12, 1968, 0536 GMT, International Service, Viet Nam News Agency, radio transcripts, National Archives Center 1, Hanoi.

[20] Clandestine broadcast in Vietnamese, July 7, 1968, 1430 GMT, Liberation Radio, radio transcripts, National Archives Center 1, Hanoi; and *Far Eastern Economic Review*, July 4, 1968, 7.

[21] Broadcast from Hanoi, in English, October 12, 1968, 1616 GMT, Viet Nam News Agency, radio transcripts, National Archives Center 1, Hanoi; and "NLF Opens Stockholm Office,"document no. 001545, Pike Collection.

[22] Broadcast from Paris, in French, September 2, 1968, Agence France-Presse, radio transcripts, National Archives Center 1, Hanoi.

[23] "AFP Report, 11 October 1968," document no. 001541, Pike Collection.

[24] Broadcast from Paris, in French, October 11, 1968, Agence France-Presse, radio transcripts, National Archives Center 1, Hanoi.

[25] Broadcast from Hanoi, in English, October 28, 1968, 1625 GMT, Viet Nam News Agency, radio transcripts, National Archives Center 1, Hanoi; and "More on the NFLSV Information Bureau Reception," document no. 001542, Pike Collection.

[26] *Vietnam Press*, October 13, 1968.

[27] *Washington Post*, October 12, 1968.

[28] "The Front in Paris Achieves Its Goals," document no. 002352, Pike Collection.

[29] Averill Harriman to Dean Rusk, October 31, 1968 (memo), National Security Files, Country File Vietnam, Box 124, Lyndon Baines Johnson Presidential Library, Austin, Tex.

[30] Viet Nam News Agency in Moscow to Viet Nam News Agency in Hanoi, telex in Vietnamese, October 28, 1968, 1240 GMT, telex transcripts, National Archives Center 1, Hanoi.

[31] "NLF Information Bureau Set Up in Sweden," document no. 001545, Pike Collection.

[32] Broadcast from Hanoi, in English, December 16, 1968, 0203 GMT, Viet Nam News Agency, radio transcripts, National Archives Center 1, Hanoi.

[33] *Washington Post*, October 15, 1968.

[34] Broadcast from Hanoi, in Vietnamese, October 28, 1968, 2400 GMT, Viet Nam News Agency, radio transcripts, National Archives Center 1, Hanoi.

[35] Interview with Le Mau Han, historian, Hanoi, July 1992.

[36] See the following documents in Pike Collection: "NLF Permanent Representation to Be Set, 31 October 1968," document no. 002362; "NLFSV Representations Abroad Enumerated," document no. 001546; "The NLF Demands Four-Sided Negotiations," document no. 02343. See also broadcast from Paris, in French, October 25, 1968, Agence France-Presse, and broadcasts from Hanoi, in Vietnamese, December 3, 1968, 0747 GMT, and October 31, 1968, 0830 GMT, Viet Nam News Agency, all in radio transcripts, National Archives Center 1, Hanoi.

[37] Broadcast from Moscow, in English, December 4, 1968, 0619 GMT, Viet Nam News Agency, radio transcripts, National Archives Center 1, Hanoi.

[38] *New York Times*, October 29, 1968; *Washington Post*, October 31, 1968; *Wall Street Journal*, October 30, 1968; *Christian Science Monitor*, October 30, 1968; *Far Eastern Economic Review*, November 1, 1968.

[39] *Le Monde*, February 9, 1968.

[40] *Tribune* (London), March 3, 1968.

[41] Dag Ryen, "The Trauma of Vietnam as Revealed in European Newspapers" (master's thesis, Department of History, University of Kentucky, 1992).

[42] *Svenska Dagbladet* (Stockholm), January 8, 1968.

[43] *Chicago Daily News*, November 5, 1968.

[44] *New York Times*, November 11, 1968.

[45] Larry Berger to President Johnson, November 1, 1968, in National Security Files, Country File Vietnam, Box 125, Lyndon Baines Johnson Presidential Library; Ambassador Bunker to Secretary of State Dean Rusk, October 15, 1968, Box 124, ibid.; U.S. Embassy, Saigon, to Rusk, October 21, 1968, ibid.; and broad-

cast in English, December 7, 1968, 1541 GMT, Radio Hanoi, radio transcripts, National Archives Center 1, Hanoi

[46] *Christian Science Monitor*, November 12, 1968; *Chicago Daily News*, November 5, 1968; *Washington Post*, November 17, 1968.

[47] Bui Diem, *In the Jaws of History* (Boston: Houghton-Mifflin, 1987), 243.

[48] *New York Times*, November 14, 1968; and Personal Papers of Clark Clifford, Box 6, Lyndon Baines Johnson Presidential Library.

[49] Diem, *In the Jaws of History*, 250.

[50] Bo, *Hanoi-Paris*, 173.

[51] Tran Van Tra, *Ket thuc cuoc chien tranh 30 nam* [Concluding the thirty-year war] (Ho Chi Minh City: Van Nghe, 1982), 35.

[52] H. R. Haldeman, *The Ends of Power* (New York: Times Books, 1978), 82.

[53] Quoted in Gareth Porter, *A Peace Denied: The United States, Vietnam, and the Paris Agreement* (Bloomington: Indiana University Press, 1975), 80.

[54] Quoted in Richard Whalen, *Catch the Falling Flag: A Republican's Challenge to His Party* (Boston: Houghton-Mifflin, 1972), 139.

[55] Patrick Anderson, "Confidence of the President," *New York Times Magazine*, June 1, 1969.

[56] Herring, *America's Longest War*, 226.

[57] *Mot so van kien cua Dang ve chong My, cuu nuoc* [Selected Party documents relating to the anti-U.S. resistance war for national salvation of the fatherland], vol. 2, *1965–1970* (Hanoi: Nha Xuat Ban Su That, 1986), 112.

[58] Interview with Vu Huy Phuoc, historian, Hanoi, July 1992.

[59] *Lich su Quan Doi Nhan Dan Viet Nam* [History of the People's Army of Viet Nam], vol. 2, pt. 2 (Hanoi: Nha Xuat Ban Quan Doi Nhan Dan, 1990), 73–76.

[60] Interview with Tuyet Thi Vanh, former NLF official, Ho Chi Minh City, July 1989.

[61] Huong Nam, "Keo dai va Mo rong chien tranh xam luoc of Dong-duong, Nich-xon, cang lam cho nhung kho khan cua nuoc My them tram trong" [The protraction and escalation of the U.S. involvement in Indochina, designed by Nixon, aggravated the U.S. problem], *Hoc Tap* 16 (October 1970): 82–89; and *Cuoc khang chien chong My*, 202.

[62] *Chu Tich Ho Chi Minh voi cong tac ngoai giao*, 231–33.

[63] "From the Daybook of V. Z. Zorin," secret copy no. 2, February 28, 1969, *Bulletin* (Woodrow Wilson International Center for Scholars, Washington, D.C.) 3 (1995): 69.

[64] Sol Stern, "A Talk with the Front," *Ramparts*, November 1967.

[65] Interview with Tuyet Thi Vanh, Ho Chi Minh City, July 1992.

[66] Douglas Pike, *Viet Cong: The Organization and Techniques of the National Liberation Front of South Vietnam* (Cambridge: MIT Press, 1966), 320, 343.

[67] Nguyen Khac Vien, "South Viet Nam: From the NLF to the Provisional Revolutionary Government," *Vietnamese Studies* 23 (June 1969): 3–6; and "Nguyen tac va noi dung chu yeu cua giai phap toan bo ve van de mien Nam Viet Nam, gop phan lap lai hoa binh o Viet Nam" [The principal and important facts of a settlement in South Viet Nam, contributions in rebuilding the peace in Viet Nam], *Hoc Tap* 15 (June 1969): 27–29.

[68] Broadcast from Hanoi, in Vietnamese, May 8, 1969, 2314 GMT, Viet Nam News Agency, radio transcripts, National Archives Center 1, Hanoi.

[69] *Cuoc khang chien chong My*, 116–17.

[70] Broadcast from Hanoi, in Vietnamese, May 10, 1969, 2130 GMT, Viet Nam News Agency, radio transcripts, National Archives Center 1, Hanoi.

[71] *Giai Phong*, May 14, 1969.

[72] *New York Times*, May 15, 1969.

[73] Tang, *Viet Cong Memoir*, 147.

[74] *Mot so van kien cua Dang ve chong My*, 2:128.

[75] *Cuoc khang chien chong My*, 117.

[76] Broadcast from Hanoi, in English, June 15, 1969, 1702 GMT, Viet Nam News Agency, radio transcripts, National Archives Center 1, Hanoi; *South Vietnam in Struggle*, July 15, 1969; and "PRG Earns Recognition," document no. 001572, Pike Collection.

[77] Broadcast in Russian, June 13, 1969, Domestic Service, Radio Moscow, radio transcripts, National Archives Center 1, Hanoi.

[78] *Vietnam Studies* 23 (June 1969) and "List of Countries Having Recognized the Provisional Revolutionary Government of the Republic of South Vietnam," document no. 001519, Pike Collection.

[79] Haldeman, *Ends of Power*, 86–93. The words represent not a direct quote but a concept current among Nixon officials.

[80] "Harriman Suggests Way Out of Vietnam," *New York Times Magazine*, August 24, 1969, 24; *Congressional Record*, May 11, 1972, E5025; and Porter, *Peace Denied*, 87.

[81] Christa Runge, "A Clever Lady Ambassador of Her Nation," *Horizont* 29 (July 1969): 14–15.

[82] Interview with Tuyet Thi Vanh, Ho Chi Minh City, July 1989.

[83] *Nhan Dan*, July 16, 1969.

[84] *Jakarta Times*, June 14, 1969; and "World's Progressive Peoples Claim Support for the PRG," document no. 002387, Pike Collection.

[85] *Vietnam Studies* 23 (June 1969).

[86] Report from Kyodo-Reuters, June 16, 1969, Middle East News Agency, radio transcripts, National Archives Center 1, Hanoi.

[87] "Viet Red Recognition Considered by India," document no. 001570, Pike Collection; and *Washington Post*, July 11, 1969.

[88] *Le Monde*, August 17, 1969.

[89] Clandestine broadcast in Vietnamese, July 25, 1969, 1530 GMT, Liberation Radio, radio transcripts, National Archives Center 1, Hanoi.

[90] Lan was assassinated in early 1968 after he revealed his NLF contacts and thus was responsible for the arrest of several of the Party's leading officials in the South.

[91] Tang, *Viet Cong Memoir*, 131.

[92] Clandestine broadcast to Eastern Europe and the Far East, in English, July 22, 1969, 1530 GMT, Liberation Press Agency, radio transcripts, National Archives Center 1, Hanoi; and "Former Bao Dai Premier Hails PRG Formation," document no. 002394, Pike Collection

[93] Clandestine broadcast to Europe and East Asia, in Vietnamese, August 2,

1969, 1530 GMT, Liberation Radio, radio transcripts, National Archives Center 1, Hanoi.

[94] Nguyen Duy Trinh, *Tren mat tran ngoai giao* [The diplomatic front] (Hanoi: Nha Xuat Ban Su That, 1972), 124.

[95] *Giai Phong*, August 23, 1969.

[96] *Washington Post*, August 3, 1969; "Saigon Fights Back," document no. 001576, Pike Collection.

[97] Interview with Douglas Pike, Berkeley, Calif., October 1992.

[98] Interview with Nguyen Dinh Ngo, vice president of Fatherland Front of Thua-Thien–Hue province, Hue, July 1989.

[99] Thomas Latimer, "Hanoi's Leaders and Their South Vietnam Policies, 1954–1968" (Ph.D. diss., Georgetown University, 1972), 256–57.

[100] Foreign Relations Commission, *Personalities of the South Vietnam Liberation Movement*, 22.

[101] *Vietnam Courier*, June 16, 1969.

[102] Runge, "Clever Lady Ambassador," 14.

[103] Stanley Karnow, *Vietnam: A History* (New York: Penguin, 1983), 599.

[104] Interviews with Abbie Hoffman, 1983 and 1984, Kingston, R.I.

[105] Interview with David Dellinger, Castleton, Vt., July 1990.

[106] Karnow, *Vietnam*, 599.

[107] Viet Nam's Ministry of Labor, War Invalids, and Social Affairs released these figures on April 3, 1995. A copy of this report is in my possession.

[108] Tang, *Viet Cong Memoir*, 157–58.

[109] Interview with Le Thi Hai, former Alliance member, Ho Chi Minh City, July 1989.

[110] Interview with a former NLF official who requested anonymity, Ho Chi Minh City, March 1996.

6. Fighting while Negotiating, 1970–1973

[1] "General Nguyen Van Vinh's speech before COSVN as summarized in the Joint U.S. Public Affairs Office, 'The Position of North Viet-Nam on Negotiations,' " *Vietnam Documents and Research Notes* 8 (October 1967): 4.

[2] Tran Huy Licu, "Danh va dam" [Fighting and talking], *Nghicn Cuu Lich Su* 111 (June 1968): 1–2, 14.

[3] Allan E. Goodman, "Fighting while Negotiating: The View from Hanoi," in Joseph J. Zasloff and MacAlister Brown, eds., *Communism in Indochina* (Lexington, Mass.: D. C. Heath, 1975), 83.

[4] *Chu Tich Ho Chi Minh voi cong tac ngoai giao* [President Ho Chi Minh and the diplomatic works] (Hanoi: Nha Xuat Ban Su That, 1990), 135.

[5] Truong Nhu Tang, *A Viet Cong Memoir: An Inside Account of the Vietnam War and Its Aftermath* (New York: Vintage, 1985), 87.

[6] *Cuoc khang chien chong My cuu nuoc, 1954–1975: Nhung su kien quan su* [The anti-U.S. resistance war for national salvation of the Fatherland, 1954–1975: Military events] (Hanoi: Nha Xuat Ban Quan Doi Nhan Dan, 1988), 124.

[7] Interview with Le Mau Han, historian and former NLF political writer, Hanoi, July 1992.

[8] Clandestine radio Broadcast in Vietnamese, April 20, 1970, 1400 GMT, Liberation Radio, radio transcripts, National Archives Center 1, Hanoi.

[9] "PRG's Peace Plan," document no. 001588, Douglas Pike Collection, NLF Documents, Indochina Archive, University of California at Berkeley (hereafter Pike Collection); *New York Times*, May 9, 1969.

[10] Interview with Tuyet Thi Vanh, former NLF official, Ho Chi Minh City, July 1989.

[11] George McT. Kahin, *Intervention: How America Became Involved in Vietnam* (New York: Doubleday/Anchor, 1986), 182–96, 199–201.

[12] Interview with Tran Van Dong, former NLF member, Hanoi, March 1996; Tang, *Viet Cong Memoir*, 203.

[13] Clandestine radio broadcast in Vietnamese, September 17, 1970, 1400 GMT, Liberation Radio, radio transcripts, National Archives Center 1, Hanoi; *New York Times*, September 18, 1970.

[14] Luu Van Loi and Nguyen Anh Vu, *Le Duc Tho–Kissinger Negotiations in Paris* (Hanoi: Gioi, 1996), 153–55.

[15] "Nguyen Thi Binh Addresses Non-Aligned Nations Conference," document no. 001592, Pike Collection.

[16] Broadcast from Moscow, in English, September 10, 1970, TASS International Service.

[17] "Professor Tours Asia," document no. 003389, Pike Collection.

[18] Nguyen Van Hieu, *Ban be ta khap nam chau* [Our friends around the world] (Hanoi: Nha Xuat Ban Van Hoc, 1963).

[19] Interview with a former NLF official who requested anonymity, Ho Chi Minh City, July 1989.

[20] Clandestine broadcast in Vietnamese to South Viet Nam, October 14, 1970, 1400 GMT, Liberation Radio, radio transcripts, National Archives Center 1, Hanoi.

[21] Bui Diem, *In the Jaws of History* (Boston: Houghton-Mifflin, 1987), 281.

[22] Interview with a former NLF official who requested anonymity, Ho Chi Minh City, March 1996.

[23] "NLF Political Strategy and Course of Action." This document was given to me by members of the Vietnamese Committee on Social Sciences in Ho Chi Minh City in July 1989. I confirmed its contents in interviews with several former NLF strategists in Ho Chi Minh City three years later.

[24] Clandestine broadcast in Vietnamese, June 13, 1971, 1400 GMT, Liberation Radio, radio transcripts, National Archives Center 1, Hanoi.

[25] Diem, *In the Jaws of History*, 290.

[26] Clandestine broadcasts in Vietnamese, July 12, 1971, 1400 GMT, and August 10, 1971, 1530 GMT, Liberation Radio, radio transcripts, National Archives Center 1, Hanoi; *Giai Phong*, August 7, 1971.

[27] Clandestine broadcast in Vietnamese, July 1, 1971, 1400 GMT, Liberation Radio, radio transcripts, National Archives Center 1, Hanoi; Gareth Porter, *A Peace Denied: The United States, Vietnam, and the Paris Agreement* (Bloomington: Indiana University Press, 1975), 98.

[28] Interview with Tran Quynh Cu, former NLF political writer and historian,

Hanoi, July 1992; and George McT. Kahin, "Negotiations: The View from Hanoi," *New Republic*, November 6, 1971, 14–15.

[29] Clandestine broadcast in Vietnamese, July 9, 1971, 1420 GMT, Liberation Radio, radio transcripts, National Archives Center 1, Hanoi.

[30] Interview with a former NLF official who requested anonymity, Hanoi, March 1996.

[31] "Upcoming Elections, Thieu's Last Days," document no. 003741, Pike Collection.

[32] Tad Szulc, "Behind the Vietnam Cease-Fire Agreement," *Foreign Policy* 15 (Summer 1974): 29–30.

[33] George C. Herring, *America's Longest War: The United States and Vietnam, 1950–1975*, 2d ed. (New York: Knopf, 1986), 243.

[34] Clandestine broadcast in Vietnamese, August 19, 1971, 1430 GMT, Liberation Radio, radio transcripts, National Archives Center 1, Hanoi.

[35] Marilyn B. Young, *The Vietnam Wars, 1945–1990* (New York: HarperCollins, 1991), 265.

[36] Interview with David Dellinger, Castleton, Vt., July 1990.

[37] *New York Times*, August 14, 1971.

[38] Herring, *America's Longest War*, 243.

[39] Interview with Tran Quynh Cu, Hanoi, July 1992.

[40] Clandestine broadcast in Vietnamese, August 14, 1971, 1530 GMT, Liberation Radio, radio transcripts, National Archives Center 1, Hanoi; *Nhan Dan*, August 17, 1971.

[41] Frances FitzGerald, *Fire in the Lake: The Vietnamese and the Americans in Vietnam* (New York: Vintage, 1972), 561.

[42] Clandestine broadcast in Vietnamese, August 1, 1971, 1400 GMT, Liberation Radio, radio transcripts, National Archives Center 1, Hanoi.

[43] Interview with a former NLF official who requested anonymity, Ho Chi Minh City, March 1996; Tang, *Viet Cong Memoir*, 203.

[44] *Giai Phong*, September 4, 1971.

[45] Clandestine broadcast in Vietnamese, August 26, 1971, 1530 GMT, Liberation Radio, radio transcripts, National Archives Center 1, Hanoi.

[46] *Burlington* (Vt.) *Free Press*, October 7, 1971.

[47] Clandestine broadcast in Vietnamese, October 28, 1971, 1530 GMT, Liberation Radio, radio transcripts, National Archives Center 1, Hanoi.

[48] "Washington Refuses to Negotiate," document no. 009387, Pike Collection.

[49] "Our Support among the Progressive Peoples of the World," document no. 009340, Pike Collection.

[50] *Viet Nam: Nhung su kien, 1945–1986* [Viet Nam: Historical events, 1945–1986] (Hanoi: Nha Xuat Ban Khoa Hoc Xa Hoi, 1990), 550.

[51] "Excerpts from the Report to the Third National Assembly, Sixth Session, June 1970," in Pham Van Dong, *Selected Writings* (Hanoi: Foreign Languages Publishing House, 1977), 240–61.

[52] *Cuoc khang chien chong My*, 138.

[53] Szulc, "Behind the Vietnam Cease-Fire Agreement," 31.

[54] *New York Times*, January 26, 1972.

[55] *Washington Post*, January 26, 1972.

[56] Interview with Le Mau Han, historian, Hanoi, July 1992.

[57] Remarks by Nguyen Thi Binh, vice president of the Socialist Republic of Viet Nam and former NLF foreign minister, Hanoi, November 1995, in Critical Oral History Project transcripts, Watson Institute for International Studies, Brown University and Institute for International Relations, Hanoi.

[58] Szulc, "Behind the Vietnam Cease-Fire Agreement," 34.

[59] Stanley Karnow, *Vietnam: A History* (New York: Penguin, 1983), 638.

[60] *The Truth about Vietnam-China Relations over the Last Thirty Years* (Hanoi: Ministry of Foreign Affairs, 1979).

[61] Interview with Dang Nhiem Bai, head of the American Department, Foreign Ministry, Hanoi, July 1989. The Party had felt betrayed by China's insistence that it accept the 1954 Geneva Accords.

[62] Porter, *Peace Denied*, 111.

[63] *Van tai quan su chien luoc tren Duong Ho Chi Minh trong khang chien chong My* [Strategic military transport on the Ho Chi Minh Trail during the anti-U.S. resistance war for national salvation of the fatherland] (Hanoi: Tong Cuc Hau Can, Nha Xuat Ban Quan Doi Nhan Dan, 1988), 312–20; *Quan Doan 2: So luoc lich su* [Second Corps: Historical sketch], vol. 1 (Hanoi: Cuc Chinh Tri Quan Doan 2 Xuat Ban, 1979); *Su doan chien thang su doan 312, Ky su* [The victory division, 312th Division, a chronicle], vol. 1 (Hanoi: Nha Xuat Ban Quan Doi Nhan Dan, 1980); and "Chien truong Tri-Thien-Hue trong cuoc khang chien chong My, cuu nuoc toan thang, du thao" [The Tri-Thien-Hue battlefield/military region during the victorious anti-U.S. resistance war for the national salvation of the fatherland, draft], National Archives Center 1, Hanoi.

[64] *Cuoc khang chien chong My*, 145–47.

[65] Remarks by General Hoang Minh Thao, Hanoi, November 1995, Critical Oral History Project transcripts, Watson Institute for International Studies, Brown University and Institute for International Relations, Hanoi.

[66] *New York Times*, April 7, 1972.

[67] Bernard Kalb and Marvin Kalb, *Kissinger* (Boston: Little, Brown, 1974), 293–95.

[68] Szulc, "Behind the Vietnam Cease-Fire Negotiations," 36.

[69] Kalb and Kalb, *Kissinger*, 209, 293–95.

[70] *Washington Star*, June 20, 1972.

[71] Remarks by Nguyen Co Thach, former foreign minister of the Socialist Republic of Viet Nam, Hanoi, November 1995, Critical Oral History Project transcripts, Watson Institute for International Studies, Brown University and Institute for International Relations, Hanoi.

[72] *Cuoc khang chien chong My*, 147.

[73] Szulc, "Behind the Vietnam Cease-Fire Agreement," 38.

[74] Porter, *Peace Denied*, 110; *New York Times*, May 3, 1972.

[75] Jim Peck, "Why China Turned West," *Ramparts*, May 1972, 34–41.

[76] *Lich su Quan Doi Nhan Dan Viet Nam* [History of the People's Army of Viet Nam] (Hanoi: Nha Xuat Ban Quan Doi Nhan Dan, 1990), 2:218.

[77] Szulc, "Behind the Vietnam Cease-Fire Negotiations," 47.

[78] *New York Times*, October 26, 1972.

[79] Ibid., September 12, 1972.

[80] *Washington Star*, September 14, 1972.

[81] Porter, *Peace Denied*, 121.

[82] Huong Nam, "Hai lap truong dam, chan doi lap" [At the peace talks, two opposing negotiating positions], *Hoc Tap* 18 (September 1972): 70–76.

[83] Interview with Dang Nghiem Bai, Hanoi, July 1989.

[84] Interview with a former NLF official who requested anonymity, Ho Chi Minh City, March 1996.

[85] *New York Times*, October 27, 1972.

[86] *Washington Post*, October 27, 1972.

[87] Broadcast to Europe and East Asia, in English, October 26, 1972, 1600 GMT, Radio Hanoi, radio transcripts, National Archives Center 1, Hanoi.

[88] Porter, *Peace Denied*, 125.

[89] Szulc, "Behind the Vietnam Cease-Fire Negotiations," 48–49.

[90] Interview with a former NLF official who requested anonymity, Hue, March 1996.

[91] "Thieu's Role in Saigon," document no. 002871, Pike Collection.

[92] Interview with Nguyen Khac Huynh, former DRV ambassador, Hanoi, November 1995.

[93] "Release of Political Prisoners, Our Needs Must Be Met," document no. 003468, Pike Collection.

[94] Interview with Nguyen Thi Hai Giau and Pham Thi Tu Thanh, Women's Union of Tien Giang Province, My Tho, July 1989.

[95] *Nhan Dan*, December 12, 1972.

[96] Interview with a former NLF official who requested anonymity, Ho Chi Minh City, March 1996.

[97] *New York Times*, October 16, 1972.

[98] *Baltimore Sun*, November 11, 1972.

[99] "Kissinger-Tho Peace Draft," document no. 003470, Pike Collection.

[100] Nguyen Tien Hung and Jerrold Schecter, *The Palace File* (New York: Harper & Row, 1986), 83, 88.

[101] Szulc, "Behind the Vietnam Cease-Fire Negotiations," 55–56.

[102] Viet Nam News Agency, November 5, 1972, press release transcript, National Archives Center 1, Hanoi. The Lao Dong paraphrased Kissinger's remarks but gave the comment significant attention.

[103] *New York Times*, November 2, 1972.

[104] Broadcast to Europe and East Asia, in English, October 26, 1972, 1600 GMT, Radio Hanoi, radio transcripts, National Archives Center 1, Hanoi.

[105] Interview with Nguyen Van Dieu, head of External Affairs, People's Committee of Thua-Thien-Hue Province, Hue, July 1989.

[106] Richard Nixon, *RN: The Memoirs of Richard Nixon* (New York: Vintage, 1978), 701.

[107] Broadcast to Europe and East Asia, in English, October 26, 1972, 1600 GMT, Radio Hanoi. Xuan Thuy also made a public statement from Paris on October 26.

[108] *New York Times*, October 27, 1972.

[109] Viet Nam News Agency, October 31, 1972, press release transcript, National Archives Center 1, Hanoi.

[110] Interview with a former NLF official who requested anonymity, Hanoi, November 1995.

[111] Interview with Nguyen Thi Hanh, former civilian prisoner of the Republic of Viet Nam, Berkeley, Calif., October 1992.

[112] Interview with Tuyet Thi Vanh, former NLF official, Ho Chi Minh City, July 1989.

[113] Tang, *Viet Cong Memoir*, 194–95, 187.

[114] "Chien truong Tri-Thien-Hue trong cuoc khang chien chong My," 198.

[115] Szulc, "Behind the Vietnam Cease-Fire Agreement," 53.

[116] Porter, *Peace Denied*, 115.

[117] Herring, *America's Longest War*, 250.

[118] Dai Tuong Hoang Van Thai, *Nhung nam thang quyet dinh hoi ky* [The decisive years, memoirs] (Hanoi: Nha Xuat Ban Quan Doi Nhan Dan, 1990), 12.

[119] Szulc, "Behind the Vietnam Cease-Fire Agreement," 53.

[120] Tang, *Viet Cong Memoir*, 214–17.

[121] Interview with Le Phuong, former Lao Dong official, Hanoi, July 1992.

[122] Tang, *Viet Cong Memoir*, 193.

[123] *Giai Phong*, November 17, 1972.

[124] *New York Times*, November 3, 1972.

[125] Porter, *Peace Denied*, 151.

[126] Louis Wiznitzer, "Peace: What Went Wrong?" *American Report*, January 1–15, 1973, 7.

[127] Agence France-Presse, Paris, December 8, 1972.

[128] *New York Times*, December 10, 1972.

[129] Interview with Luu Van Tru, former Lao Dong official, Ho Chi Minh City, March 1996.

[130] Interview with Le Phuong, former Lao Dong official, Hanoi, July 1992.

[131] *New York Times*, December 17, 1972.

[132] Interview with Luu Doan Huynh, former Foreign Ministry official, Hanoi, 1995.

[133] In 1992, my wife and I lived in the Bach Mai district of Hanoi with a medical doctor from the hospital. He took me on a walking tour of the area to show me the considerable damage that still remains from the Christmas bombings.

[134] Herring, *America's Longest War*, 254.

[135] Richard Dudman, "The Lesson of Vietnam," *Congressional Record*, February 26, 1973, S3275.

[136] Mai Van Bo, *Hanoi-Paris: Hoi ky ngoai giao cua* [Hanoi-Paris: Personal memories of the secret diplomacy] (Ho Chi Minh City: Nha Xuat Ban Van Nghe, 1993), 216–17.

[137] *Washington Post*, December 21, 1972. Sweden, Denmark, Belgium, Italy, Canada, Australia, New Zealand, Finland, and Japan openly criticized the U.S. bombing raids. See ibid., December 24 and 30, 1972; *Christian Science Monitor*, December 26, 1972.

[138] *Washington Post*, December 22, 1972.

[139] *Baltimore Sun*, December 30, 1972.

[140] "The Vietnam Bombing: Senate Opposition Grows," *Congressional Quarterly —Weekly Reports*, December 23, 1972, 3171.

[141] Herring, *America's Longest War*, 254.

[142] *New York Times*, December 30, 1972.

[143] "The Vietnam Agreement and Protocols, Signed January 27, 1973: Agreement on Ending the War and Restoring Peace to Vietnam," in *Weekly Compilation of Presidential Documents*, January 29, 1973, 4564.

[144] *Baltimore Sun*, January 7, 1973.

7. The Ceaseless Fire, 1973–1975

[1] *Giai Phong*, February 2, 1974.

[2] *Lich su khang chien chong My cuu nuoc* [History of the anti-American resistance war for national salvation of the fatherland], 2 vols. (Hanoi: Nha Xuat Ban Su That, 1990); *Cuoc khang chien chong My cuu nuoc, 1954–1975: Nhung su kien quan su* [The anti-American resistance war for national salvation of the fatherland, 1954–1975: Military events] (Hanoi: Nha Xuat Ban Quan Doi Nhan Dan, 1988); *Lich su Dang Cong San Viet Nam* [History of the Vietnamese Communist Party] (Hanoi: Nha Xuat Ban Su That, 1980); *Chu Tich Ho Chi Minh voi cong tac ngoai giao* [President Họ Chi Minh and the diplomatic works] (Hanoi: Nha Xuat Ban Su That, 1990); Dai Tuong Van Tien Dung, *Buoc ngoat lon cua cuoc khang chien chong My* [The big turning point in the war against the Americans] (Hanoi: Nha Xuat Ban Su That, 1989); and *Lich su Quan Doi Nhan Dan Viet Nam* [History of the People's Army of Viet Nam], vol. 1, *Du thao tom tat* [Draft summary] (Hanoi: Nha Xuat Ban Quan Doi Nhan Dan, 1977).

[3] "Dong chi Le Duc Tho noi ve mot so van de tong ket chien tranh va bien soan lich su quan su" [Comrade Le Duc Tho discusses a number of questions on the general assessment of the war and the writing of military history], *Tap Chi Lich Su Quan Su*, March 1988, 1–10.

[4] Art. 12 of chap. 4 of the Paris peace agreement states:

> (a) Immediately after the cease fire, the two South Vietnamese parties shall hold consultations in a spirit of national reconciliation and concord, mutual respect, and mutual nonelimination to set up a National Council of National Reconciliation and Concord of three equal segments. The Council shall operate on the principle of unanimity. After the National Council of National Reconciliation and Concord has assumed its functions, the two South Vietnamese parties will consult about the formation of councils at lower levels. The two South Vietnamese parties shall sign an agreement on the internal matters of South Vietnam as soon as possible and do their utmost to accomplish this within ninety days after the cease-fire comes into effect, in keeping with the South Vietnamese people's aspirations for peace, independence, and democracy.
>
> (b) The National Council of National Reconciliation and Concord shall have the task of promoting the two South Vietnamese parties' implementation of this Agreement, achievement of national reconciliation and concord, and guarantees of democratic liberties. The National Council of National Reconciliation and

Article 9b shall decide the procedures and modalities of these general elections. The institutions for which the general elections are to be held will be agreed upon through consultations between the two South Vietnamese parties. The National Council of National Reconciliation and Concord will also decide the procedures and modalities of such local elections as the two South Vietnamese parties agree upon.

[5] Gareth Porter, *A Peace Denied: The United States, Vietnam, and the Paris Agreement* (Bloomington: Indiana University Press, 1975), 188.

[6] *Su doan dong bang, su doan 320B-quan doan 1* [The Delta Division, 320B Division, 1st Corps] (Hanoi: Nha Xuat Ban Quan Doi Nhan Dan, 1983), 295.

[7] *Far Eastern Economic Review*, February 26, 1973, 14–15.

[8] Clandestine broadcast in Vietnamese, March 20, 1973, 1430 GMT, Liberation Radio, radio transcripts, Trung Tam Luu Tru Quoc Gia-1 (hereafter National Archives Center 1, Hanoi).

[9] "One Year of Fruitless Negotiations," Fact Sheet no. 06/74, March 19, 1974, Embassy of the Republic of Viet Nam, Paris, 6.

[10] Clandestine broadcast in Vietnamese, March 22, 1973, 1530 GMT, Liberation Radio, radio transcripts, National Archives Center 1, Hanoi.

[11] Broadcast to Europe and East Asia, in English, April 20, 1973, 1530 GMT, Radio Hanoi, radio transcripts, National Archives Center 1, Hanoi.

[12] "Text of Statement by PRG Chief of State, Nguyen Van Hieu," *Vietnam News and Reports* 16–17 (April–May 1973): 9.

[13] Interview with a former NLF official who requested anonymity, Ho Chi Minh City, March 1996.

[14] "COSVN Directive 3," *Vietnam Documents and Research Notes*, no. 115 (September 1973), 12.

[15] Broadcast to Europe and East Asia, in English, May 4, 1973, 1530 GMT, Radio Hanoi, radio transcripts, National Archives Center 1, Hanoi.

[16] Interview with a former NLF official who requested anonymity, Ho Chi Minh City, March 1996.

[17] *One Year of Communist Violations of the Paris Agreement* (Saigon: Ministry of Foreign Affairs, 1974), 17–19.

[18] Broadcast in Vietnamese, July 30, 1973, 1200 GMT, Domestic Service, Radio Saigon, radio transcripts, National Archives Center 1, Hanoi.

[19] "Preliminary Accord on Principles Between the Two South Vietnamese Parties to the La Celle St-Cloud Conference," in *One Year of Communist Violations*, 17–19.

[20] Interview with Nguyen Van Le, former Saigon official, Ho Chi Minh City, March 1996.

[21] *Viet Nam News and Reports* 16–17 (April–May 1973): 9; and clandestine broadcast in Vietnamese, April 25, 1973, 1400 GMT, Liberation Radio, radio transcripts, National Archives Center 1, Hanoi.

[22] Interview with a Lao Dong official who requested anonymity, Hanoi, November 1995.

[23] "COSVN's Directive 02/73: On Policies Related to the Political Settlement and Cease-Fire," *Vietnam Documents and Research Notes*, no. 113 (June 1973), 4.

[24] Interview with Dang Nghiem Bai, head of the American Department, Foreign Ministry, July 1989, Hanoi; and *Far Eastern Economic Review*, March 26, 1973, 23.

[25] Interview with a former NLF official who requested anonymity, Ho Chi Minh City, March 1996.

[26] Nguyen Van Tien to Tuyet Thi Vanh, July 28, 1988, in my possession.

[27] Interview with Ba Chu, former NLF official, Ho Chi Minh City, March 1996.

[28] Tran Van Tra, *History of the Bulwark B-2 Theatre*, vol. 5, *Concluding the Thirty-Year War*, publication no. 82783 (Springfield, Va.: Joint Publications Research Service, 1983), 53. This book was originally published by the Van Nghe Publishing House in Ho Chi Minh City and was confiscated by Party officials immediately.

[29] Interview with a former NLF official who requested anonymity, Ho Chi Minh City, March 1996.

[30] Tra, *History of the Bulwark B-2 Theatre*, 33.

[31] Interview with a Lao Dong official who requested anonymity, Hanoi, November 1995. See also Tra, *History of the Bulwark B-2 Theatre*, 53.

[32] William J. Duiker, "Waging Revolutionary War: The Evolution of Hanoi's Strategy in the South, 1959–1965," in Jayne S. Werner and Luu Doan Huynh, eds., *The Vietnam War: Vietnamese and American Perspectives* (Armonk, N.Y.: M. E. Sharpe, 1993), 24–36; and Le Duan, *Thu vao Nam* [Letters to the South] (Hanoi: Nha Xuat Ban Su That, 1986).

[33] General Hoang Van Thai, *How South Vietnam Was Liberated* (Hanoi: Gioi, 1992), 46, 49.

[34] Ibid., 65, 67, 68; Duan, *Thu vao Nam*, 358, 362.

[35] *Cuoc khang chien chong My*, 159.

[36] Tra, *History of the Bulwark B-2 Theatre*, 33.

[37] Broadcast to Europe and East Asia, in English, July 2, 1973, 1530 GMT, Radio Hanoi, radio transcripts, National Archives Center 1, Hanoi.

[38] *Far Eastern Economic Review*, August 6, 1973, 15.

[39] "North Vietnam: Reconstruction and Vigilance," *International Bulletin* 6 (March 25–April 17, 1974): 16.

[40] Nguyen Khanh Toan, "Ho Chu Tich va tinh doan ket quoc te" [President Ho Chi Minh and international solidarity], *Hoc Tap* 18 (November 1972): 16.

[41] Interview with a former NLF official who requested anonymity, Ho Chi Minh City, March 1996.

[42] Interview with Tran Van Dong, former NLF official, Ho Chi Minh City, March 1996.

[43] *Communiqué of the Representatives of the Republic of South Vietnam at the Conference of Non-aligned Nations in Algiers*, pamphlet published by the Embassy of the Republic of South Viet Nam in Cuba. A copy is in my possession.

[44] *Far Eastern Economic Review*, September 10, 1973, 20, and October 1, 1973, 27–28. The three nations that did not vote for the resolution were Indonesia, Malaysia, and Singapore.

[45] *Communiqué of the Representatives.*

[46] "Results of the 21st Plenum," Liberation News Agency, October 22, 1973. Although the plenum was held in mid-June, its resolutions were not approved until October, and there was much debate before the final draft report was recorded.

[47] *Cuoc khang chien chong My*, 161; and Tra, *History of the Bulwark B-2 Theatre*, 45.

[48] Interviews with the curators of Party documents in the National Archives of Viet Nam, Hanoi, July 1992 and November 1995.

[49] "Dong chi Le Duc Tho," 4.

[50] *Cuoc khang chien chong My*, 162; *Lich su Quan Doi Nhan Dan Viet Nam* [History of the People's Army of Viet Nam], vol. 2, bk. 2 (Hanoi: Nha Xuat Ban Quan Doi Nhan Dan, 1990), 297–302; *Su doan 303: Doan Phuoc Long* [The 303d Division: Phuoc Long group] (Hanoi: Nha Xuat Ban Quan Doi Nhan Dan, 1989), 9–12; and Dai Tuong Hoang Van Thai, *Nhung nam tam thang quyet dinh: Hoi ky* [The decisive years: Memoirs] (Hanoi: Nha Xuat Ban Quan Doi Nhan Dan, 1990), 274.

[51] Remarks by Nguyen Thi Binh, former NLF foreign minister and current vice president of the Socialist Republic of Viet Nam, Hanoi, November 1995, Critical Oral History Project transcripts, Watson Institute for International Studies, Brown University and Institute for International Relations, Hanoi.

[52] *Washington Post*, January 5, 1974.

[53] Porter, *Peace Denied*, 260.

[54] George C. Herring, *America's Longest War: The United States and Vietnam, 1950–1975*, 2d ed. (New York: Knopf, 1986), 261.

[55] Remarks by General Hoang Minh Thao, Hanoi, November 1995, Critical Oral History Project transcripts, Watson Institute for International Studies, Brown University and Institute for International Relations, Hanoi.

[56] Remarks by Lieutenant General Nguyen Dinh Uoc, Hanoi, November 1995, Critical Oral History Project transcripts, Watson Institute for International Studies, Brown University and Institute for International Relations, Hanoi.

[57] Clandestine broadcast in Vietnamese, August 8, 1974, 1400 GMT, Liberation Radio, radio transcripts, National Archives Center 1, Hanoi.

[58] Stanley Karnow, *Vietnam: A History* (New York: Penguin, 1983), 661.

[59] *Dai Dan Toc* [The greater national community], August 8, 1974.

[60] Ngo Vinh Long, "Post-Paris Agreement Struggles and the Fall of Saigon," in Werner and Huynh, *Vietnam War*, 209.

[61] *Dai Dan Toc*, September 30, 1974.

[62] *Dong Phuong*, September 27, 1974.

[63] Long, "Post-Paris Agreement Struggles," 211.

[64] *Chinh Luan* [Official discussion], November 5, 1974; *Dien Tin* [Telegraph], September 6, 1974; and *Dai Dan Toc*, September 30, 1974.

[65] John C. Donnell, "South Vietnam in 1975: The Year of the Communist Victory," *Asian Survey* 16 (January 1976): 1–13.

[66] *Washington Post*, November 2, 1974; *Hoa Binh* [Peace], September 27, 1974.

[67] *Washington Post*, October 22, 1974.

[68] *Cuoc khang chien chong My*, 165.

[69] Tra, *History of the Bulwark B-2 Theatre*, 92.

[70] *Cuoc khang chien chong My*, 165–67.

[71] Thai, *How South Vietnam Was Liberated*, 133.

[72] Clandestine broadcast in Vietnamese, October 8, 1974, 1400 GMT, Liberation Radio, radio transcripts, National Archives Center 1, Hanoi.

[73] *Dieu Tin*, October 22, 1974; *Dai Dan Toc*, October 14, 1974; *Hoa Binh*, October 29, 1974.

[74] *Dai Dan Toc*, October 28, 1974.

[75] The U.S. Congress appropriated $450 million in economic aid to Saigon on December 17, 1974, for fiscal year 1975, representing a $100 million increase over the amount authorized for fiscal 1974. In addition, PAVN divisions in the South had remained near the same level (fourteen to fifteen main force divisions) throughout 1974, and only in early 1975 did three additional PAVN divisions cross the DMZ. In March, of course, almost all of PAVN's main force units were sent south, bringing the total to twenty. See Carlyle A. Thayer, "Vietnam: Republic of Vietnam," in Richard Staar, ed., *Yearbook on International Communist Affairs* (Stanford: Hoover Institution Press, 1975), 451–52.

[76] Thai, *Nhung nam thang quyet dinh*, 42.

[77] *Su Doan 303*, 93.

[78] Tra, *History of the Bulwark B-2 Theatre*, 94–100.

[79] Thai, *How South Vietnam Was Liberated*, 156.

[80] *Luc luong vu trang nhan dan Tay nguyen trong khang chien chong My, cuu nuoc* [The people's armed forces of the western highlands during the anti-U.S. resistance war for national salvation] (Hanoi: Nha Xuat Ban Quan Doi Nhan Dan, 1980), 280–320; *Su Doan 10, binh doan Tay nguyen* [Tenth Division, Western Highlands group] (Hanoi: Nha Xuat Ban Quan Doi Nhan Dan, 1987), 175–201; and *Lich su Quan Doi Nhan Dan Viet Nam*, 2:278–300.

[81] *Luc luong vu trang nhan dan Tay nguyen*, 310–20.

[82] Thai, *How South Vietnam Was Liberated*, 166, 169.

[83] Duan, *Thu vao Nam*, 399.

[84] *Su Doan 304: Ky Su* [304th Division: Chronology], vol. 2 (Hanoi: Nha Xuat Ban Quan Doi Nhan Dan, 1990), 298–320.

[85] *Cuoc khang chien chong My*, 176.

[86] *Lich su Quan Doi Nhan Dan Viet Nam*, 2:324.

[87] Clandestine broadcast in Vietnamese, April 4, 1975, 1400 GMT, Liberation Radio, radio transcripts, National Archives Center 1, Hanoi.

[88] *Cuoc khang chien chong My*, 179.

[89] *Time*, May 5, 1975, 12; Gareth Porter, "The Paris Agreement and Revolutionary Strategy in South Vietnam," in Joseph Zasloff and MacAlister Brown, eds., *Communism in Indochina: New Perspectives* (Lexington, Mass.: D. C. Heath, 1975), 72.

[90] Donnell, "South Vietnam in 1975," 4.

[91] Clandestine broadcast in Vietnamese, April 30, 1975, 1400 GMT, Liberation Radio, radio transcripts, National Archives Center 1, Hanoi.

Epilogue

[1] Broadcast in Vietnamese, May 15, 1975, 1530 GMT, Radio Hanoi, radio transcripts, Trung Tam Luu Tru Quoc Gia-1 (hereafter National Archives Center 1, Hanoi).

[2] Truong Nhu Tang, *A Viet Cong Memoir: An Inside Account of the Vietnam War and Its Aftermath* (New York: Vintage, 1985), 264–65.

[3] Broadcast in Vietnamese, May 5 1975, 1400 GMT, Radio Saigon, radio transcripts, National Archives Center, Hanoi.

[4] Broadcast in Vietnamese, November 15, 1975, 1400 GMT, Radio Hanoi, radio transcripts, National Archives Center, Hanoi.

[5] Interview with a former NLF official who requested anonymity, Ho Chi Minh City, July 1989.

[6] *Nhan Dan*, November 29, 1975.

[7] *Far Eastern Economic Review*, December 5, 1975, 23.

[8] Interview with Nguyen Van Khanh, former member of the Alliance for Democratic and Peace Forces, Berkeley, Calif., October 1992.

[9] Nguyen Van Canh, *Vietnam under Communism, 1975–1982* (Stanford: Hoover Institution Press, 1983), 16–17; Doan Van Toai, "The Fate of the National Liberation Front," *Asian Affairs* 8 (March–April 1981): 217.

[10] Joan Baez circulated "An Open Letter to the Socialist Republic of Viet Nam" in 1979, deploring the mistreatment of prisoners of conscience being held in Hanoi's reeducation camps. See *New York Times*, May 30, 1979.

[11] Interview with a Cambodian official who requested anonymity, Phnom Penh, July 1989.

[12] William Duiker, *Vietnam: Revolution in Transition*, 2d ed. (Boulder, Colo.: Westview, 1995), 109–10.

BIBLIOGRAPHY

VIETNAMESE SOURCES

Documents

Declaration of the First Congress of the South Viet Nam National Front for Liberation. Hanoi: Foreign Languages Publishing House, 1962.

Documents Related to the Implementation of the Geneva Agreements Concerning Viet Nam. Hanoi: Press and Information Department, Ministry of Foreign Affairs, 1956.

"Duong loi cach mang mien Nam" [The revolutionary path in the South]. Hanoi: Lao Dong, 1956. Trung Tam Luu Tru Quoc Gia-1 [National Archives Center 1], Hanoi.

Foreign Relations Commission. *Personalities of the South Vietnam Liberation Movement.* Tran Phu: South Vietnam National Front for Liberation, 1965.

Mot so van kien cua Dang ve chong My, cuu nuoc [Selected Party documents related to the anti-U.S. resistance war for national salvation of the fatherland]. 2 vols. Hanoi: Nha Xuat Ban Su That, 1985.

Nguyen Ngoc Thong. *Documents of the First Congress of the People's Front for the Liberation of South Viet Nam.* Ben Tre: Victory Publishing House, 1962.

South Viet Nam Congress of People's Representatives for the Formation of the Provisional Revolutionary Government of the Republic of Viet Nam. Saigon: Giai Phong, 1969.

South Viet Nam National Front for Liberation: Documents. Saigon: Giai Phong, 1968.

Third National Congress of the Viet Nam Workers' Party: Documents. 3 vols. Hanoi: Foreign Languages Publishing House, 1961.

Tinh hinh phong trao dau tranh chinh tri o Nam Bo tu hoa binh lap lai den hien nay [The situation of the political struggle movement in Nam Bo from the restoration of peace to the present]. Ca. 1960. Trung Tam Luu Tru Quoc Gia-1 [National Archives Center 1], Hanoi.

"Tinh hinh va nhiem vu 59" [The situation and tasks for 1959]. Ca. 1959. Trung Tam Luu Tru Quoc Gia-1[National Archives Center 1], Hanoi.

Tran Huy Lieu et al. *Tai lieu tham khao lich su cach mang can dai Viet Nam* [Research materials on the history of the contemporary Vietnamese revolution]. 12 vols. Hanoi: Van Su Dia, 1955–58.

Viet Nam nhung su kien lich su [Viet Nam's historical events]. Hanoi: Nha Xuat Ban Su That, 1990.

Xu Uy Nam Bo [Southern Regional Committee]. "Ban so ket hoc tap ve 'duong loi cach mang mien Nam' " [Preliminary report on the study of "the path of revolution in the South"]. Ca. 1956. Trung Tam Luu Tru Quoc Gia-1[National Archives Center 1], Hanoi.

——. "Chanh sach dien dia" [Policy on land]. Ca. 1957. Trung Tam Luu Tru Quoc Gia-1[National Archives Center 1], Hanoi.

——. "Tinh hinh Nam Bo tu sau hoa binh lap lai den hien nay" [The situation in Nam Bo from the restoration of peace to the present]. Ca. 1960. Trung Tam Luu Tru Quoc Gia-1[National Archives Center 1], Hanoi.

Memoirs and Collections

Bui Diem. *In the Jaws of History.* Boston: Houghton Mifflin, 1987.

Bui Tin. *From Cadre to Exile: The Memoirs of a North Vietnamese Journalist.* Changmai: Silkworm Books, 1995.

Dai Tuong Van Tien Dung: Buoc ngoat lon cua cuoc khang chien chong My [Senior General Van Tien Dung: The big turning point in the anti-U.S. resistance war]. Hanoi: Nha Xuat Ban Quan Doi Nhan Dan, 1989.

Dang Van Viet, Colonel. *Highway 4: The Border Campaign, 1947–1950.* Hanoi: Foreign Languages Publishing House, 1990.

Duong mon tren bien: Ky su Nguyen Tu Duong [Road upon the seas: Memoirs of Nguyen Tu Duong]. Hanoi: Nha Xuat Ban Quan Doi Nhan Dan, 1986.

Ho Chi Minh. *Nhung chang duong lich su ve van* [Glorious historic episodes]. Hanoi: Nha Xuat Ban Quan Doi Nhan Dan, 1973.

——. *Selected Writings, 1920–1969.* Hanoi: Foreign Languages Publishing House, 1973.

——. *Toan tap* [Complete works]. 10 vols. Hanoi: Nha Xuat Ban Su That, 1969–90.

Hoang Minh Thao. *The Victorious Tay Nguyen Campaign.* Hanoi: Foreign Languages Publishing House, 1979.

Hoang Van Hoan. *Giot nuoc trong bien ca: Hoi ky cach mang* [A drop in the ocean: Memoirs of the revolution]. Peking: Foreign Language Press, 1988.

Hoang Van Thai. *How South Vietnam Was Liberated.* Hanoi: Gioi, 1992.

Le Duan. *Thu vao Nam* [Letters to the South]. Hanoi: Nha Xuat Ban Su That, 1986.

Mai Van Bo. *Hanoi-Paris: Hoi ky ngoai giao cua* [Hanoi-Paris: Personal memories of the secret diplomacy]. Ho Chi Minh City: Nha Xuat Ban Van Nghe, 1993.

Nguyen Duy Trinh. *In the Enemy's Net.* Hanoi: Foreign Languages Publishing House, 1962.

Nguyen Thi Dinh. *Khong con duong nao khac* [No other road to take]. Hanoi: Nha Xuat Ban Phu Nu, 1968.

Nguyen Van Hieu. *Ban be ta khap nam chau* [Our friends around the world]. Hanoi: Nha Xuat Ban Van Hoc, 1963.

Pham Van Dong. *Selected Writings.* Hanoi: Foreign Languages Publishing House, 1977.

Tran Van Don. *Our Endless War Inside Vietnam.* San Rafael, Calif.: Presidio Press, 1978.

Tran Van Tra. *History of the Bulwark B-2 Theatre.* Vol. 5: *Concluding the Thirty-Year War.* Document no. 82783. Springfield, Va.: Joint Publications Research Service, 1983.

Truong Nhu Tang. *A Viet Cong Memoir: An Inside Account of the Vietnam War and Its Aftermath.* New York: Vintage, 1985.

Vien Tien Dung. *Dai thang mua xuan* [The great spring victory]. Hanoi: Nha Xuat Ban Quan Doi Nhan Dan, 1977.

——. *South Vietnam. U.S. Defeat Inevitable.* Hanoi: Foreign Languages Publishing House, 1967.

Viet Tran. *Viet Nam: J'ai choisi l'exil* [Viet Nam: I chose exile]. Paris: Seuil, 1979.

Vo Nguyen Giap. *Unforgettable Days.* 3d ed. Hanoi: Gioi, 1994.

——. *Once Again, We Will Win.* Hanoi: Foreign Languages Publishing House, 1966.

——. *People's War, People's Army.* Hanoi: Foreign Languages Publishing House, 1961.

Official Histories

30 nam Duong Ho Chi Minh, 19-5-1959–19-5-1989 [Thirty years on the Ho Chi Minh Trail, May 19, 1959–May 19, 1989]. Hanoi: Binh Doan Truong Son Xuat Ban, 1989.

Bac Ho voi luc luong vu trang nhan dan [Uncle Ho with the people's armed forces]. Hanoi: Nha Xuat Ban Quan Doi Nhan Dan, 1976.

"Bang ke khai tong so can bo va thuong Dan Viet Nam Cong hoa bi Cong San bat giu ke tu 1954" [List of the civil servants, cadres, and civilians of the Republic of Vietnam abducted by the Communists since 1954]. Saigon: Co So An Luat Trung Uong Phu Tong Uy Dan Van, 1973. Document no. 000379, Douglas Pike Collection, NLF Documents, Indochina Archive, University of California at Berkeley.

Ban roi tai cho may bay B.52 [Shooting down B-52 aircraft]. Hanoi: Nha Xuat Ban Quan Doi Nhan Dan, 1978.

Binh doan Cuu Long (Quan Doan 4) [The Mekong/Cuu Long military group (4th Corps)]. Vol. 1. Hanoi: Nha Xuat Ban Quan Doi Nhan Dan, 1989.

Binh doan Huong Giang [The Huong Giang battle group]. Hanoi: Nha Xuat Ban Quan Doi Nhan Dan, 1985.

Bon muoi lam nam hoat dong cua Dang Lao Dong Viet Nam [Forty-five years of activities of the Viet Nam Workers' Party]. Hanoi: Nha Xuat Ban Su That, 1976.

Chien dich phan cong Duong 9, Nam Lao 1971 [The 1971 Southern Laos, Route 9, counteroffensive campaign]. Hanoi: Vien Lich Su Quan Su Viet Nam, Bo Quoc Phong, 1987.

Chien dich phong ngu: Canh dong chum mua mua nam 1972 [Defensive campaigns: The 1972 rainy season in the Plain of Jars]. Ho Chi Minh City: Khoa Nghe Thuat Quan Su, Vien Khoa Hoc Quan Su, 1977.

Chien dich Tay: Nguyen dai thang [The Western Highlands campaign: The great victory]. Hanoi: Nha Xuat Ban Quan Doi Nhan Dan, 1977.

Chien dich tien cong Ba Gia, he 1965 [The Ba Gia offensive campaign, summer 1965]. Hanoi: Vien Lich Su Quan Su Viet Nam, Bo Quoc Phong, 1987.

Chien dich tien cong Binh Gia (Binhl Giax), dong xuan 1964–1965 [The winter–spring Binh Gia offensive campaign, 1964–1965]. Hanoi: Vien Lich Su Quan Su Viet Nam, Bo Quoc Phong, 1988.

Chien dich tien cong Duong 9, Khe Sanh xuan he 1968 [The spring–summer 1968 Khe Sanh Route 9 offensive campaign]. Hanoi: Vien Lich Su Quan Su Viet Nam, Bo Quoc Phong, 1987.

Chien dich tien cong Nguyen Hue, 1972 [The Nguyen Hue offensive campaign, 1972]. Hanoi: Vien Lich Su Quan Su Viet Nam, Bo Quoc Phong, 1988.

Chien dich tien cong tong hop quan khu 8 (Dong Bang Song Cuu Long) 1972 [The combined general offensive in military region 8 (Mekong River Delta), 1972]. Hanoi: Vien Lich Su Quan Su Viet Nam, Bo Quoc Phong, 1987.

Chien thuat phao phong khong [Anti-aircraft artillery tactics]. Vol. 1: *Cap phan doi* [Small unit level]. Hanoi: Nha Xuat Ban Quan Doi Nhan Dan, 1987.

Chien tranh giai phong va chien tranh giu nuoc [Wars of liberation and national salvation]. Vol. 1. Hanoi: Nha Xuat Ban Quan Doi Nhan Dan, 1974.

"Chien truong Tri-Thien-Hue trong cuoc khang chien chong My, cuu nuoc toan thang: Du thao" [The Tri-Thien-Hue battlefield/military region during the victorious anti-U.S. resistance war for national salvation of the fatherland: Draft]. Trung Tam Luu Tru Quoc Gia-1 [National Archives Center 1], Hanoi.

Chong My, cuu nuoc thien anh hung ca vi dai [National salvation against the U.S., a great and courageous chapter]. Hanoi: Nha Xuat Ban Quan Doi Nhan Dan, 1985.

Chu Tich Ho Chi Minh voi cong tac ngoai giao [President Ho Chi Minh and the diplomatic works]. Hanoi: Nha Xuat Ban Su That, 1990.

Cong tac hau can: chien dich Duong 9 Khe Sanh xuan he 1968 [Rear services operations: Spring–summer Khe Sanh Route 9 campaign of 1968]. Hanoi: Tong Cuc Hau Can, 1988.

Cuoc khang chien chong My, cuu nuoc, 1954–1975: Nhung su kien quan su [The anti-U.S. resistance war for national salvation of the fatherland, 1954–1975: Military events]. Hanoi: Nha Xuat Ban Quan Doi Nhan Dan, 1988.

Dang Thai Mai. *Van tho cach mang Viet Nam dau the ky XX* [Revolutionary Vietnamese literature from the early twentieth century]. 3d ed. Hanoi: Van Hoc Giai Phong, 1976.

Dien Bien Phu: Trang su anh hung [Dien Bien Phu: A courageous page of history]. Hanoi: Nha Xuat Ban Quan Doi Nhan Dan, 1984.

Ho Chi Minh. *Against U.S Aggression for National Salvation.* Hanoi: Foreign Languages Publishing House, 1967.

Ho Chi Minh Trail, The. Hanoi: Red River Press, 1982.

Ho Chi Minh ve cong tac Dang cong tac chinh tri trong luc luong vu tran nhan dan [Ho Chi Minh on Party tasks and political tasks in the people's army]. Hanoi: Nha Xuat Ban Quan Doi Nhan Dan, 1990.

Hop tuyen thao van yeu nuoc va cach mang [Collection of patriotic and revolutionary literature]. 2d ed. Hanoi: Van Hoc, 1976.

Huong tien con Sai Gon–Gia Dinh, 1968 [The Saigon–Gia Dinh offensive, 1968]. Hanoi: Vien Lich Su Quan Su Viet Nam, Bo Quoc Phong, 1988.

Huong tien cong va noi day Tet Mau Than o Tri-Thien-Hue (Nam 1968) [The general offensive and uprising of Tet Mau Than (Tet 1968) in Tri-Thien-Hue]. Hanoi: Vien Lich Su Quan Su Viet Nam, 1988.

Huynh Kim Khanh. *Vietnamese Communism, 1925–1945*. Ithaca: Cornell University Press, 1982.

The Indochinese Peoples Will Win. Hanoi: Foreign Languages Publishing House, 1970.

Indomitable South Vietnam. Hanoi: Foreign Languages Publishing House, 1964.

Ky hieu quan doi [Military symbols]. Hanoi: Bo Tong Tham Muu, Quan Doi Nhan Dan, 1975.

Le Duan. *Cach mang xa hoi chu nghia o Viet Nam: Tac pham chon loc* [The socialist revolution in Viet Nam: Selected writings]. Vol. 4. Hanoi: Nha Xuat Ban Su That, 1984.

——. *On Some Present International Problems*. 2d ed. Hanoi: Foreign Languages Publishing House, 1964.

——. *On the Socialist Revolution in Viet Nam*. 3 vols. Hanoi: Foreign Languages Publishing House, 1965–67.

——. *Some Questions Concerning the International Tasks of Our Party: Speech at the Ninth Party Plenum of the Third Central Committee Meeting of the Viet Nam Workers' Party, December, 1963*. Peking: Foreign Language Press, 1964.

——. *Ta nhat dinh thang, dich nhat dinh thua* [We will certainly win, the enemy will certainly be defeated]. Hanoi: Nha Xuat Ban Tien Phong, 1966.

Le Trong Tan. *May van de chi dao va chi huy tac chien* [A few issues concerning directing and commanding combat]. Hanoi: Nha Xuat Ban Quan Doi Nhan Dan, 1979.

Le Van Chat. *The Undeclared War in South Vietnam*. Hanoi: Foreign Languages Publishing House, 1962.

Lich su bo doi bien phong [History of the border defense troops]. Vol. 1: "1959–1979." Hanoi: Nha Xuat Ban Cong An Nhan Dan, 1990.

Lich su bo doi dac cong [History of the army sappers]. Vol. 1. Hanoi: Nha Xuat Ban Quan Doi Nhan Dan, 1987.

"Lich su bo doi hoa hoc: Du thao" [History of the chemical forces: Draft]. Vol. 1: "1958–1975." Trung Tam Luu Tru Quoc Gia-1 [National Archives Center 1], Hanoi.

"Lich su bo doi thong tin lien lac: So thao" [History of the communications and liaison troops: Draft]. 2 vols. Trung Tam Luu Tru Quoc Gia-1 [National Archives Center 1], Hanoi.

"Lich su cong an nhan dan Viet Nam" [Draft history of the Vietnamese people's public security]. Vol. 2: "1954–1965." Trung Tam Luu Tru Quoc Gia-1 [National Archives Center 1], Hanoi.

Lich su cong binh Viet Nam, 1945–1975 [History of the Vietnamese engineer corps, 1945–1975]. Hanoi: Nha Xuat Ban Quan Doi Nhan Dan, 1991.

Lich su Dang Cong San Viet Nam [History of the Vietnamese Communist Party]. Hanoi: Nha Xuat Ban Su That, 1980.

Lich su Hai Quan Nhan Dan Viet Nam [History of the People's Navy of Viet Nam]. Hanoi: Nha Xuat Ban Quan Doi Nhan Dan, 1985.

Lich su khang chien chong My, cuu nuoc [History of the anti-U.S. resistance war for national salvation of the fatherland]. 2 vols. Hanoi: Nha Xuat Ban Su That, 1990.

Lich Su Quan Doi Nhan Dan Viet Nam: Du thao tom tat [History of the People's Army of Viet Nam: Draft summary]. Pt. 1. Hanoi: Nha Xuat Ban Quan Doi Nhan Dan, 1977.

Lich su Quan Doi Nhan Dan Viet Nam [History of the People's Army of Viet Nam]. Vol. 2, bks. 1 and 2. Hanoi: Nha Xuat Ban Quan Doi Nhan Dan, 1988–90.

Lich Su Viet Nam [History of Viet Nam]. Hanoi: Khoa Hoc Xa Hoi, 1971.

Luat Su Nguyen Huu Tho [Lawyer Nguyen Huu Tho]. Saigon: Nha Xuat Ban Van Hoc, 1995.

Luc luong vu trang nhan dan Tay nguyen trong khang chien chong My, cuu nuoc [The people's armed forces of the Western Highlands during the anti-U.S. resistance war for national salvation of the fatherland]. Hanoi: Nha Xuat Ban Quan Doi Nhan Dan, 1980.

"Luoc su, Ba muoi nam chien dau va xay dung cua phao binh Quan Doi Nhan Dan Viet Nam" [Draft history, thirty years of combat and development of the People's Army of Viet Nam artillery corps]. Trung Tam Luu Tru Quoc Gia-1 [National Archives Center 1], Hanoi.

Luu Van Loi and Nguyen Anh Vu. *Tiep xuc bi mat Viet Nam-Hoa Ky truoc hoi nghi Pa-ri* [Secret contacts between Viet Nam and the United States before the Paris talks]. Hanoi: Vien Quan He Quoc Te, 1990.

Mau Than Saigon [The Tet Offensive in Saigon]. Ho Chi Minh City: Nha Xuat Ban Van Nghe, 1988.

May van de tong ket chien tranh va viet lich su quan su [Selected issues related to the conclusions and the writing of the military history of the war]. Hanoi: Vien Lich Su Quan Su Viet Nam, 1987.

Mien Dong Nam Bo khang chien, 1945–1975 [The war in Eastern Nam Bo Region, 1945–1975]. Vol. 1. Hanoi: Nha Xuat Ban Quan Doi Nhan Dan, 1990.

50 nam dau tranh kien cuong cua Dang bo va nhan dan thanh pho [Fifty years of steadfast struggle of the city Party organization and the people]. Ho Chi Minh City: Nha Xuat Ban Thanh Pho Ho Chi Minh, 1981.

New Facts: Phu Loi Mass Murder in South Viet Nam. Hanoi: Foreign Languages Publishing House, 1959.

Nghiem Ke To. *Viet Nam mau lau* [Viet Nam in blood and fire]. Saigon: Mai Linh, 1954.

Nguyen Chi Thanh. *Who Will Win in South Viet Nam?* Peking: Foreign Languages Press, 1963.

Nguyen Duy Trinh. *Mat tran ngoai giao thoi ky chong My, cuu nuoc, 1965–1975* [The diplomatic front during the anti-U.S. resistance war for national salvation of the fatherland, 1965–1975]. Hanoi: Nha Xuat Ban Su That, 1979.

——. *Tren mat tran ngoai giao* [The diplomatic front]. Hanoi: Nha Xuat Ban Su That, 1972.

Nguyen Khac Vien. *The Long Resistance, 1858–1975*. 2d ed. Hanoi: Foreign Languages Publishing House, 1978.

Nguyen Quyet. *Quan Khu ba, nhung nam danh My* [Military region 3, the years of fighting the Americans]. Hanoi: Nha Xuat Ban Quan Doi Nhan Dan, 1989.

Nguyen Sinh and Vu Ky Lan. *Fighting at the Seventeenth Parallel.* Hanoi: Foreign Languages Publishing House, 1982.

Nguyen Viet Phuong. *Van tai quan su chien luoc tren Duong Ho Chi Minh trong khang chien chong My* [Strategic military transport on the Ho Chi Minh Trail during the war against the Americans]. Hanoi: Nha Xuat Ban Quan Doi Nhan Dan, 1988.

Nhung hoat dong pha hoai va lat do cua CIA o Viet Nam [CIA subversion and sabotage in Viet Nam]. Hanoi: Nha Xuat Ban Cong An Nhan Dan, 1990.

One Year of Communist Violations of the Paris Agreement. Saigon: Ministry of Foreign Affairs, 1974.

Ong co van: Ho so mot diep vien [Mister adviser: A spy's file]. 3 vols. Hanoi: Nha Xuat Ban Quan Doi Nhan Dan, 1988.

An Outline History of the Viet Nam Workers' Party. Hanoi: Foreign Languages Publishing House, 1970.

Pham Van Bach et al. *Fascist Terror in South Viet Nam: Law 10/59.* Hanoi: Foreign Languages Publishing House, 1961.

The Phu Loi Massacre in South Vietnam. Hanoi: Foreign Languages Publishing House, 1959.

The Problems Facing the Democratic Republic of Viet Nam in 1961. Hanoi: Foreign Languages Publishing House, 1961.

Quan doan 2: So luoc lich su [Second corps: Historical sketch]. Vol. 1. Hanoi: Cuc Chinh Tri Quan Doan 2 Xuat Ban, 1979.

Quan doan canh Bac: Hoi ky Cua Thieu Tuong Hung Phung [Northern wing corps: Memoirs of Major General Hung Phung]. Hanoi: Nha Xuat Ban Quan Doi Nhan Dan, 1981.

Quang Loi. *Growing Oppression, Growing Struggle.* Hanoi: Foreign Languages Publishing House, 1961.

——. *South of the 17th Parallel.* Hanoi: Foreign Languages Publishing House, 1959.

Quan khu ba: Nhung nam danh My [Military region 3: The years of fighting the Americans]. Hanoi: Nha Xuat Ban Quan Doi Nhan Dan, 1989.

Quan khu nam: Thang loi va nhung bai hoc trong khang chien chong My [Military region 5: Successes and lessons learned during the war against the Americans]. 2 vols. Hanoi: Nha Xuat Ban Quan Doi Nhan Dan, 1981–82.

Suc manh Viet Nam [The strength of Viet Nam]. Hanoi: Nha Xuat Ban Quan Doi Nhan Dan, 1976.

Su doan 2 [The 2d division]. Da Nang: Nha Xuat Ban Da Nang, 1989.

Su doan 7 [The 7th division]. 2 vols. Hanoi: Nha Xuat Ban Quan Doi Nhan Dan, 1986–90.

Su doan 9 [The 9th division]. Hanoi: Nha Xuat Ban Quan Doi Nhan Dan, 1990.

Su doan 10, binh doan Tay nguyen [The 10th division, Western Highlands battle group]. Hanoi: Nha Xuat Ban Quan Doi Nhan Dan, 1987.

Su doan 303: Doan Phuoc Long [The 303d division: The Phuoc Long group]. Hanoi: Nha Xuat Ban Quan Doi Nhan Dan, 1989.

Su doan 304: Ky su [304th division: Chronology]. 2 vols. Hanoi: Nha Xuat Ban Quan Doi Nhan Dan, 1980–90.

Su doan 316 [316th division]. 2 vols. Hanoi: Nha Xuat Ban Quan Doi Nhan Dan, 1981–86.

Su doan 325, 1954–1975 [325th division, 1954–1975]. Vol. 2. Hanoi: Nha Xuat Ban Quan Doi Nhan Dan, 1986.

Su doan chien thang su doan 312: Ky su [The victory division, 312th division: A chronicle]. Vols. 1 and 2. Hanoi: Nha Xuat Ban Quan Doi Nhan Dan, 1980.

Su doan dong bang: Binh doan Tay nguyen [The delta division: The Western Highlands military group]. Vol. 3. Hanoi: Nha Xuat Ban Quan Doi Nhan Dan, 1984.

Su doan dong bang, su doan 320B, quan doan 1 [The delta division, 320B division, 1st corps]. Hanoi: Nha Xuat Ban Quan Doi Nhan Dan, 1983.

Su doan phong khong 367: Lich su [The 367th air defense division: A history]. Vol.1. Hanoi: Quan Binh Chung Phong Khong Xuat Ban, 1988.

Su doan quan tien phong (su doan 308) [The vanguard division (308th division)]. Vol. 3: "Ky su" [Memoir]. Hanoi: Nha Xuat Ban Quan Doi Nhan Dan, 1979.

Su doan sao vang (su doan 3) binh doan Chi Lang quan khu 1: Ky su [Yellow star division (3d division), Chi Lang military group, military region 1: Memoir]. Hanoi: Nha Xuat Ban Quan Doi Nhan Dan, 1984.

Su doan Song Lam (su doan 341) [The Lam River division (341 division)]. Hanoi: Nha Xuat Ban Quan Doi Nhan Dan, 1984.

Tang cuong suc chien dau cua Dang [Strengthening the Party's combat capability]. Hanoi: Nha Xuat Ban Su That, 1988.

Ten Years of the PLAF. Saigon: Giai Phong, 1971.

Tet Mau Than 68 [Tet 1968]. Hanoi: Ban Tuyen Huan Trung Uong, 1988.

Thanh Nam. *In the Shadow of the American Embassy.* South Viet Nam: Giai Phong, 1973.

Thu do Ha Noi: Lich su khang chien chong My, cuu nuoc, 1954–1975 [The capital of Hanoi: The anti-U.S. resistance war for national salvation of the fatherland, 1954–1975]. Hanoi: Nha Xuat Ban Quan Doi Nhan Dan, 1991.

Thu Trang. *Nhung hoat dong cua Phan Chu Trinh tai Phap, 1911–1925* [Phan Chu Trinh's activities in France, 1911–1925]. Paris: Sudestasie, 1983.

Tong ket cong tac Dang cong tac chinh tri trong cuoc khang chien chong My, cuu nuoc, 1954–1975 [Writing the history of Party tasks and political tasks during the anti-U.S. resistance war for national salvation of the fatherland]. Hanoi: Nha Xuat Ban Quan Doi Nhan Dan, 1990.

Tong ket cong tac hau can: Chien truong Nam Bo-cuc Nam Trung Bo (B-2) trong khang chien chong My [Rear services operations report: Southern Region battlefield—Southern Central Region department (B-2) during the war against the Americans]. Hanoi: Tong Cuc Hua Can, Quan Doi Nhan Dan, 1986.

Tong ket tac chien phao binh [Artillery tactical operations reports]. Hanoi: Binh Chung Phoa Binh, Quan Doi Nhan Dan Viet Nam, 1985.

Tram hoa dua no tren dat Bac [The blooming of the hundred flowers in the North]. Saigon: Mat Tran Bao Ve Tu Do Van Hao, 1959.

Tran Cong Tuong and Pham Thanh Vinh. *The NLF, Symbol of Independence, Democracy, and Peace in South Viet Nam.* Hanoi: Foreign Languages Publishing House, 1962.

Tran Kim Tuyen. "Study of the National Liberation Front of South Vietnam." Saigon, 1972. Document no. 0009888, Douglas Pike Collection, NLF Documents, Indochina Archive, University of California at Berkeley.

Tran Van Giau and Le Van Chat. *The South Viet Nam Liberation National Front.* Hanoi: Foreign Languages Publishing House, 1962.

Trung Nam et al. *On the Highway 9 Front.* South Viet Nam: Giai Phong, 1971.

Truong Buu Lam. *Patterns of Vietnamese Response to Foreign Intervention: 1858–1900.* Monograph Series no. 11. New Haven: Yale University, Southeast Asian Studies, 1967.

Truong Chinh. *Cach mang dan toc dan chu nhan dan Viet Nam: Tac pham chon loc* [The Vietnamese people's national democratic revolution: Selected works]. Hanoi: Nha Xuat Ban Su That, 1976.

——. *The Resistance Will Win.* 3d ed. Hanoi: Foreign Languages Publishing House, 1966.

——. *Ve cong tac mat tran hien nay* [On the front work at present]. Hanoi: Nha Xuat Ban Su That, 1972.

The Truth about Vietnam–China Relations over the Last Thirty Years. Hanoi: Ministry of Foreign Affairs, 1979.

Van tai quan su chien luoc tren Duong Ho Chi Minh trong khang chien chong My [Strategic military transport on the Ho Chi Minh Trail during the anti-U.S. resistance war for national salvation of the fatherland]. Hanoi: Nha Xuat Ban Quan Doi Nhan Dan, 1988.

"Viet Bac: 30 nam chien tranh cach mang, 1945–1975" [Viet Bac military region: Thirty years of revolutionary war, 1945–1975]. Vol. 1. Hanoi: Nha Xuat Ban Quan Doi Nhan Dan, 1990.

Vu Can. *North Vietnam: A Daily Resistance.* Hanoi: Foreign Languages Publishing House, 1975.

Vu Van Thai. *Fighting and Negotiating in Vietnam: A Strategy.* Santa Monica: Rand Corporation, October 1969.

We Open the File. Hanoi: Foreign Languages Publishing House, 1961.

Essays

An Bao Minh. "Uprisings in Ben Tre." *Vietnamese Studies* 18/19 (1968): 130–50.

"Bai phat bieu cua dong chi Le Duan, truong doan dai bieu Dang Lao Dong Viet Nam tai Dai Hoi lan thu 23 cua Dang Cong San Lien-Xo" [Speech by Comrade Le Duan, head of the Viet Nam Lao Dong Party delegation, to the 23d Congress of the Communist Party of the Soviet Union]. *Hoc Tap* 12 (May 1966): 4–9.

"Bon xam luoc My da bi trung tri dich dang, xa luan" [U.S. aggressors were appropriately punished, editorial]. *Hoc Tap* 11 (April 1965): 8–9.

"Dong Chi Le Duc Tho noi ve mot so van de tong ket chien tranh va bien soan lich su quan su" [Comrade Le Duc Tho discusses a number of questions on the general assessment of the war and writing of military history]. *Tap Chi Lich Su Quan Su* 25 (March 1988): 1–10.

Ha Van Lu. "That bai va khung hoang tram trong cua de quoc My va be lu tay sai o mien Nam" [Serious failure and crisis of the U.S. imperialists and their henchmen in the South]. *Hoc Tap* 10 (October 1964): 58–65.

——. "Van de giai phong dan toc trong thoi dai hien nay" [The question of national liberation in the present era]. *Hoc Tap* 10 (March 1964): 1–12.

Ho Chi Minh. "Hai muoi nam dau tranh thang loi cua Cach Mang Viet Nam" [Twenty years of successful struggle of the Viet Nam Revolution]. *Hoc Tap* 11 (September 1965): 1–3.

Ho Si Than. "Quyet tam danh thang giac My xam luoc, quan va dan Vinh-linh vuot moi kho khan de san xuat va chien dau tot" [Determined to defeat the American invader, Vinh-linh military and civilians overcome all difficulties to produce and fight well]. *Hoc Tap* 11 (June 1965): 26–29.

Hoang Minh Thao. "Duong loi xay dung luc luong vu trang nhan dan cua Dang" [The Party line on building the people's armed forces]. *Hoc Tap* 13 (February 1967): 62–72.

——. "Quan diem chien tranh nhan dan cua Dang ta" [Our Party's viewpoint on people's war]. *Hoc Tap* 12 (December 1966): 26–38.

Hoang Nam, Linh Vien, Phong Hien, et al. "U.S. Neo-colonialism in South Viet Nam: The Vietnamization of the War." *Vietnamese Studies* 42 (1975): 1–294.

Hoang Quoc Viet. "Giai cap cong nhan Viet Nam can nang cao hon nua tinh tien phong chien dau cach mang, cung toan dan quyet danh thang de quoc My xam luoc" [The Vietnamese workers' class must further raise its vanguard revolutionary spirit and together with all people defeat the U.S. imperialists]. *Hoc Tap* 11 (May 1965): 38–41.

——. "Nen tang va nguon goc suc manh cua mat tran dan toc thong nhat" [The basis and the source of strength of the unified national front]. *Hoc Tap* 11 (September 1965): 32–37.

——. "Phong trao dau tranh cua nhan dan My va cuoc khang chien chong My, cuu nuoc cua nhan dan ta" [Struggle movement of the American people and the anti-U.S. resistance war for national salvation of the fatherland of our people]. *Hoc Tap* 12 (June 1966): 51–60.

Hoang Van Thai. "Am muu xam luoc cua de quoc My va qua trinh chien dau thang loi cua nhan dan ta" [The American aggressors' conspiracy and the development of the victorious struggle of our people]. *Hoc Tap* 11 (September 1965): 38–47.

——. "Cung co va tang cuong quoc phong nhan dan, dua su nghiep chong My, cuu nuoc den toan thang" [Consolidate and strengthen the people's national defense and lead the anti-U.S. resistance war for national salvation of the fatherland to complete victory]. *Hoc Tap* 12 (January 1966): 37–49.

——. "Gop phan nghien cuu su thanh hinh va phat trien cua duong loi quan su cua Dang ta—khoi nghia vu trang gianh chinh quyen va chien tranh nhan dan" [To help study the formation and development of the military strategy of our Party: Armed uprising for seizure of power and people's war]. *Hoc Tap* 11 (June 1965): 14-21.

——. "Toan Dang, toan dan va toan quan ta hay nang cao khi the cach mang, quyet tam danh thang giac My xam luoc" [Let our party, people, and army heighten our revolutionary strength and defeat the American aggressors]. *Hoc Tap* 11 (May 1965): 7–13.

——. "Tu tuong chien luoc chien thuat cua chien tranh nhan dan—duong loi xay dung luc luong vu trang nhan dan" [Thoughts on tactics and strategy of people's war: The direction to build the armed forces]. *Hoc Tap* 11 (July 1965): 44–51.

Hoang Xuan Binh, Hoang Nguyen, Phan Thai, and Ton Vy. "The Year 1968." *Vietnamese Studies* 22 (1970): 1–354.

"Hoc tap quan diem van hoa, van nghe cach mang cua Ho Chu Tich" [Study the revolutionary literature and cultural viewpoint of President Ho Chi Minh]. *Hoc Tap* 11 (May 1965): 23–31.

Hong Chuong. "35 nam dau tranh anh dung va thang loi ve vang" [35 years of a brave and glorious successful struggle]. *Hoc Tap* 11 (February 1965): 36–44.

——. "Kien quyet danh thang cuoc chien tranh pha hoai cua giac My o mien Bac nuoc ta" [Let us resolutely defeat the American war of destruction in the North of our country]. *Hoc Tap* 11 (September 1965): 48–55.

——. "Lanh tu va quan chung" [Leaders and the masses]. *Hoc Tap* 13 (May 1967): 61–66.

——. "Su nghiep giai phong dan toc cua chung ta nhat dinh se thang loi hoan toan" [Our efforts to liberate the people will be completely successful]. *Hoc Tap* 10 (July 1964): 16–29.

Hong Vu. "Dang Nhan Dan Cach Mang Viet Nam voi su mang lich su giai phong mien Nam" [The Viet Nam People's Revolutionary Party and its historic mission to liberate the South]. *Hoc Tap* 12 (January 1966): 31–36.

Huong Nam. "Am muu cua My truoc sau van nham pha hoai hiep nghi Gio-ne-vo 1954 ve Viet Nam" [The U.S. conspiracy before and after its violations of the 1954 agreement on Viet Nam]. *Hoc Tap* 15 (July 1969): 61–74.

——. "Hai lap truong dam, phan doi lap" [At the peace talks, two opposing negotiating positions]. *Hoc Tap* 18 (September 1972): 70–76.

——. "Keo dai va Mo rong chien tranh xam luoc o Dong-duong, Nich xon, cang lam cho nhung kho khan cua nuoc My them tram trong" [The protraction and escalation of the U.S. involvement in Indochina, designed by Nixon, aggravated the U.S. problems]. *Hoc Tap* 16 (October 1970): 82–89.

——. "Nhan dan 3 nuoc Dong-duong tang cuong doan ket chong de quoc My va bon tay sai" [The people of the three Indochina countries were united against the American imperialists and their followers]. *Hoc Tap* 16 (July 1970): 47–52.

La Con. "Su phat trien manh me cua phong trao nhan dan the gioi ung ho Viet Nam danh thang de quoc My xam luoc" [To develop the strongest movement of the peoples of the world to support Viet Nam and defeat the imperialist American invasion]. *Hoc Tap* 14 (August 1968): 84–89.

Le Duan. "Cuu nuoc la nghia vu thieng lieng cua ca dan toc ta" [National salvation is the sacred mission of our people]. *Hoc Tap* 12 (December 1966): 7–13.

——. "On the South Vietnamese Revolution." *Vietnamese Studies* 18/19 (1968): 7–15.

——. "Xay dung tu tuong lam chu tap the tren lap truong giai cap vo san" [Let us build the collective ownership concept on the proletariat standpoint]. *Hoc Tap* 11 (June 1965): 1–13.

Le Duc Tho. "Chuyen huong va tang cuong cong tac xay dung Dang de bao dam hoan thanh thang loi su nghiep chong My, cuu nuoc" [Change direction and build up the Party to complete the victory in the anti-U.S. resistance war for national salvation of the fatherland]. *Hoc Tap* 12 (February 1966): 8–24.

——. "Cung co moi lien he giua to chuc co so cua Dang va quan chung nhan dan" [The relationship between basic Party organizations and the masses must be consolidated]. *Hoc Tap* 12 (November 1966): 6–15.

——. "Day manh phe binh va tu phe binh, khac phuc mau thuan trong Dang, de cung co doan ket va tang cuong suc chien dau cua Dang" [Raise criticism and self-criticism, resolve conflicts in our Party to consolidate and strengthen the combative spirit of our Party]. *Hoc Tap* 11 (February 1965): 7–17.

——. "Tang cuong vai tro lanh dao cua Dang o cac xi nghiep" [Strengthening the role of the Party's leadership in enterprises]. *Hoc Tap* 11 (April 1965): 42–56.

Le Tan Danh. "The South Vietnam National Front for Liberation, 1961–1965." *Vietnamese Studies* 11 (1966): 154–82.

Le Thanh Nghi. "Phat huy cao do chu nghia anh hung cach mang, day manh cao trao thi dua chong My, cuu nuoc, quyet tam danh thang giac My xam luoc" [Promote revolutionary heroism, enhance the anti-U.S. resistance movement for national salvation, determine to defeat the U.S. aggressors]. *Hoc Tap* 13 (January 1967): 21–45.

Le The Son. "May kinh nghiem ve chien dau va sanx uat cua quan va dan Thanh-hoa." [Several production and combat experiences of the army and people of Thanh-hoa]. *Hoc Tap* 11 (June 1965): 44–48.

Luu Qui Ky. "Cang ngoan co va gian doi, de quoc My cang them co lap!" [The more persistent and deceitful, the more isolated the U.S. imperialists became!]. *Hoc Tap* 14 (July 1968): 74–81.

"Mot vai van de trong nhiem vu quoc te cua Dang ta" [Some issues regarding our Party's international works]. *Hoc Tap* 10 (February 1964): 1–20.

"Nghi quyet co ban cua Dai hoi dai bieu quoc dan mien Nam Viet Nam"

[Statement by the Provisional Revolutionary Government of the Republic of South Viet Nam]. *Hoc Tap* 15 (June 1969): 12–15.

Nguyen Chi Thanh. "Cang thuoc tu tuong cong viec giua luc luong vu trang va nhan dan o mien Nam va 1965–66 kho mua thang loi" [The ideological task among the armed forces and people of our South and the 1965–66 dry season victories]. *Hoc Tap* 12 (July 1966): 1–10.

——. "Hoc tap cai moi, ung ho cai moi, thuc day cai moi phat trien" [Learn new ideas, support new ideas, and push for new ideas]. *Hoc Tap* 7 (June 1961): 1–4.

——. "May kinh nghiem ve hop tac hoa nong nghiep cua chung ta" [A few experiences on agricultural collectivization]. *Hoc Tap* 10 (November 1964): 1–20.

Nguyen Duy Trinh. "Chu Tich Ho Chi Minh, nguoi con uu tu cua giai cap cong nhan va cua dan toc Viet Nam" [President Ho Chi Minh, the brilliant son of the workers' class and Viet people]. *Hoc Tap* 11 (May 1965): 14–22.

——. "Lap Truong Bon Diem, ngon co doc lap va hoa binh cua chung ta hien nay" [The Four-Point Stand, our banner of independence and peace at the present time]. *Hoc Tap* 13 (April 1967): 10–22.

——. "Nang cao trinh do lanh dao to chuc va chi dao thuc hien, phan dau hoan thanh thang loi ke hoach 5 nam thu nhat" [Improving our leadership in the organization and guidance of plan implementation, and striving to achieve the first five-year plan]. *Hoc Tap* 11 (March 1965): 6–14.

——. "Tang cuong nha nuoc dan chu nhan dan de lam tot nhiem vu vua san xuat vua chien dau" [Let us strengthen the people's democratic state to fulfill the task of production and combat]. *Hoc Tap* 11 (September 1965): 24–31.

Nguyen Hoang, Hoang Xuan Binh, et al. "Indochina, 1971–72." *Vietnamese Studies* 33 (1972): 1–211.

Nguyen Khac Vien. "Nguyen tac va noi dung chu yeu cua giai phap toan bo ve van de mien Nam Viet Nam, gop phan lap lai hoa binh o Viet Nam" [The principal and important facts of a settlement in South Viet Nam, contributions to rebuilding the peace in Viet Nam]. *Hoc Tap* 15 (June 1969): 27–29.

——, ed. "South Viet Nam: From the NLF to the Provisional Revolutionary Government." *Vietnam Studies* 23 (1969–70): 11–428.

Nguyen Khanh Toan. "Ho Chu Tich va tinh doan ket quoc te" [President Ho Chi Minh and international solidarity]. *Hoc Tap* 18 (November 1972): 14–19.

Nguyen Minh Vy. "Phong trao cong nhan va nhan dan trong cac thanh thi o mien Nam Viet Nam" [Workers' and citizens' movement in the cities of the South]. *Hoc Tap* 10 (July 1964): 40–47.

Nguyen Ninh. "Chinh quyen tay sai moi cua My o mien Nam Viet Nam khong tranh khoi that bai tham hai" [Inevitable failure ahead for the new American lackey government in the South]. *Hoc Tap* 10 (May 1964): 44–51.

Nguyen Si Que. "Dang Bo Nghe-an lanh dao san xuat va chien dau" [The Nghe-an Party segment provides leadership in production and combat]. *Hoc Tap* 11 (June 1965): 40–43.

Nguyen Thi Binh. "Phu nu mien Nam dau tranh anh dung chong de quoc My va tay sai" [Women in the South are bravely fighting the American imperialists and their lackeys]. *Hoc Tap* 12 (March 1966): 22–27.

Nguyen Thi Thap. "Van De Phu Nu va Cach Mang" [Women and the Revolution]. *Hoc Tap* 11 (March 1965): 25–30.

Nguyen Tho Chan. "Quang-ninh day manh san xuat va san sang chien dau" [Quang-ninh steps up production and combat readiness]. *Hoc Tap* 11 (April 1965): 64–69.

Nguyen Tien. "Ke hoach Gion-xon McNamara khong the cuu de quoc My va tay sai thoat khoi su that bai tham hai" [Johnson-McNamara plan can't bail the U.S. imperialists and their lackeys out of their miserable failure]. *Hoc Tap* 10 (April 1964): 35–39.

Nguyen Tu Thoan. "Quang-binh vua san xuat vua chien dau thang loi" [Quang-binh both produces and fights successfully]. *Hoc Tap* 11 (June 1965): 30–35.

Nguyen Van Tien. "Vung giai phong mien Nam Viet Nam va su nghiep dau tranh chong My, cuu nuoc" [The South Vietnamese liberated zones and the anti-U.S. resistance war for national salvation of the fatherland]. *Hoc Tap* 13 (July 1967): 42–48.

Nguyen Xuan Linh. "Chien thang tran dau" [The initial victory]. *Hoc Tap* 11 (June 1965): 36–39.

Pham Hung. "Giai quyet dung dan moi quan he giua dong vien cao do suc nguoi, suc cua va boi duong suc dan de tang cuong tiem luc kinh te va quoc phong" [Let us properly solve the relation between mobilizing manpower and resources and increasing the people's strength to strengthen economic and defense potentials]. *Hoc Tap* 13 (March 1967): 13–32.

Pham Thanh Bien et al. "Ve cuoc Khoi Nghia Tra-Bong va mien Tay Quang Ngai mua thu 1959" [The Tra Bong and western Quang Ngai uprisings, 1959]. *Nghien Cuu Lich Su* 146 (September–October 1972): 11–22.

Pham Van Dong. "Giuong cao ngon co Cach Mang Thang Tam, phat huy thang loi cua 20 nam qua, tien len chien thang de quoc My xam luoc, bao ve mien Bac, giai phong mien Nam" [Raise the August Revolution flag, promote the victory of the last twenty years, advance to defeat the U.S.

aggressors, protect the North and liberate the South]. *Hoc Tap* 11 (September 1965): 4–17.
——. "Mot so van de ve viec tiep tuc cai tao xa hoi chu nghia, nhat la trong nhung nganh, nghe lao dong thu cong" [A few problems concerning the reform of socialism, especially in the field of handicrafts]. *Hoc Tap* 11 (March 1965): 1–5.
——. "Phat huy chu nghia anh hung cach mang, day manh su nghiep chong My, cuu nuoc den thang loi hoan toan" [Promote revolutionary heroism, strengthen the anti-U.S. resistance for national salvation of the fatherland to lead to complete victory]. *Hoc Tap* 13 (January 1967): 17–20.
Phan Hanh. "Ket hop dau tranh chinh tri voi dau tranh vu trang la hinh thuc dau tranh sang tao cua cach mang mien Nam" [A combination of political struggle with armed struggle is the creative form of the revolution in the South]. *Hoc Tap* 11 (July 1965): 30–38.
——. "Muoi nam dau tranh, muoi nam thang loi" [Ten years of struggle, ten years of victory]. *Hoc Tap* 10 (July 1964): 48–55.
Phan Hien. "Vau danh, vua dam trong chong My, cuu nuoc" [Fighting while negotiating during the anti-U.S. resistance war for national salvation of the fatherland]. *Tap Chi Lich Su Quan Su* 25 (January 1988): 74–82, 95.
Quang Loi. "Nhan dan My phan doi chien tranh xam luoc Viet Nam cua de quoc My" [The American people protest the U.S. imperialists' war of aggression in Viet Nam]. *Hoc Tap* 12 (March 1966): 83–91.
Quang Thai. "Dua linh danh thue sang nam Viet Nam, Bon Pac Chung Hy dang di vao con duong chet cung voi chu My" [In bringing mercenaries to Viet Nam, the Chung Hee Park clique is entering the path of death with its American master]. *Hoc Tap* 13 (March 1967): 82–91.
"Ra suc phat trien san xuat tang cuong chien dau, gianh them nhieu thang loi trong nam 1965, xa luan" [Endeavor to develop production, strengthen the fighting, and win many more victories in 1965]. *Hoc Tap* 11 (July 1965) 1–6.
Song Hao. "Lanh dao Quan Doi Nhan Dan la nhiem vu lich su cua Dang ta" [Guiding our People's Army is the historic mission of our Party]. *Hoc Tap* 10 (December 1964): 17–36.
——. "Phat huy truyen thong quyet chien quyet thang cua cac luc luong vu trang nhan dan danh thang giac My xam luoc" [Promote the tradition of determination of our people's armed forces to defeat the U.S. aggressors]. *Hoc Tap* 12 (December 1966): 14–25.
"Su nghiep chong My, cuu nuoc cua nhan dan ta nhat dinh thang loi, xa luan" [Our people's anti-U.S. resistance war for national salvation of the fatherland shall be successful, editorial]. *Hoc Tap* 11 (May 1965): 1–6.

Ta Xuan Linh. "Cuoc Dong Khoi Tra Bong, 28-8-59" [The Tra Bong uprising of August 28, 1959]. *Nghien Cuu Lich Su* 138 (May–June 1971): 2–27.

——. "South Vietnam at the Time of Dien Bien Phu." *Vietnamese Studies* 42 (1976): 53–78.

Thai Ha. "De quoc My dung chien luoc quan su nao cung deu bi that bai nhuc nha" [The U.S. shall be defeated shamefully for any of its strategies]. *Hoc Tap* 10 (August 1964): 72–81.

"Thu Ho Chu Tich gui Luat Su Nguyen Huu Tho, Chu Tich Doan Chu Tich, va Cac Vi Trong Uy Ban Truong Uong Mat Tran Dan Toc Giai Phong mien Nam" [Letter from Chairmen Ho to Lawyer Nguyen Huu Tho, chairman of the Presidium, and to distinguished members of the Central Committee of the National Front for the Liberation of South Viet Nam]. *Hoc Tap* 13 (July 1967): 3–5.

To Minh Trung. "The Students' and Pupils' Struggle." *Vietnamese Studies* 8 (1966): 112–80.

Ton Vy. "The Workers' Struggle." *Vietnamese Studies* 8 (1966): 78–111.

Ton Vy, Tom Vu, To Minh Trung, and Le Tan Danh. "The Failure of the Special War, 1961–1965." *Vietnamese Studies* 11 (1967): 1–198.

Tran Bach Dang. "Mau Than: cuoc tong dien tap chien tuoc" [Tet Offensive: A strategic rehearsal]. *Tap Chi Lich Su Quan Su*, special issue, February 1988, 23–90.

Tran Duc Thao, Bui Tin, Vu Quy, et al. "In Face of American Aggression, 1965–67." *Vietnamese Studies* 16 (1968): 1–182.

Tran Huu Ta. "Doc hoi ky cach mang, nghi ve ve dep cua nguoi chien si Cong San Viet Nam" [Reading revolutionary memoirs and thinking of the splendid appearance of Vietnamese Communist militants]. *Tap Chi Van Hoc* 2 (1977): 40–54.

Tran Huy Lieu. "Danh va Dam." [Fighting while negotiating]. *Nghien Cuu Lich Su* 111 (June 1968): 1–2, 14.

——. "Gan lien cuoc chien tranh nhan dan vi dai cua ta voi su ung ho to lon cua cac ban quoc te" [Link our great people's war with the great support from international friends]. *Nghien Cuu Lich Su* 109 (April 1968): 1–4.

Tran Quoc Tu. "Hoa Binh va Cach Mang" [Peace and revolution]. *Hoc Tap* 10 (January 1964): 41–55.

Tran Quynh Cu. "May net ve mat tran nhan dan the gioi chong My ung ho cuoc dau tranh giai phong cua nhan dan mien Nam" [A sketch of the peoples of the world opposing the U.S. and supporting the southern people's liberation movement]. *Nghien Cuu Lich Su* 99 (June 1967): 10–22.

——. "Phong trao nhan dan My phan doi cuoc chien tranh xam luoc my o mien Nam Viet Nam" [The American antiwar movement against U.S. aggression in South Viet Nam]. *Nghien Cuu Lich Su* 91 (October 1966): 5–16.

Truong Chinh. "De thau suot nghi quyet cua dai hoi toan quoc lan thu III cua Dang" [To thoroughly understand the resolution of the Third Party Congress]. *Hoc Tap* 7 (April 1961): 10–36.

——. "Nam vung moi quan he giua chien tranh va cach mang o Viet Nam de hoan thanh thang loi su nghiep chong My, cuu nuoc" [Let us fully understand the relationship between war and revolution in our anti-U.S. resistance war for national salvation of the fatherland]. *Hoc Tap* 11 (September 1965): 18–23.

Truong Ngoc Khang et al. "Dan toc Cor Tra Bong truoc cuoc Khoi Nghia Ngay 28-8-1959" [The Cor peoples of Tra Bong before the uprising of August 28, 1959]. *Nghien Cuu Lich Su* 148 (January–February 1973): 11-25.

Van Tien Dung. "Dang thang lon ve quan su, quan va dan mien Nam nhat dinh danh bai chien tranh xam luoc cua de quoc My" [Being greatly victorious in the military field, the southern armed forces and people will surely defeat the U.S. imperialists' aggressive war]. *Hoc Tap* 13 (April 1967): 27–42.

——. "People's War against Air War of Destruction." *Vietnamese Studies* 20 (1968): 65–86.

——. "Quan va dan ta da thang, dang thang va nhat dinh se danh thang hoan toan giac My xam luoc" [Our armed forces and the people have won, are winning, and will surely and completely win over the American aggressors]. *Hoc Tap* 12 (February 1966): 40–50.

——. "Thau suot duong loi chien tranh nhan dan cua Dang, kien quyet danh bai de quoc My xam luoc" [Thoroughly understand the people's war line of the Party, be determined to defeat the imperialist American aggressors]. *Hoc Tap* 11 (August 1965): 12–23.

Viet Hong. "Vai net va dau tranh vo trang va luc luong vo trang o Nam Bo truoc cuoc dong Khoi, 1959–1960" [A sketch of the armed struggle and the armed forces of Nam Bo before the 1959–1960 General Uprising]. *Nghien Cuu Lich Su* 155 (March–April 1974): 39–55.

Vo Nguyen Giap. "Ca nuoc mot long day manh chien tranh yeu nuoc vi dai kien quyet danh thang giac My xam luoc" [The people of the entire country are of one mind in stepping up the great patriotic war and are determined to fight and vanquish the American aggressors]. *Hoc Tap* 12 (January 1966): 11–30.

——. "The Liberation War in South Vietnam: Its Essential Characteristics." *Vietnamese Studies* 8 (1966): 5–36.

——. "Quyet tam danh thang giac My xam luoc" [We are determined to defeat the U.S. aggressors]. *Hoc Tap* 11 (July 1965): 7–16.

Vu Can. "The People's Struggles against the U.S.-Diem Regime from 1954 to 1960." *Vietnam Studies* 18/19 (1968): 16–34.

Vu Lac. "Chong chien tranh tam ly cua de quoc My" [Against the imperialist American psychological warfare]. *Hoc Tap* 11 (September 1965): 56–60.

Newspapers and Radio

Chin Luan [Official discussion]
Dia Dan [Greater national community]
Dien Tien [Telegraph]
Giai Phong [Liberation]
Nhan Dan [The people]
South Vietnam in Struggle
Vietnam Advances
Vietnam Courier
Liberation Radio, Trung Tam Luu Tru Quoc Gia-1 [National Archives Center 1], Hanoi
Radio Hanoi, Trung Tam Luu Tru Quoc Gia-1 [National Archives Center 1], Hanoi

WESTERN SOURCES

Documents

"Bloc Support of the Communist Effort against the Government of Vietnam." Document no. 53–2-6–1. Central Intelligence Agency, October 5, 1961. Document no. 0007693, Douglas Pike Collection, NLF Documents, Indochina Archive, University of California at Berkeley.

"COSVN Directive 3." *Vietnam Documents and Research Notes*, no. 115, September 1973.

"COSVN Directive 08." *Vietnamese Documents and Research Notes*, no. 118, February 1975.

Dudman, Richard. "The Lesson of Vietnam." *Congressional Record*, February 26, 1973.

Foreign Relations of the United States, 1955–1957, Southeast Asia. Vol. 22. Washington D.C.: Government Printing Office, 1989.

Foreign Relations of the United States, 1958–1960, Vietnam. Vol. 1. Washington, D.C.: Government Printing Office, 1986.

Foreign Relations of the United States, 1961–1963: Vietnam, 1961. Vol. 1. Washington, D.C.: Government Printing Office, 1988.

Foreign Relations of the United States, 1961–1963: Vietnam, 1962. Vol. 2. Washington, D.C.: Government Printing Office, 1992.

Foreign Relations of the United States, 1961–1963: Vietnam, August–December, 1963. Vol. 4. Washington, D.C.: Government Printing Office, 1991.

Foreign Relations of the United States, 1964–1968: Vietnam, 1964. Vol. 1. Washington, D.C.: Government Printing Office, 1992.

Gettleman, Marvin E. *Vietnam: History, Documents, and Opinions on a Major World Crisis.* New York: Fawcett, 1965.

"Hanoi's Strategy for Conquest: The Liberation Front." Tokyo: United States Mission, June 21, 1965. Document no. 0000382, Douglas Pike Collection, NLF Documents, Indochina Archive,University of California at Berkeley.

Herring, George C., ed. *The Secret Diplomacy of the Vietnam War: The Negotiating Volumes of the Pentagon Papers.* Austin: University of Texas Press, 1983.

McGee, Gale. "South Vietnam's National Liberation Front: Creation of Hanoi." United States Information Agency. March 1966. Document no. 0007003, Douglas Pike Collection, NLF Documents, Indochina Archive, University of California at Berkeley.

"The Organization, Activities, and Objectives of the Communist Front in South Vietnam." United States Department of State, September 22, 1965. Document no. 000015, Douglas Pike Collection, NLF Documents, Indochina Archive, University of California at Berkeley.

The Pentagon Papers: The Defense Department History of United States Decisionmaking on Vietnam. Senator Gravel ed. 4 vols. Boston: Beacon, 1971–72.

Pohle, Victoria. *The Viet Cong in Saigon: Tactics and Objectives during the Tet Offensive.* Santa Monica: Rand Corporation, November 1969.

Porter, Gareth, ed. *Vietnam: A History in Documents.* New York: New American Library, 1981.

Raskin, Marcus, and Bernard Fall. *The Viet Nam Reader.* New York: Random House, 1965.

Sheehan, Neil, Hedrick Smith, E. W. Kenworthy, and Fox Butterfield. *The Pentagon Papers as Published by the New York Times.* New York: Bantam, 1971.

"A Threat to Peace: North Viet Nam's Effort to Conquer South Viet Nam." United States Department of State, December 1961. Document no. 000358, Douglas Pike Collection, NLF Documents, Indochina Archive, University of California at Berkeley.

United States-Vietnam Relations, 1945–1967. 12 vols. Department of Defense. Washington, D.C.: Government Printing Office, 1971.

"The Viet Cong: The Front Technique." Document no. R-13–67. United States Information Agency, April 20, 1967. Document no. 000391, Douglas Pike Collection, NLF Documents, Indochina Archive, University of California at Berkeley.

"The Vietnam Agreement and Protocols, Signed January 27, 1973: Agreement on Ending the War and Restoring Peace to Vietnam." *Weekly Compilation of Presidential Documents,* January 29, 1973.

"The Vietnam Bombing: Senate Opposition Grows." *Congressional Quarterly: Weekly Reports*, December 23, 1972.

"Working Paper on the North Vietnamese Role in the War in South Viet Nam." Document no. 52. United States Department of State, 1968. Document no. 000329, Douglas Pike Collection, NLF Documents, Indochina Archive, University of California at Berkeley.

Memoirs and Collections

Ball, George. *The Past Has Another Pattern: Memoirs*. New York: Norton, 1982.

Colby, William. *Lost Victory*. Chicago: Contemporary Books, 1989.

Cooper, Chester. *The Lost Crusade*. Rev. ed. Greenwich, Conn.: Fawcett, 1972.

Dellinger, David. *Vietnam Revisited: Covert Action to Invasion to Reconstruction*. Boston: South End Press, 1986.

Haldeman, H. R. *The Ends of Power*. New York: Times Books, 1978.

——. *The Haldeman Diaries: Inside the Nixon White House*. New York: Putnam, 1994.

McNamara, Robert S., with Brian VanDeMark. *In Retrospect: The Tragedy and Lessons of Vietnam*. New York: Times Books, 1995.

Nixon, Richard. *RN: The Memoirs of Richard Nixon*. New York: Vintage, 1978.

Rusk, Dean. *As I Saw It: A Secretary of State's Memoirs*. New York: Norton, 1990.

Salisbury, Harrison. *Behind the Lines: Hanoi*. New York: Harper & Row, 1967.

Histories

Anderson, David. *Shadow on the White House: Presidents and the Vietnam War*. Lawrence: University Press of Kansas, 1993.

——. *Trapped by Success: The Eisenhower Administration and Vietnam, 1953–1961*. New York: Columbia University Press, 1991.

Andrews, William. *The Village War: Vietnamese Communist Revolutionary Activities in Dinh Tuong Province*. Columbia: University of Missouri Press, 1973.

Bergerud, Eric. *The Dynamics of Defeat: The Vietnam War in Hau Nghia Province*. Boulder: Westview, 1991.

Berman, Paul. *Revolutionary Organization, Institution-Building within the People's Liberation Armed Forces*. Lexington, Mass.: Lexington Books, 1974.

Blaufarb, Douglas. *The Counterinsurgency Era: U.S. Doctrine and Performance, 1950 to the Present*. New York: Free Press, 1977.

Burchett, Wilfred. *Vietnam: Inside Story of the Guerrilla War*. New York: International Publishers, 1965.

Butler, David. *The Fall of Saigon*. New York: Dell, 1985.

Buttinger, Joseph. *A Defiant Dragon*. New York: Praeger, 1972.

——. *Vietnam: A Political History*. New York: Praeger, 1969.

Chen, King. *Vietnam and China, 1938–1954.* Princeton: Princeton University Press, 1969.

Christopher, Renny. *The Vietnam War/The American War: Images and Representations in Euro-American and Vietnamese Exile Narratives.* Amherst: University of Massachusetts Press, 1995.

Duffy, Dan. *Not a War: American Vietnamese Fiction, Poetry, and Essays.* Viet Nam Forum no. 16. New Haven: Yale University Council on Southeast Asia Studies, 1997.

Duiker, William. *The Communist Road to Power in Vietnam.* Boulder: Westview, 1981.

——. *The Rise of Nationalism in Vietnam.* Ithaca: Cornell University Press, 1976.

——. *Vietnam: Revolution in Transition.* 2d ed. Boulder: Westview, 1995.

Duncanson, D. J. *Government and Revolution in Vietnam.* Oxford: Oxford University Press, 1968.

Fall, Bernard. *Hell in a Very Small Place: The Siege of Dien Bien Phu.* New York: Vintage, 1966.

——. *Street without Joy.* Harrisburg: Stackpole, 1961.

——. *The Two Viet Nams: A Military and Political Analysis.* 2d ed. New York: Praeger, 1967.

——. *Vietnam Witness, 1953–1966.* New York: Praeger, 1966.

FitzGerald, Frances. *Fire in the Lake: The Vietnamese and the Americans in Vietnam.* New York: Vintage, 1972.

Floyd, David. *Mao against Khrushchev: A Short History of the Sino-Soviet Conflict.* New York: Praeger, 1963.

Ford, Ronnie E. *Tet 1968: Understanding the Surprise.* Portland, Ore. : F. Cass, 1995.

Freeman, James. *Hearts of Sorrow: Vietnamese-American Lives.* Stanford: Stanford University Press, 1989.

Gallucci, Robert. *Neither Peace nor Honor.* Baltimore: Johns Hopkins University Press, 1975.

Gardner, Lloyd C. *Approaching Vietnam: From World War II through Dien Bien Phu.* New York: Norton, 1988.

——. *Pay Any Price: Lyndon Johnson and the Wars for Vietnam.* Chicago: Ivan Dee, 1995.

Gibbons, William Conrad. *The U.S. Government and the Vietnam War: Executive and Legislative Roles and Relationships.* 4 vols. Princeton: Princeton University Press, 1986–94.

Gilbert, Marc, and William Head, eds. *The Tet Offensive.* Westport, Conn.: Praeger, 1996.

Goldman, Eric. *The Tragedy of Lyndon Johnson.* New York: Dell, 1968.

Goldstein, Martin. *American Policy toward Laos.* Rutherford, N.J.: Fairleigh Dickinson University Press, 1973.

Gurtov, Melvin. *The First Vietnam Crisis.* New York: Columbia University Press, 1967.

Hammer, Ellen J. *The Struggle for Indochina, 1940–1955: Viet Nam and the French Experience.* Stanford: Stanford University Press, 1955.

Henderson, William D. *Why the Viet Cong Fought.* Westport, Conn.: Greenwood, 1979.

Herring, George C. *America's Longest War: The United States and Vietnam, 1950–1975.* 2d ed. New York: Knopf, 1986.

——. *LBJ and Vietnam: A Different Kind of War.* Austin: University of Texas Press, 1994.

Hickey, Gerald C. *Village in Vietnam.* New Haven: Yale University Press, 1964.

Hunt, Richard. *Pacification: The American Struggle for Vietnam's Hearts and Minds.* Boulder: Westview, 1995.

Jamieson, Neil. *Understanding Vietnam.* Berkeley: University of California Press, 1993.

Kahin, George McT. *Intervention: How America Became Involved in Vietnam.* New York: Doubleday/Anchor, 1986.

Kahin, George McT., and John Lewis. *The United States in Vietnam: An Analysis in Depth of the History of America's Involvement in Vietnam*, Rev. ed. New York: Dell, 1969.

Kail, F. M. *What Washington Said: Administration Rhetoric and the Vietnam War, 1949–1969.* New York: Harper Torchbooks, 1973.

Kalb, Bernard, and Marvin Kalb. *Kissinger.* Boston: Little, Brown, 1974.

Karnow, Stanley. *Vietnam: A History.* New York: Penguin, 1983.

Kinnard, Douglas. *The War Managers.* New York: Da Capo, 1991.

Kolko, Gabriel. *Vietnam: Anatomy of a War.* New York: Pantheon, 1985.

Kraslow, David, and Stuart Loory. *The Secret Search for Peace in Vietnam.* New York: Random House, 1968.

Krepinevich, Andrew. *The Army and Vietnam.* Baltimore: Johns Hopkins University Press, 1986.

Lanning, Michael Lee, and Dan Cragg. *Inside the VC and the NVA: The Real Story of North Vietnam's Armed Forces.* New York: Ivy, 1992.

Lewy, Guenter. *America in Vietnam.* New York: Oxford University Press, 1978.

Lockhart, Greg. *Nation in Arms: The Origins of the People's Army of Vietnam.* Sydney/Boston: Allen & Unwin, 1989.

Lynd, Staughton, and Thomas Hayden. *The Other Side.* New York: New American Library, 1966.

Marr, David. *Vietnam, 1945: The Quest for Power.* Berkeley: University of California Press, 1995.

——. *Vietnamese Tradition on Trial, 1925–1945.* Berkeley: University of California Press, 1981.

McAlister, John. *Viet Nam: Origins of Revolution.* New York: Knopf, 1969.

McDonald, Peter. *Giap: The Victor in Vietnam.* New York: Norton, 1993.

Moss, Donnelson. *Vietnam: An American Ordeal.* Englewood Cliffs, N.J.: Prentice-Hall, 1990.

Oberdorfer, Don. *Tet!* New York: Avon, 1971.

Olsen, Mari. *Solidarity and National Revolution: The Soviet Union and the Vietnamese Communists, 1954–1960.* Oslo: Institutt for Forsvarsstudier, 1997.

Palmer, Bruce, Jr. *The 25-Year War: America's Military Role in Vietnam.* Lexington: University of Kentucky Press, 1984.

Pike, Douglas. *PAVN: People's Army of Vietnam.* Novato, Calif.: Presidio, 1986.

——. *Viet Cong: The Organization and Techniques of the National Liberation Front of South Vietnam.* Cambridge: MIT Press, 1966.

——. *War, Peace, and the Viet Cong.* Cambridge: MIT Press, 1969.

Podhoretz, Norman. *Why We Were in Vietnam.* New York: Simon & Schuster, 1982.

Porter, Gareth. *A Peace Denied: The United States, Vietnam, and the Paris Agreement.* Bloomington: Indiana University Press, 1975.

——. *Vietnam: The Politics of Bureaucratic Socialism.* Ithaca: Cornell University Press, 1993.

Prados, John. *The Hidden History of the Vietnam War.* Chicago: Ivan Dee, 1995.

Race, Jeffrey. *War Comes to Long An: Revolutionary Conflict in a Vietnamese Province.* Berkeley: University of California Press, 1972.

Rotter, Andrew. *The Path to Vietnam: Origins of the American Commitment to Southeast Asia.* Ithaca: Cornell University Press, 1987.

Schell, Jonathan. *The Military Half.* New York: Vintage, 1968.

Scigliano, Robert. *South Vietnam: Nation under Stress.* Boston: Houghton Mifflin, 1964.

Shaplen, Robert. *The Lost Revolution: The U.S. in Vietnam, 1944–66.* New York: Harper & Row, 1966.

——. *The Road from War: Vietnam, 1965–1971.* New York: Harper & Row, 1971.

Smith, Ralph. *An International History of the Vietnam War.* Vol. 2. New York: St. Martin's Press, 1987.

Spector, Ronald H. *After Tet: The Bloodiest Year in Vietnam.* New York: Free Press, 1993.

Stebbins, Richard P. *The United States in World Affairs, 1963.* New York: Council on Foreign Relations, 1964.

Summers, Harry. *On Strategy: A Critical Analysis of the Vietnam War.* Rev. ed. New York: Dell, 1984.

Thayer, Carlyle A. *War by Other Means: National Liberation and Revolution in Viet-Nam, 1954–1960.* Sydney/Boston: Allen & Unwin, 1989.

Thies, Wallace. *When Governments Collide: Coercion and Diplomacy in the Vietnam Conflict, 1964–1968.* Berkeley: University of California Press, 1980.

Turley, William. *The Second Indochina War: A Short Political and Military History, 1954–1975.* New York: Signet, 1986.

Werner, Jayne, and Luu Doan Huynh, eds. *The Vietnam War: Vietnamese and American Perspectives.* Armonk, N.Y.: M. E. Sharpe, 1993.

Whalen, Richard. *Catch the Falling Flag: A Republican's Challenge to His Party.* Boston: Houghton Mifflin, 1972.

Wirtz, James. *The Tet Offensive: Intelligence Failure in War.* Ithaca: Cornell University Press, 1991.

Woods, Randall Bennett. *Fulbright: A Biography.* New York: Cambridge University Press, 1995.

Woodside, Alexander. *Community and Revolution in Modern Vietnam.* Boston: Houghton Mifflin, 1976.

Young, Marilyn. *The Vietnam Wars, 1945–1990.* New York: HarperCollins, 1991.

Zagoria, Donald. *Vietnam Triangle: Moscow/Peking/Hanoi.* New York: Pegasus, 1967.

Zasloff, Joseph, and MacAlister Brown, eds. *Communism in Indochina: New Perspectives.* Lexington, Mass.: D. C. Heath, 1975.

Essays

Bain, Chester. "Viet Cong Propaganda Abroad." *Foreign Service Journal,* October 1968, 12–16.

Brigham, Robert K. "Vietnamese-American Peace Negotiations: The Failed 1965 Initiatives." *Journal of American-East Asian Relations* 4 (Winter 1995): 377–95.

Carver, George. "The Faceless Viet Cong." *Foreign Affairs* 44 (April 1966): 347–72.

Chafford, Georges. "Inside Viet Cong Territory." *Viet Report,* July 1965, 3–11.

Chen Jian. "China's Involvement in the Vietnam War, 1964–1969." *China Quarterly* 142 (June 1995): 356–87.

Crawford, Curtis. "Aggression from the North?" Pt. 2. *Viet Report,* October 1966, 24–33.

Devillers, Philippe. "The Struggle for Unification in Vietnam." *China Quarterly* 9 (January–March 1962): 2–23.

Duiker, William. "Waging Revolutionary War: The Evolution of Hanoi's Strategy in the South, 1959–1965." In Jayne S. Werner and Luu Doan Huynh, eds., *The Vietnam War: Vietnamese and American Perspectives*, 24–36. Armonk, N.Y.: M. E. Sharpe, 1993.

Fall, Bernard. "South Viet Nam at the Crossroads." *International Journal* 19 (Spring 1964): 139–54.

——. "Unrepentant and Unyielding." *New Republic*, February 4, 1967, 19–24.

Goodman, Allan. "Fighting while Negotiating: The View from Hanoi." In Joseph Zasloff and MacAlister Brown, eds., *Communism in Indochina: New Perspectives*, 81–107. Lexington, Mass.: D. C. Heath, 1975.

Herring, George C. "The Truman Administration and the Restoration of French Sovereignty in Indochina." *Diplomatic History* 1 (Spring 1977): 97–117.

Herring, George C., and Richard H. Immerman. "Eisenhower, Dulles, and Dien Bien Phu: The 'Day We Didn't Go To War' Revisited." *Journal of American History* 72 (September 1984): 343–63.

Honey, P. J. "The National United Front in Vietnam." *Studies in Comparative Communism* 2 (January 1969): 69–95.

Joiner, Charles. "Patterns of Political Behavior in South Vietnam." *Journal of Southeast Asian History* 8 (March 1967): 83–98.

Kahin, George McT. "Negotiations: The View from Hanoi." *New Republic*, November 6, 1971, 13–16.

——. "The NLF's Terms for Peace." *New Republic*, October 14, 1967, 13–17.

Lacouture, Jean. "The Face of the Viet Cong." *War/Peace Report*, July 1966, 7–8.

——. "Viet Cong: Who Are They, What Do They Want?" *New Republic*, March 6, 1965, 21–24.

Ladd, Jonathan. "Viet Cong Portrait." *Military Review* 15 (July 1964): 2.

Logevall, Fredrik. "De Gaulle, Neutralization, and American Involvement in Vietnam, 1963–1964." *Pacific Historical Review* 61 (February 1992): 69–102.

——. "The Swedish-American Conflict over Vietnam." *Diplomatic History* 17 (Summer 1993): 421–46.

Ngo Vinh Long. "Post-Paris Agreement Struggles and the Fall of Saigon." In Jayne S. Werner and Luu Doan Huynh, eds., *The Vietnam War: Vietnamese and American Perspectives*, 203–15. Armonk, N.Y.: M. E. Sharpe, 1993.

Pike, Douglas. "How Strong Is the NLF?" *Reporter*, February 24, 1966, 20–24.

Porter, Gareth. "The Paris Agreement and Revolutionary Strategy in South Vietnam." In Joseph Zasloff and MacAlister Brown, eds., *Communism in Indochina: New Perspectives*, 57–75. Lexington, Mass.: D. C. Heath, 1975.

Rose, Jerry. "The Elusive Viet Cong." *New Republic*, May 4, 1963, 19–26.

Scalapino, Robert. "Moscow, Peking, and the Communist Parties of Asia." *Foreign Affairs* 41 (January 1963): 323–43.

Stern, Sol. "A Talk with the Front." *Vietnam Roundup*, November 1967, 12–16.

Szulc, Tad. "Behind the Vietnam Cease-Fire Agreement." *Foreign Policy* 15 (Summer 1974): 21–69.

Van der Kroef, Justus. "What Are the Aims of the NLF?" *Vietnam Roundup*, November 1967, 3–20.

"Viet Cong Documents on the War." Pt. 1. *Communist Affairs*, September–October 1967, 18–34.

"Viet Nam's Liberation Front." *Interpreter*, February 1967, 25–28.

Warner, Denis. "Ho's Underground in South Vietnam." *Vietnam Roundup*, November 1967, 1–3.

——. "The NLF's New Program." *Vietnam Roundup*, October 1967, 1, 10–11.

"What Is the National Liberation Front of South Vietnam?" *SANE*, June 1965, 1–6.

Newspapers and Radio

Agence France-Presse

Baltimore Sun

British Broadcasting Company

Chicago Daily News

Christian Science Monitor

Far Eastern Economic Review

London Times

Le Monde

New York Times

Wall Street Journal

Washington Post

Washington Star

Special Collections

Johnson Papers, Meeting Notes File, Lyndon Baines Johnson Presidential Library, Austin, Tex.

National Security Files, Country File Vietnam, Lyndon Baines Johnson Presidential Library, Austin, Tex.

Douglas Pike Collection, NLF Documents, Indochina Archive, University of California at Berkeley.

Jeffrey Race Collection, Captured Documents, Center for Research and University Libraries, Chicago.

INDEX